T0369271

Harsh Vineyard

A History of Catholic Life in the Russian Far East

Miroslava Efimova

Order this book online at www.trafford.com
or email orders@trafford.com

Most Trafford titles are also available at major online book retailers.

Translated by: Geraldine H. Kelley

Print information available on the last page.

ISBN: 978-1-4251-6803-2 (sc)

Trafford rev. 07/29/2020

www.trafford.com

North America & international
toll-free: 1 888 232 4444 (USA & Canada)
fax: 812 355 4082

Translated for the benefit of Mary Mother of God Mission Society
St. Paul, Minnesota, USA
Geraldine H. Kelley, Ph.D.

Originally published as *Vera skvoz' veka* [Faith Through the Ages],
2007.

Introduction to the English Edition

By V. Rev. Myron Effing, C.J.D.

For people in the English-speaking world, the "Russian Far East" does not exist because cartographers continue to use the word "Siberia" for everything east of the Urals, even though there were centuries between Russia's acquisition of Siberia and its acquisition of the Russian Far East. At one time the Russian Far East extended from Lake Baikal to San Francisco. Precious little is known by English speakers about the human history of these huge land masses—maybe a little about the Russian background of Alaska, about volcanoes on Kamchatka, and perhaps the phrase "Trans-Siberian Railroad." The first time I flew into Khabarovsk I reprimanded myself before landing that I—a long-time teacher of geography—did not have the faintest idea of what the land and the people would be like.

I have lived fifteen years in Vladivostok—in the heart of the Roman Catholic Diocese of Vladivostok, the "Eastern capital," and the "back door" of Russia. They say that, with its hills and valleys, its gulfs and islands and its ever-present fog, the city is somewhat like San Francisco. It has yet another similarity to San Francisco: it is the end of the Trans-Siberian Railroad. But while San Francisco was the embodiment of the American dream, and all yearnings strained toward the West with hope for the future, Vladivostok was never thus—because all the power and all the resources were swallowed up by Moscow and St. Petersburg. Perhaps now in the twenty-first century Vladivostok and the Russian Far East may have a promising future as a new territory with great potential.

In the present work we see the tragic story of those people who were first sent to settle this land, to build the railroads and defend the borders. And more important, we see the story of those who tried to serve, meeting the spiritual and cultural needs of the resettled peoples. After great beginnings, their hopes were crushed by the cruel blows of militant atheism, which forbade God to exist and forbade the people to remember Him under the penalty of death. Such was the monstrous death-dealing machine, demanding human sacrifices—and there were many sacrifices.

Miroslava Igorevna has done us all a huge favor by opening up to the light of day the stories of some of those who lived and suffered in this land, stories which would never have been told had she not persevered in her search. I am sure some will be critical, but then Miroslava is not an historian but a geologist! She has traveled these lands and examined the territory like no one else. And when traveling in the wild was no longer possible for her, she continued to explore it—now in the rich veins of its human history. As a geologist she could not possibly be everywhere, and as an historian she could not research everything. But the human hope and human tragedy show themselves on every page.

We express our gratitude to Miroslava Igorevna for her research and the collection of "pieces" of this tragic story into a single whole. She could not end her work without a happy ending. We all hope that religious freedom and the establishment of economic possibilities in the Russian Far East will lay the foundation of a great rebirth of the Faith and well-being for the peoples living in the eastern region of Russia.

Translator's Introduction

It is to be expected that most readers of this English translation of Miroslava Efimova's work will be unfamiliar with the history and geography of the Russian Far East. As I proceeded with the translation I added explanatory notes to passages where I thought some clarification would be helpful, but there are topics that could be more beneficially explained at the outset.

The first of these is the prominence of the archdiocese of Mogilev. The city of Mogilev dates back to 1267. Located 500 miles southwest of Moscow, the city is presently in Belarus, but in times past it has been part of Russia, Poland and Lithuania. The archdiocese of Mogilev was erected in 1782 by Catherine II after the First Partition of Poland. After discussions with the Russian government, the Vatican recognized the archdiocese in 1783. Right up to the end of tsarist rule in 1918, the Russian government continued to interfere with and strictly regulate the administrative affairs of the Roman Catholic Church on Russian territory. Under the 1847 Concordat between Nicholas I and the Vatican, the Mogilev archdiocese was expanded to include Finland, Siberia and Turkestan. It became the largest Roman Catholic jurisdiction in the world, covering 5,400,000 square miles.

The episcopal see, including the administrative offices and the archdiocesan seminary, was located in St. Petersburg. Most of the priests whose lives are described in this work were Belorussian priests of the Mogilev archdiocese, and the people they served were Poles, Ukrainians and Lithuanians as well as Belorussians.

The Roman Catholic Diocese of Vladivostok, erected in 1922, has been vacant since 1933. Roman Catholics in the Russian Far East Federal District are presently under the jurisdiction of the Diocese of St. Joseph in Irkutsk.

A second topic for consideration is that of the sheer magnitude of the territory. The following are some of the cities that figure in our story, with distances from Moscow given in parentheses: Tambov (260 miles), Omsk (1,392 miles), Novosibirsk (1,750 miles), Tomsk (1,789 miles), Irkutsk (2,615 miles), Chita (2,945 miles), Blagoveshchensk (3,491 miles), Khabarovsk (3,817 miles), Vladivostok (3,988 miles), Petropavlovsk (4,200 miles). How did one travel out to Vladivostok from European Russia? There are travelogues written in the seventeenth and eighteenth centuries describing overland journeys taking several weeks. Travel by sea—from Kronstadt then either around the Horn and across the Pacific, or around the Cape of Good Hope and through the Indian Ocean—was undertaken from the end of the seventeenth century. Once the Suez Canal was completed in 1869 steamers could leave Odessa and proceed through the Canal, across the Indian Ocean and then north. Work on the Trans-Siberian Railroad was begun in the 1890s and by 1904 one could go all the way to Vladivostok, by way of Harbin, Manchuria (a parallel route on Russian territory was completed in 1916).

Another topic of interest is that of the settlement of Siberia and the Far East. Vladivostok was established in 1860, roughly the same time as Denver, Colorado. One might be tempted to think that American westward expansion approximately coincided with Russian eastward expansion. But this is not so. By the time Russia acquired the Chinese port of Haishenwei and renamed it Vladivostok, it had already abandoned its settlement in California, where for almost thirty years (1812-1841) Russia had attempted to grow provisions for its settlements in Alaska. “Russian America” (Alaska and California) was a venture that had begun in the 1780s and came to an end with the sale of Alaska in 1867. Russian settlement of the Far East dates back to the 1600s.

The plan of the work is very simple: the author presents the story of Catholic life in the Russian Far East by compiling a series of biographical sketches of the priests who were assigned to the Far East. The sketches are presented in chronological order, but since many of the priests were nearly contemporaries, the narrative moves forward, then returns to begin again with the story of the next priest. Within any particular sketch the author might come across an interesting fact in the archival record, and then a fascinating digression ensues.

The work is not meant as a comprehensive study, the final word on the topic of Catholic life in the Russian Far East—rather it is offered as a foundation for future work on a topic that was largely ignored during the 70-year reign of atheistic communism. The author personally endured that period, and through her friendships with those of a generation that has now almost died, she knew of the existence of this unrecorded history. Rather than letting it slip away into oblivion, she has in her late years done yeoman's work in bringing it to light, so that perhaps another generation of students and scholars will be inspired to explore more deeply any of a number of topics that will occur to the careful reader.

Readers may find useful some information about the present-day population and governmental administration of the Russian Far East Federal District, and that is provided in Appendix A. A list of present-day Roman Catholic parishes is provided as Appendix B.

On these and other topics the reader will of course find a wealth of information on the internet. For those wishing a recommendation for further reading, John J. Stephan's *The Russian Far East: A History* (Stanford: Stanford Univ. Press, 1994) is a fine work with a very comprehensive bibliography. Current events in the Vladivostok Catholic Deanery are reported in *Vladivostok Sunrise*, the newsletter of the Mary Mother of God Mission Society, which can be found on its website www.vladmission.org

Russian units of measure have not been converted to English units, but a list of equivalents is provided just before Appendix A. The reader may also find useful a website that easily converts various units of measure: www.convert-me.com

A note on transliteration. For Russian names I have used the Library of Congress transliteration system, except where there is a more commonly used spelling. I have used the Anglicized form of given names for members of the Russian imperial family. For names that were originally in a language other than Russian, I have attempted to use the original name, rather than a transliteration of a transliteration. In some cases the number of possible variants made it difficult to ascertain the original spelling. The name Ejsymontt, for example, comes in at least a half dozen variants.

And finally, a word of caution—with respect to events occurring prior to February 14, 1918, when the Soviet Union adopted the Gregorian calendar, the manuscript rarely noted whether dates were according to the Julian or Gregorian calendar. The Gregorian calendar was adopted at different times in the various western lands where much of the archival information was gathered. Thus a closcr investigation of specific dates would be recommended in any case where the difference (12 days in the nineteenth century) would be significant to the reader.

I share the hope of Fr. Myron Effing, the Mary Mother of God Mission Society, and all Catholics of the Russian Far East that this translation will reach a wide audience and that it will foster an interest in this part of the world that remains unfamiliar to most Americans. I wish to express my gratitude to my family, friends and co-workers who over the past year have graciously let my interest in the Russian Far East become one of their interests as well.

Geraldine H. Kelley, Ph.D.
March 2008

Foreword

The purpose of the present monograph is the study of the history of, and the reasons for the rise of, the Roman Catholic Church in the Russian Far East, and it is this question that the first chapter of the monograph treats in some detail. As seen from the historical evidence presented, Poland, a central European government, found itself seriously dependent upon neighboring governments, primarily upon the Russian Empire. There were practically no borders between Poland and Russia and the Russian army was able to move freely across Polish lands in any direction. This situation naturally provoked Polish patriots, who established secret societies for the purpose of organizing rebellions. But all rebellions were cruelly suppressed by Russian forces and hundreds and thousands of rebels, bound in chains, were sent to harsh outposts where they expanded the contingents of prisoners who worked the Siberian mines. If the rebels were military men, they were whipped (in the best cases) or beaten (in the worst cases), then dressed in the uniform of the Russian army and sent to serve in the so-called "Siberian battalions."

Since the Poles were Catholic, they needed contact with Catholic priests. Efforts of tsarist officials to convert Catholics to the Orthodox faith were unsuccessful. Polish Catholic priests of various religious orders voluntarily went to Siberia, where they served as chaplains in Polish military units as well as in prisoner settlements, thus bringing spiritual consolation to these Catholics. The best known of these volunteer priests was Fr. Krzystóf Szwermicki, who tended to the spiritual needs of both Polish military and Polish civilian prisoners.

After treaties with China, Russia acquired territories along the left and right banks of the Amur River; Polish artillery battalions were then sent to these newly acquired lands, and the new city of Nikolaevsk-on-Amur became their main base.

The appearance in the Far East of these "ready-made Catholics" was an unspeakably joyous event for the French Catholic missions that had been established in China in the fifteenth century. French missionaries now hastened to take advantage of the opportunity to make contact with these Polish Catholics. It was this development that prompted both tsarist officials and the Russian emperor himself to send "their own" Catholic priests to the Far East. Thus was the basis laid for the establishment of Roman Catholic parishes on the distant borders of Russia. In the present monograph the activity of practically all Catholic priests who served in the Far East of the Russian Empire is described.

We obtained historical documents and the names of Catholic priests who served in the Far East from the Moscow State Archive, the St. Petersburg State Archive, and the archives in Minsk and Vitebsk, Belarus. Thanks to the spiritual care of Pope John Paul II and the primate of Poland as well as the practical concern of the Warsaw Bureau of Aid to the Churches in the East, valuable historical documents concerning Polish priests who served in the Russian Far East were made available to us, and representatives of the archives of the Bernadine Fathers and the Ursuline Sisters in Kraków were also gracious to us. In addition, we also acquired very valuable historical data from our research of historical materials in the library of Jagellonian University in Kraków and the National Library in Warsaw. The author expresses her deepest gratitude to all benefactors, to all who helped make it possible for this monograph to be brought forth into the world.

No less interesting, in our opinion, are the materials that tell of the rebirth of the Roman Catholic parish of Vladivostok. It must be noted that this rebirth became possible only because of the selfless assistance of Catholic organizations in the USA, which organized in 1992 the delivery of food, medicine and clothing for the people of the Russian Far East. But it was the arrival of Fr. Myron Effing and Fr. Daniel Maurer that marked the re-establishment of the Catholic parish, which for all practical purposes had been annihilated in 1937. Because the church building itself was then occupied by the Regional Archive, the newly revived parish took shelter, like a "poor relative," in various meeting halls, renting space at clubs and "Palaces of Culture."

When the Archive moved to its new building, the Catholics had the opportunity to return to their "native" house. But this house was in a terrible condition. It immediately needed major repairs, which meant large sums of money. The Vladivostok parishioners, of course, had no means of raising such monies—so Fr. Effing turned once again to American Catholics. Vladivostok Catholics worshipped for ten years in a partially restored church, while grand plans for the reconstruction of their church were being carried out. The church has now taken on its original majestic appearance, with groups of snow-white columns. The windows, which had been screened and barred up like prison windows, now show beautiful stained glass work, like "pages" of Biblical scenes well known to all Catholics.

The cathedral was joyfully rededicated February 3, 2008—one hundred years after the cornerstone had been laid and eighty years after the execution of five parishioners, which effectively suppressed the Roman Catholic Church in the Russian Far East until religious freedom was restored in 1991.

Miroslava Teresa Efimova

I

Historical Background

In the first half of the eighteenth century, during the reigns of Augustus II (1697-1733) and Augustus III (1736-1763), the Polish government fell into complete disarray. When most of the nobility urged the king to an alliance with Sweden instead of Russia, 18,000 Russian troops set foot upon Polish soil under the leadership of Prince Iurii Dolgorukii. The Polish Sejm (Parliament) was forced to enter into the "Warsaw Treaty" (1717), under which Russia received the right to be the guarantor of Poland's internal affairs. Then in 1732 the three neighbors of Poland—Prussia, Austria and Russia—signed the "Treaty of the Black Eagles," under which they agreed not to allow any changes in the structure of the Polish government. Thereafter the boundaries of Poland became "slippery," and Russian troops began to move freely about the territory of Poland and beyond. The Poles tried to protest, but in answer to their protests Russia began to construct military bases on Polish lands, bases that became part of the typical Polish landscape.

Augustus III died in 1763 after nearly 30 years on the throne,[1] and the election of the new king by the Sejm was conducted un-

1 Translator's Note: He is poorly regarded in Polish history. "… he neither spoke Polish nor liked Poland. Apart from the period 1733-1736 and his unwill-

der the strict surveillance of Russian troops. The vote went to the Lithuanian nobleman, Stanisław August Poniatowski, the candidate favored by Catherine II (1762-1796).

Soon after his coronation King Stanisław August took measures leading to the improvement of the governmental apparatus. In the Sejm, Prince Andrzej Zamoyski initiated a program of new reforms, including adoption of the "rule of the majority," in place of the "rule of unanimity," a change that was expected to give the work of the Sejm a collegial character.[2]

The Sejm demanded the integrity of Polish territories, the expulsion of Russian troops, and increasing the Polish Army to 100,000. (The Treaty of Warsaw had limited the Polish Army to 24,000.)

The Prussian king Frederick II was hostile to any reforms that might stabilize Poland, and in keeping with ideas she had long nurtured, Catherine II protested in general against all the reforms contemplated by the Poles. "From the archives" came forth the idea of the rule of the Russian tsar over the Orthodox in Poland. This meant that Catherine was able to deport Orthodox residents of Poland deep into Russia, beyond Lake Baikal—including Old Believers.

The stifling presence of Russia in all aspects of Polish life eventually resulted in a broad resistance movement that centered in Bar, Podolia. The dissidents became known as the Confederates of Bar. The ideas of the Confederates quickly spread through all of

---

ing stay in Warsaw during the Seven Years War (1756-1763), he spent in Poland altogether about two years. A dullard, with no interests outside the fine arts and only one passion—hunting, . . ." *The New Cambridge Modern History—Vol. VII - The Old Regime, 1713-63*, p. 381.

2 Translator's Note: The *liberum veto*, or "free vote," was instituted in 1652. It allowed the wrecking of any legislation if even one vote were cast against it and thus became a means of paralyzing the Sejm. In the twenty-eight Sejms that had occurred during the preceding sixty years, twenty-three were wrecked. Foreign powers (Prussia, France, Russia) were implicated in seventeen of these cases. The policy of Poland's neighbors was to ensure paralysis and anarchy. *Ibid.*, p. 389.

Poland and Ukraine. Even Russia's allies supported the Confederate movement: for example, the Confederates had depots, camps and hospitals in Austria and Saxony, and France provided instructors for the Confederates. But the very well trained Russian troops marched against the Confederates, and in heavy bloody fighting the Confederates were roundly beaten—and immediately thereafter began reprisals against those partisans taken prisoner. Catherine II directed that "rank and file soldiers be sent to the army of General Rumiantsev and dispersed in the provinces of Kazan, Orenburg, Ufa, Tobolsk and deep into Russia," i.e., into Siberia.

At the same time, those rank and file Confederates who agreed to convert to Orthodoxy were freed from Siberian exile, awarded eighteen rubles, and released at the Polish border. Old and sick officers, invalids, were also released from Siberian exile and returned to Poland. Young and healthy Confederates, however, were sent as "Cossack settlers," i.e., they were sent to Siberia in order to populate the empty land and to form "Cossack villages" there that would serve as border defense.

After they had exiled and punished the Bar Confederates, Austria, Prussia and Russia came to an agreement concerning the partition of Polish lands, and in 1772, in St. Petersburg, they signed an agreement that became known as the First Partition of Poland. Austria took the southern Polish lands (Galicia), which included approximately 83,000 square km with a population of 2.6 million. Prussia took the mouth of the Vistula River (the Gdańsk Coast with Varmia), part of Greater Poland and Kuiava, which amounted to 36,000 sq km and 580,000 people. Russia took the greatest territory, to the east of the Dvina and Dnieper—92,000 sq km and 1.3 million people. With these divisions, Poland was now cut off from the Baltic. The land grabbers then demanded that the Polish Sejm confirm this division of Polish lands!

But even though Poland lost a third of its territory and thirty percent of its population, it remained a European government and the spirit of the Polish people did not die out—on the contrary, it flourished. The king came to terms with the fate of the Bar Confederates and "revolutionary passions" calmed down.

In the autumn of 1788, the "Great Sejm" was convened in Warsaw. The participants were primarily young people, completely lacking in political experience. Thus the Sejm undertook bold resolutions—for example, the young deputies again demanded the expulsion of Russian troops from Polish lands, the increase of the Polish army to 100,000 troops, and the establishment of Poland's independence from Russia.

Finally, on May 3, 1791, a new Constitution was adopted, laying the foundation for a modern constitutional monarchy with a Parliament and an efficiently working government.

These innovations alarmed Catherine II, and thus once again the Russian army marched 100,000 troops onto Polish soil and quickly smashed the opposition of the 60,000 Polish troops. There then immediately occurred what has become known as the Second Partition of Poland. In the winter of 1793 Prussian troops occupied Gdańsk, Torun, part of Mazovia, Częstochowa and other cities, and Russia again "sliced off" for herself the eastern lands of Poland, east of the Drui and Zbruch Rivers. Austria did not participate in the Second Partition. For the confirmation of the results of this robbery, it was nevertheless necessary for the consent of the Polish Sejm, which was convened in Grodnensk Castle by force and intimidation. But the Sejm remained silent the whole night. Then the marshal of the Sejm, Stanisław Belinski, was forced to acknowledge the silence of the Sejm as its "silent agreement" to the partition of the fatherland....

After this shameful act, patriotic elements of Polish society accused King Stanisław August of treason, and on March 24, 1794, a new uprising broke out in Poland, headed by a Polish officer, a hero in the War of American Independence, Tadeusz Kościuszko.[3]

3 *Polskie dzieje* [Polish History], Warszawa: Wydawnictwo Naukowe, 1994, p. 158.

Kościuszko's troops comprised approximately 2,000 peasants, armed with knives and picks, but despite such primitive weaponry this peasant force in battle outside Racławice broke the Russian contingents and batteries. The military activities of Kościuszko's forces spread even into Lithuania, where insurgents under the leadership of the Polish colonel Jakub Jaśiński seized the city of Vilnius.

Desite its successes, the Insurrection gradually died down and soon the city of Vilnius was retaken, then contingents fighting at the Bug River suffered defeat. On October 10, 1794, Russian troops completely defeated Kościuszko's forces outside the village of Macewicz. The wounded Kościuszko was taken prisoner and imprisoned in the bastion of the Peter Paul Fortress in St. Petersburg and threatened with the death penalty. But the unexpected death of Catherine II in 1796 brought her son Paul I (1796-1801) to the throne. He granted clemency to Kościuszko and allowed him to go into emigration, thus joining a large number of Polish officers abroad.

All Polish officers taken prisoner were supposed to have been sent to Ekaterinoslav *gubernia*, but in 1797 Paul I transferred these officers to the Hussar squadron of the St. Petersburg Guard. In addition, some Polish officers of well-known families were released from prison "upon their word of honor," and they all isolated themselves on their estates. As for the rank and file soldiers of the Polish army, they were flogged, issued Russian army uniforms, and dispersed through the very most distant eastern provinces of Imperial Russia. In the tsar's Order they were referred to as "Poles—residents of former Russian provinces which now have been returned to the Empire."

During the course of military activities against the Kościuszko forces, Austria, Prussia and Russia in 1795 came to an agreement about a new and final partition of the Polish lands. Prussia took a large part of Mazovia along with Warsaw, as well as Lithuanian lands along the Neman River. Austria took Little Poland and Liublinshch up to the Pilits and Bug Rivers; and Russia took the lands east of the Bug and Neman Rivers, including Courland. This was the Third Partition of Poland, whereby Poland completely lost its independence and was removed from the political map of the world for more than a hundred years. On the Polish lands seized by Russia, Prussia and Austria, the occupiers immediately established their laws, they introduced their language, they designated their officials and leaders, they increased taxes, and they began to conscript young Poles into their national armies.

Stanisław August Poniatowski, the last Polish king, was taken to Grodno where they forced him to sign an act of abdication of the throne. For three years the former Polish monarch lived in oblivion in the Grodno castle, then Paul I invited him to St. Petersburg. On his first evening in St. Petersburg, he was invited to dine in the Imperial Palace—and that night the former Polish king suddenly died....

All strata of the Polish population felt the loss of the independence of the Polish government—all Poles were deprived of their political and civil rights. Courts were closed, organs of local self-government were dispersed, and the Catholic clergy suffered as well, since Lutheranism was the predominant religion in Prussia, and Orthodoxy in Russia, and the Catholic Church in Austria strictly controlled the activity of Polish priests, forbidding them any direct contact with the Vatican.

And nevertheless over this long period of time, not one generation of Poles acknowledged the legality of this partition of the Polish land and these foreign powers! Many patriotic Poles protested the grabbing actions of Russia, Prussia and Austria, and a large number of them joined the Polish legions of General Henryk Dombrowski that were quartered in northern Italy together with the French forces of Napoleon Bonaparte. In ten years, approximately 25,000 Poles were enlisted in the ranks of these Polish legions.

In 1812 Napoleon began his war with Russia, and because he promised them he would return all their lands, the Poles agreed to fight on his side in the Polish Corps. But Napoleon lost the war with Russia. Russian troops took many captives—and the fate of the Polish captives was a foregone conclusion: they were all sent to distant Siberian provinces. After victory over Napoleon in 1815, at the Congress of Vienna, the monarchs of Prussia and Austria attempted to grab all the Polish lands for themselves, but Alexander I also wanted to seize for himself as much of the land of the Republic as he could—as the result of lengthy negotiations, most of the Polish lands remained part of the Russian Empire, to be known as the "Congress Kingdom of Poland."

In 1815, Alexander I (1801-1825) came to Warsaw to sign the Constitution of the Congress Kingdom of Poland. The new Constitution of the Congress Kingdom of Poland guaranteed the existence of the Polish Sejm, the Polish government, a Polish army and also the inviolability of person and property, and the freedom and equality of religious faiths. But even though the Constitution guaranteed Poles personal and civil freedoms, in fact things turned out differently: censorship was introduced, the secret police and spies became quite active and the Sejm was not convened. Religious freedoms were not observed either—for example, Catholic priests were required to submit all their sermons to the censor and many Catholic feasts were forbidden.

These constraints led to the growth of dissatisfaction in the Polish Army, and eventually to a hidden dissatisfaction at absolutely all levels of the population. It gave birth to underground circles and societies. Clearly a storm was brewing.

In the summer of 1830 the French overthrew the Bourbon dynasty, and then the Belgians ceded from Holland and established themselves as an independent government. These events were very unsettling to Nicholas I (1825-1855) because they disturbed the order that had been established by the Congress of Vienna, and he decided to send Polish troops into Belgium for "pacification." But the Poles had no desire to be the "gendarmes of Europe"[4] and they staged an uprising which has become known in history as the "November Insurrection." On the evening of November 29, 1830, the conspirators attacked the Belvidere Palace, the residence of the Grand Duke Constantine. But the conspirators were not successful—the viceroy,

4 Regarded from 1812 to 1815 as the "savior of Europe," Russia under Nicholas I became known as the "gendarme of Europe."

having been warned about the danger, had managed to flee with his family from Warsaw.

The Insurrection encompassed the lands of Lithuania, Ukraine and Belorussia. To crush such an expansive insurrection, Russia would need a large force—and Russia indeed had adequate troops at the places of conflict. Therefore, despite the unlimited self-sacrifice of the Polish people of all levels of society, the supremacy of the Russian military was unarguable. After Warsaw was taken, the remaining Polish Army and its commander-in-chief with 20,000 officers and soldiers fled abroad. Many very well-known Poles emigrated at that time—Joachim Lelewel, Adam Mickiewicz, Juliusz Slowacki, Zigmunt Krasinski, Cyprian Norwid, Frederic Chopin, and many other Polish patriots.

Nicholas I tried to establish that the Catholic Church had organized the uprising in order to lay his evidence before the Pope and thus justify his repression of the Catholic Church. He did not like Catholics and he did not like Poles. He often said that he wanted to dedicate his reign and government to the "struggle with Polishness." In reality the Catholic Church was not involved in the organization of the Insurrection. As for the participation of individual members of the Catholic hierarchy, most of the bishops took a negative attitude toward the Insurrection, as they believed it was doomed to fail.

Inasmuch as the parish priests were not well off, being paid only 200 złotys a year, those that were supportive of the rebels were only able to contribute small sums to the Insurrection—twenty to thirty zlotys, or in some cases as little as one or two złotys. These priests collected contributions for the Insurrection among their parishioners in the form of family valuables—but given the poverty of their congregations these collections were also very meager. The most productive collection turned out to be that of extra or damaged bells in the counties of Kraków, Lublin, Mazovetsk, and Polotsk—which yielded 240 tons of bells. From these it was possible to make approximately sixty-five cannons! The priests also collected unused church linens which were sent to the hospitals to be used as bandaging materials for the wounded. Almost all the religious orders engaged in the charitable care of wounded rebels.

Some priests joined the political club of Warsaw, the Patriotic Society: Aleksandr Puławski, Ignacij Szynglarski, Jósef Gazki, Pawel Rzymski, Ludwig Tencerowski and others. This club did not promote any political slogans, but when it came to the defense of Warsaw, the priests called upon everyone to take up arms.

Polish Eastern Rite Catholics found themselves in an interesting position with respect to the November Insurrection. Catherine II had absolished the Eastern Rite and Paul I was also antagonistic toward Eastern Rite Catholics—thus vis-à-vis the Russian Empire they were neither this nor that, neither fish nor fowl, neither Catholic nor Orthodox.

The reaction of the Russian government to the Insurrection was harsh: the autonomy of the Kingdom of Poland was abolished, the Sejm and the Polish Army were dispersed, the Constitution was changed, and for twenty-seven years the Kingdom was on a military standing. The property of 3,000 estates that belonged to participants in the Insurrection was confiscated, and approximately 50,000 families of the lower level of Polish nobility were exiled deep into Russia, to Siberia....

Thus once again several hundreds of thousands of Catholics experienced this coercive and painful expansion of the lands of the Russian Empire and the majority of them never returned to Poland. It was these political exiles who formed the first Catholic parishes in the European part of Russia and in her distant Asian *gubernia*s.[5] In addition, several tens of thousands of Polish soldiers were inducted into the ranks of the Russian Army and dispatched to the Caucasus or Siberia. Over the course of twenty years, Russian authorities recruited approximately 200,000 young Poles into the Russian Army where, under the most severe discipline, they served twenty-five years! On the territory of the former Kingdom of Poland, all educational institutions were closed, all centers of learning, all scholarly

5 Bolesław Kumor, "Niedziela," No. 2, 1992.

libraries—and in addition all the scholarly collections associated with these institutions were carted off to Russia. Poland had neither its own government nor its own army. The Eastern Rite Catholic Church was abolished. Hundreds of Catholic convents and monasteries were liquidated.

At the end of 1831, the Russian government announced an amnesty for participants of the November Insurrection, but this was a deceit because they quickly rounded up all those Poles who returned from European emigration and conscripted them into the Russian Army. Those who were imprisoned were sent under guard to Siberia and the Caucasus. Inasmuch as all these young people confessed the Catholic faith, it came to be that on the territory of an Orthodox government, its authorities had once again coercively settled a huge number of Catholics who would be in need of contact with Catholic priests. One can see that the Lord looked after those rebels, because among the participants were many clerics who were also sent to Siberia. All these priests shared the heavy lot of their co-religionists and rendered them spiritual support.

It would seem that such cruel repressions would once and for all root out the rebellious spirit of the Poles. But there gradually brewed a new insurrection—its beginning can be noted in the spring of 1863. It was very poorly planned. The forces were unequal: uncoordinated Polish brigades numbering in all 20,000 to 30,000 men were met by a force of 100,000 very well trained and completely armed Russian troops. Although the European democracies supported the uprising, sending small groups from the Czech lands, Hungary, Italy and France, they did not manage to achieve a victory on behalf of the uprising Polish patriots. The governments of England, Austria and France in general limited themselves to dispatching diplomatic notes to the Russian emperor proposing that he grant autonomy to the Poles. Naturally, Alexander II ignored these proposals.

The rebels' Temporary National Government was placed in the hands of Romuald Traugutt (1826-1864), an experienced military man who had served as a Sublieutenant in the Russian Army. The tsar's generals were convinced that the peasants would not help the rebels, and they were not mistaken—most of the peasants broke off from the rebels. Many peasants even apprehended rebels and turned them over to the gendarmes. The uprising was doomed. In April 1864, dictator Romuald Traugutt was arrested and on August 5, 1864, he was hanged near Warsaw Citadel.

After the crushing of the January Insurrection, once again tens of thousands of the petty nobility from Lithuania and Poland were exiled deep into Siberia. The estates of those participating in the Insurrection were burdened with high taxes for many years and in order to wipe away the memory of those who had died in the Insurrection, families were sternly prohibited from wearing mourning. The Catholic Church was also subjected to cruel persecution inasmuch as a large number of Catholic pastors had participated in the Insurrection. In accordance with the verdicts of military judges, hundreds of priests were sent under guard to Siberia. They were settled, just like the prisoners, throughout the Siberian steppes and the taiga villages.

After the period of the November and January Insurrections, hundreds of thousands of Polish patriots had been exiled to Siberia. All these people, forcibly relocated to Siberia and other far-away places, needed the spiritual care of Catholic priests, of whom there were very few. For this reason, after the November Insurrection of 1830, the Russian government was forced to consider supporting, at the government's expense, four Catholic priests to serve in Siberia: two for the Tobolsk and Tomsk *gubernia*s and two for the Yenisey and Irkutsk *gubernia*s.[6] In addition to these priests, who were paid a stipend by the government, Catholic priests from various religious orders were also sent to Siberia to look after the spiritual needs of their co-religionist/prisoners.

One of the most outstanding Catholic priests of Siberia was Fr. Krzystóf Szwermicki (Lithuanian, Krzystupas Szwirmickas; 1814-1894). He was born in the village of Worpuniany of the Augustinow

---

6 K. Piotrowski, *Pamiętki z pobytu na Syberji* [Memoirs from My Time in Siberia], Warsaw: Biblioteka Narodowa.

gubernia. After completing the school run by the Marians of the Immaculate Conception in Mariampole, Krzystóf entered Warsaw University. At the time of the 1830 Insurrection, the 16-year-old youth joined the ranks of the rebels and was heavily wounded in a bloody battle with the Russian Army. In 1833, after his recovery, he entered the Marianist order in Mariampole, where upon his completion of studies he was ordained June 29, 1838. In 1844 he was already serving as the Superior at the monastery. He remained there some time, teaching novices, and in addition he was involved with the establishment of a school for deaf mutes. On December 6, 1846, the tsar's secret police conducted an unexpected search of the monastery, during which a little anti-tsarist booklet was discovered. This was serious grounds for the arrest of Fr. Szwermicki.

For approximately seven years he was imprisoned in Warsaw, then he was sent to Siberia in March 1852. After some time they allowed him to take up pastoral work associated with the Catholic Church of Irkutsk. On his suggestion, the Mogilev archbishop established Roman Catholic parishes in Siberia and the Far East—in Chita, Khabarovsk and Blagoveshchensk. He recommended that two priests serve at each post. One would make the pastoral circuit of all the numerous congregations in the surroundings, and the second would serve Catholics in the central parish. Each priest would thus be able to rely on the fraternal help and support of his co-worker. The vicar priest, Fr. Tyburcyj Pawłowski, assisted Fr. Krzystóf.

According to the testimony of contemporaries, Fr. Krzystóf was a staunch priest, his heart always open to all believers and therefore both Catholics and Orthodox respected him. The life of Catholic priests in Siberia was very difficult and not all of them dedicated all of their strength to the sincere service of their co-religionists. Concerning such, Fr. Krzystóf wrote: "…some priests arrive in Siberia 'non per Spiritum Dei, sed per spiritum mundi vocati [called not by the Spirit of God but by the spirit of the world].'[7] Having

---

7 Michal Janik, *Dzieje polaków na Syberji* [History of the Poles in Siberia], Kraków, 1928, p. 237.

received in Siberia a fine situation, they have forgotten the purpose of their being here and in a very short time their hearts and thoughts have been given over to greed for plunder, drunkenness and dissolution. Such a cleric, instead of an evangelical example, has become a lousy example, evoking disgust among his own co-religionists." In Fr. Szwermicki's opinion, these priests were concerned only with their own personal situation and in their eyes there always gleamed contempt for their flock. Fortunately, the majority of priests brought to Siberia a deep spirituality, the embryo of European civilization and orderliness that softened the harsh Siberian ways of life.

Judging by historical documents, the Irkutsk Catholic Church owes much to Fr. Szwermicki. He created a committee under the leadership of Major Bolesław Kukel, which took up the construction of a brick church to replace the wooden church that had burned down. On December 8, 1884, the congregation celebrated the dedication of the beautiful new Gothic-styled Roman Catholic church, the construction of which had been financed by a 22,000 ruble contribution from the engineer Michal Kossowski. The church had a beautiful wooden Gothic altar, designed in Lithuania by Walerian Kulikowski and a wonderful organ that was brought from St. Petersburg. Adorning the steeple was a large cross, the gift of the Decembrist Mikhail Lunin who had converted to Catholicism before his death. Fr. Szwermicki urged his compatriots to good works, being convinced that a people who had neither its own government nor its own army could become strong only through achievements in culture and economics. He often brought forward the example of the cultural development of Poles who lived in the Caucasus. His sermons were always filled with appeals to love one's neighbor and with concern for the unification of the Polish people.

Zealously concerned about the Irkutsk church and its congregation, Fr. Krzystóf also willingly took up missionary work, traveling throughout all the far-flung villages of Eastern Siberia. Fr. Szwermicki left as his legacy a book of recollections that describes his difficult travels through the places of his compatriots' exile: Journal of Travels Through the Amur Regions and the Provinces of the Irkutsk Gubernias to Tend to the Spiritual Needs of Catholics, March 26, 1859—January 15, 1860.[8] It should be noted that the military governor of the province, Count Muraviev-Amursky, seriously supported the travels of the Catholic priest through the Far East. He describes them thus: "…journeys for bringing spiritual sustenance to Catholic exiles on the Amur and to those settlers who have emigrated to these lands in the last three years."

In 1863 Alexander II granted exiled Poles the same rights as all tax-paying Russians. The exiles could return to Poland, however, only under the condition that their native community would guarantee that the returning Poles would pay all the taxes on their property and land-holdings. If the community would not give such a guarantee, then those returning could settle on the permission of the authorities, but they would be deprived of the right of inheritance to the land and other property. For these and other reasons, not everyone returned to their native lands. Fr. Krzystóf visited Catholics who had remained behind in Kiakhta, Buriatia, Argun, Albazin, and then Blagoveshchensk. There was still no house of prayer in Blagoveshchensk and therefore Fr. Krzystóf celebrated Mass in the home of a Pole, a company captain. The Mass was attended by three officers, one clerk, forty-five soldiers, two women and two male civilians.

When he arrived in Nikolaevsk, Fr. Szwermicki stayed at the home of the Pole Laskowski. He then went by sea to Okhotsk and he got as far as Ayan and Yakutsk. Now winter set in and he clothed himself in appropriate winter attire: rabbit-skin socks, footwear made from deerskin, a hooded fur coat made of the skins of young deer, and over all this a huge sheepskin coat. On his head he wore a fur cap with ear muffs. Fr. Krzystóf was accompanied on this exotic and difficult journey by the Pole Rudolf Zaremba. In Yakutsk,

---

8 "Pamiętnik Relegijnie—Moralny, za 1861 [Religious and Moral Diary for 1861]."

a warm meeting with Governor Steubendorf, a Protestant, awaited him. He returned to Irkutsk January 26, 1860.[9]

In the Far East Fr. Krzystóf discovered in all 323 Catholic men and 26 Catholic women. They were primarily soldiers and clerks as well as several criminals who had been sent into exile. To his great dismay, Catholic children were being raised in Siberia without religion. But what a huge joy and religious feast it was for Catholics whom fate had dispersed into such places when a Catholic priest managed to reach them. In half an hour all the residents of the village knew of the priest's arrival and hurried to pay him a visit. Everything Polish flowed forth from trunks into the light of day—Polish holiday dress, ribbons, caps, religious books and prayer books that for a year or two had lain without use. Then they all hurried to Mass that was said in one of the more spacious homes. Naturally not everyone could fit, but no one grumbled, listening to Mass by the doors or windows. The house where the priest stayed was filled with people from morning to late evening—his arrival was a religious holiday. During his visit the children were baptized, the newlyweds were blessed and the funeral rites for the long-ago deceased were sung. Fr. Krzystóf always conducted his meetings with Catholics in a very joyous, but solemn manner. He said that he mixed his tears with those of the faithful, and that these were tears of repentance for what in his opinion was an insufficiently zealous service of God. Thus passed three or four days and then he hurried on to the next village where there awaited him still other Christian souls….

Fr. Krzystóf wanted to encompass with his pastoral visits absolutely all places where Catholics were living, but alas, the complete absence of roads did not allow him to visit all the faraway corners of the Far East taiga. After the Far East, he went also to Buriatia, where he came upon the exiled Franciszik Belewski and his com-

9 Russian settlement at Yakutsk dates back to 1632. Situated on the Lena River, it was the starting point of the rugged 650-mile trek to Okhotsk. Okhotsk was first settled in 1647; Ayan, in 1844. For more information, see James P. Gibson, *Imperial Russia in Frontier America* (New York: Oxford Univ. Press, 1976).

rade in misfortune. In Argun he came upon seventy young Catholics whom the Russian authorities had designated as Cossacks.[10] No less interesting were the encounters with Catholics in Blagoveshchensk, Khabarovsk, Mariinsk, Sofisk, and Nikolaevsk, from where he went by sea to Ayan and then to Yakutsk. The conclusions of his travel were disconcerting: the adults still remembered God, but the children were now growing up without religion....

Summing up the results of his observations during the period of his travels, he sadly wrote that the Polish nationality was melting in the sea of Russian social life, that their Catholic roots were gradually being lost, and that it was only Catholic churches and Catholic priests that would be able to save the Poles from dissolving in the Russian hinterlands. But one priest, even a very diligent priest, would not be able to solve such a fundamental problem.

Perhaps it was for this reason that Fr. Krzystóf did not take advantage of the amnesty of 1855 and return to Poland. He continued to voluntarily serve in Irkutsk in order to help his co-religionists and their offspring. Seeing the heavy lot of the exiled Polish intellectuals, he convinced the local authorities of Irkutsk to organize trade guilds. Having completed a course of study in such a guild, having acquired the ability to take up one or another trade, the exiled Catholics would then be able not only to earn their bread, but also to have a decent income that would allow them to fully support their families.

The heartfelt dedication of Fr. Szwermicki to God and the Catholics was well known to the Roman curia inasmuch as his parish came under the jurisdiction of the Congregation for the Propagation of the Faith. In 1888, in honor of the fiftieth anniversary of Fr. Szwermicki's ordination, Pope Leo XIII sent him his blessing, a chalice and a prayer book and named him the "Apostle of Siberia." It would seem that such sincere, God-pleasing activity on the part

10 Cossacks were peasants who lived in autonomous communal settlements; in return for special privileges they served in the cavalry under the tsars and provided border defense.

of the priest would have evoked the universal respect of Catholics—but in January 1894 he was brutally beaten by unknown assailants. He never recovered from his injuries, and died November 20, 1894. On the same day, November 20, 1894, the local Irkutsk newspaper, *Vostochnoe obozrenie* [The Eastern Review], in issue number 144 wrote: "Many sighs of grief and sadness were heard from the lips of Catholics and Orthodox when one of the greatest priests of the nineteenth century was laid to rest in the harsh and cold Siberian land…."

At that time many figures of the Catholic Church began to wonder aloud, what sort of future did the Catholic Church have in Russia? With a Catholic population of well over three million on lands within the Russian Empire, the Catholic Church experienced various forms of persecution through administrative decrees and penalties that seriously impeded her legitimate pastoral care for her members.

Even the matter of accurately determining the number of Catholics on Russian soil was fraught with difficulties and the numbers relied upon were often underreported. It was to the government's advantage that the number of believers with respect to number of parishes and deaneries would be lower, as this would allow it to close down the smaller parishes, expropriate Catholic churches, and decrease the number of dioceses.

As early as 1832 the Senate deprived priests of the right of ministry if any among them dared to spread Catholicism among the Russian population.

In accordance with a decree of December 16, 1839, the construction of new Catholic churches and chapels was forbidden as well as the repair of those churches already built.

The struggle against the Eastern Rite Catholics also grew in strength. As early as 1839 Nicholas I strictly forbade Eastern Rite Catholics to be allowed to receive Holy Communion in Latin Rite Catholic churches—and a decree of March 20, 1840, strictly forbade the conversion of Orthodox and Eastern Rite Catholics to the Latin Rite Catholic faith. Severe decrees such as these followed one after another. For example, on June 6, 1842, Nicholas I ordered that Catholic priests should turn over to Orthodox priests lists of those Eastern Rite Catholic families who had converted to the Latin Rite.

In 1866 a decree was issued prohibiting processions and liturgies beyond the bounds of any Catholic church and its courtyard. Violation of the prohibition would allow the authorities to seize the church. A still more dangerous innovation for the Catholic Church was the Russian government's plan to russify the Polish and Belorussian Catholics. To this end, supplemental prayers in the Russian language were literally imposed in the Catholic churches. It was supposed that after this innovation there would remain only one step toward Orthodoxy. But although there did occur isolated cases of conversion, the majority of Catholics did not desire to become Orthodox.

During the reign of Alexander II Russian authorities abolished the Kamenetsk-Podolsk and the Minsk Roman Catholic Dioceses, and the Warsaw Theological Academy as well. In 1875, the Kholmsk Diocese, the last Eastern Rite Catholic Diocese, was abolished. It had been in union with Rome since 1830. Rome then forbade Catholic bishops to participate in the work of the Russian religious Collegium. It was only around the middle of 1870 that Alexander II began leaning toward a liberalization of relations with the Catholic Church, as the result of which in 1894 diplomatic relations with the Papal See were reestablished. Nonetheless, most of the rich and powerful in St. Petersburg continued to have a suspicious attitude toward Poles, seeing them as instruments of the Roman Catholic Church, expanding Catholicism within the Russian domain.

Such was the state of affairs with respect to the Catholic Church in Russia in the second half of the nineteenth century, when the Russian Empire began to expand its holdings in the Far East, taking possession of new lands in the Amur River Basin and its tributaries.

II

The First Priest for the Russian Far East

"The Manchurian Monsignor Verrolles, Bishop of Peking, expresses his gratitude for the assistance rendered to his missionary. He was surprised, however, to learn that the missionary had been officially informed that without a special order from St. Petersburg priests of foreign faiths are not to evangelize or conduct religious services [in Primorye]. The prelate was certain that Primorye belonged to Manchuria and was thus part of his diocese, which had been established by the Apostolic See and could not be altered by any other authority."[11]

--Communiqué of the Russian Ambassador in Peking

In the first half of the nineteenth century the government of the Russian Empire developed and strengthened programs for the expansion of its possessions in the Far East. Various geographical expeditions were deployed to further these ends. As part of the work of the Amur Expedition of 1848, G. I. Nevelskoi, traveling on the transport *Baikal*, explored the northern and southern channels at

11 Primorye was only acquired by Russia in 1858; prior to that it was part of Manchuria.

the mouth of the Amur River and also determined that Sakhalin was separated from the mainland by a channel. The senior officer of the *Baikal*, Lieutenant Peter Vasilievich Kazakevich (later, from 1856 to 1865, the military governor of Primorye), was the first to set sail on the Amur River, going up as far as the settlement of Chadbakh. The first Russian settlement, "Peter's Winter Quarters," was established June 29, 1850, by G. I. Nevelskoi and D. I. Orlov on the sandy spit right near the mouth of the Amur River. It served as the base of the Amur Expedition in its early years. For the founding of Peter's Winter Quarters, Nevelskoi was awarded the St. George Medal, 4th Degree.[12]

In the following year, 1851, forty versts up the Amur River, a new outpost was established, the future city of Nikolaevsk, to which the headquarters of the Amur Expedition was then transferred. A beautiful, natural deepwater harbor, sheltered from the main channel by a natural spit, allowed sea-faring vessels to enter the harbor. The new port soon had a garrison and the beginnings of a naval squadron, the future Amur Flotilla. The soldiers of the garrison came mostly from the lower ranks of the so-called Eastern Siberian Line Battalions, which for the most part were recruits that had been gathered in the former Polish *gubernia*s. By the directive of Catherine II, such politically unreliable contingents had been sent either to the Caucasus or Eastern Siberia, as far as possible from the Polish lands. A similar situation obtained with the naval squadron. Thus in the young city of Nikolaevsk there was a concentration of persons who confessed the Catholic faith by virtue of their national heritage. They were all in need of pastoral care, sometimes waiting months or years to meet

12 The feat was so highly valued because the Russian Empire, which had established a settlement on the North Pacific as early as 1647, had been unable to locate the entry into the Amur River, which is five to six miles wide at its mouth. Access to the river would allow easier access from Irkutsk to the Pacific—and Alaska. The fact that Nevelskoi's camp was based on land that by treaty belonged to China may have been problematic, but there were no adverse consequences as China was preoccupied with other troubles.

with a Catholic priest, all the while firmly refusing to convert to the Orthodox faith.

In 1861, the foundation of the city of Blagoveshchensk was made at the confluence of the Amur and Zeya Rivers [approximately 800 miles upstream from Nikolaevsk]. A member of the Amur Expedition, Nikolai Vasilievich Busse (1828-1866), became the first governor of the center of the Amur Region. Soldiers of the Thirteenth Line Artillery Battalion under the command of Major N. Yazykov were the first builders and settlers of the new city. The settlement quickly took on an "urban appearance"—they built a two-story clubhouse, in which they had an excellent choir ensemble, a wind orchestra and an excellent conductor. There were often musical evenings in the club, which also had a fine library as well as a billiard room and snack bar. Soon the new settlement even had a boarding school for girls, similar to the Institute for Noble Girls [*Institut blagorodnykh devits*], and in 1862 the Naval *Shturmanskii* School and a grammar school for sailors also opened.

Formally Eastern Siberia and all the Far East, including Sakhalin Island, belonged to the Irkutsk parish, led by Krzystóf Szwermicki, but his isolated visits throughout the territory were clearly insufficient. French missionaries from northern Manchuria, where their mission had been active since 1650, hastened to the Far East when they learned of the settlement of European Catholics there. All the efforts of these missionaries to convert the Amur natives to Christianity had been unsuccessful and had ended in tragedy. For example, at the mouth of the Amur River the French missionary Fr. de la Brunier had been viciously killed by local natives. A similar drama had played out at the mouth of the Bureya River, where another French missionary had perished. Now these missionaries were counting on acquiring already baptized European Catholics who were settling in places that were well known to the missionaries. They ignored the fact that the Amur lands had become the possession of the Russian Empire in the late 1850s.

In a secret missive of August 3, 1865, the governor general of Eastern Siberia communicated the following to the governors of the Amur and Primorye districts:

> Catholic evangelization in China, Manchuria and Korea at the present time has taken on a very efficient organization. The French missionaries, having huge resources at their disposal and being very well acquainted with the mores and customs of the native inhabitants, have complete influence over the natives. Traveling for their purposes throughout all of China, in recent times they have begun to show up at our borders, and even within the bounds of Russia. But since in accordance with the clear precepts of our laws (See *Svod zakonov, T. XI, Ust. Dukh. Del Inostr. Ispov., St. 4* [Code of Laws, Statutes of Religious Affairs Concerning Foreign Confessions, Statute 4]), only the Orthodox Church has the right to spread its teaching within the bounds of governmental territory, I most respectfully ask Your Excellency not to allow foreign missionaries within the bounds of the district that has been entrusted to you under any circumstance, all the more so since those missionaries, given that they know the native languages, could pursue other goals as well. In particular, I ask you not to allow any dealings between political criminals and foreigners.[13]

One can imagine how seriously these words were taken by the governor general of the Amur Region who well understood that East Siberia needed its own Catholic priest. But what was he to do, since

---

13 RGIA, f. 822, op. 4, d. 683, l. 5, 6, 6 ob. RGIA is the Russian State Historical Archive, and the abbreviations f. (fond), op. (opis), d. (delo), l. (list) and ob. (obverse) are standard archival notations and are used throughout.

at that time all important government business was decided only in St. Petersburg! Governor General Korsakov dispatched messages to the Russian capital with a request that there be assigned to the Amur Region a special Catholic priest who would enjoy the same rights and stipend as those granted to the head of the Irkutsk parish, Fr. Krzystóf Szwermicki. After long consideration, the Minister of Internal Affairs expressed his support of the request, for he came to the conclusion that the head of the Irkutsk Roman Catholic parish could not possibly tend to the needs of all the Catholics of the Far East. In a letter of January 21, 1866, the Minister wrote:

> The head of the Irkutsk Roman Catholic church, by his position, is obligated to make an annual visitation of the Amur Region in order to attend to the religious needs of his co-religionists. He is not able to accomplish this, however, owing to the expansiveness of the territory as well as to the significant number of political criminals of the Catholic faith who have been transported to Eastern Siberia. For this reason, Catholics of the Amur Region have for several years been completely deprived of spiritual care.[14]

Further on he adds:

> The absence of a staff Roman Catholic priest in the Amur Region deprives the local leadership of a firm and plausible basis for prohibiting the entry [onto Russian territory] of Catholic missionaries from Manchuria and it even possibly gives rise to secret contacts between those missionaries and the inhabitants of the Catholic faith in our Amur possessions.

14 RGIA, f. 822, op. 4, d. 683, l. 80.

In the same document, the Minister of Internal Affairs concludes that it is necessary to organize a Roman Catholic parish in the Far East and he sees the possibility of paying the future Catholic priest a stipend of 600 rubles a year.

This whole assortment of convincing arguments was rightly understood and accepted at all levels of authority in St. Petersburg. It remained only to receive the consent of Alexander II, and this consent was in fact granted on February 18, 1866. By a Supreme Order, a special Roman Catholic priest was assigned to the Amur Region with the same rights and stipend of 600 rubles a year as had been granted to the head of the Irkutsk parish. Despite the Supreme Order, however, the Minister of Finance showed himself to be quite strict in his vigilance regarding monetary disbursements from the State Treasury. He directed the following remarks to Governor General Korsakov:

> Dear Sir, on the grounds of Supreme Order No. 124 dated September 29, 1865, concerning the non-allowance of the above-mentioned disbursements, I am not able to consent to the release of the designated 600 rubles from the State Treasury. I further consider it my duty to add that if you consider this disbursement necessary, then in my opinion it would be appropriate to charge it against the funds that have been assigned to the accounts of the Ministry of Internal Affairs for the stipends for Roman Catholic clergy.

After a lengthy bureaucratic correspondence, the question of the financial arrangements was resolved and now it remained only to find the place for the organization of the future parish. On the advice of the experienced missionary, Fr. Krzystóf Szwermicki, the young, quickly growing Far East port city of Nikolaevsk was selected. Lieutenant General Korsakov also supported this advice. He wrote the following: "I have the honor of informing you that from my perspective, I find the most suitable place for the location of the Roman

Catholic parish of the Amur District to be the city Nikolaevsk since the military are concentrated in this location and therefore the number of persons of the Catholic faith is much larger than elsewhere in the Amur District." Further, in accordance with the Supreme Order, the Vicar General of the Mogilev Roman Catholic Archdiocese, Bishop Maximilian Stanewski, was advised that he should select a candidate for the post of staff priest of the Amur Region. Having received such a responsible assignment, communicated by Minister of Internal Affairs P. A. Valuev, Bishop Stanewski responded that simply naming a priest to the Amur Region might turn out to be a useless proposition. He therefore proposed the post to several clergymen who might then request to be assigned to the post. As a result there was found a volunteer, the vicar of the Roman Catholic parish of the city of Ulla, Vitebsk *gubernia*, Fr. Kazimierz Ignatiewicz Radziszewski.[15]

In accordance with the rules of that time, it was necessary to verify the political reliability of the proposed candidate. The Department of Religious Affairs submitted a questionnaire to the Vitebsk *gubernia*. The chancellery of the Vitebsk governor soon issued an official statement that "the vicar priest of the Roman Catholic church of the city of Ulla, Kazimierz Radziszewski, has not been singled out with respect to his political unreliability: he enjoys the respect of his office." To this confirmation was attached a brief biographical sketch of the candidate in which it was noted that Fr. Kazimierz had been born into the family of the nobleman Ignacyj Radziszewski of the Biisk district, Grodnensk *oblast* in 1838. The boy received his early education at home and then he studied at the Grodnensk five-grade school for children of the nobility, where he completed the full course of studies. In 1858 he enrolled in the Mogilev-Minsk seminary and upon graduation and ordination Fr. Kazimierz, on April 11, 1863, was assigned to the post of vicar to the Sokolnikow parish, Vitebsk *gubernia*. Soon thereafter he was transferred to the same post in the Roman Catholic parish in Ulla.

15 RGIA, f. 892, d. 683, l. 87.

What did this young priest experience when he received an assignment to a still non-existing parish at the "end of the world"? We can suppose that he considered the fulfillment of the Supreme Order as a matter of duty, but we cannot exclude the possibility that he also felt confusion and a lack of confidence in his own strength and knowledge. Who knows? In any event, he acted very circumspectly, going right away to St. Petersburg where he would be able to familiarize himself with the documents and maps there and also to take counsel with experienced missionary priests on whose shoulders had rested many years of similar service. The preparation for his future missionary activity was lengthy. On the advice of experienced missionaries, he composed a list of all that he would need for the activities of his new parish. He submitted an estimate and upon receipt of 1,169 rubles he purchased church vessels for the furnishing of his future chapel in Nikolaevsk and also appropriate items for ministering to Catholics in all the villages of the Far East.

His list included ciboria, chalices, vessels for church wine, holy water and anointing oil; sprinklers; molds for baking bread for the offertory; poor boxes; candlesticks; little bells; crosses for the altar and sacristy; various icons, church books and many other items. The question regarding the stipend for the young priest was under discussion for some time. As a result of various agreements, he received the same compensation (600 rubles a year) as that paid to Fr. Szwermicki, as well as round-trip travel expenses and other perquisites as set forth in accordance with the laws of the Empire.

The decree concerning the appointment of Fr. Radziszewski as priest to Nikolaevsk was signed by Alexander II February 18, 1866,[16] but it was not until autumn 1867, more than a year and a half later, that the priest was able to arrive at his assignment. The first question that arose concerned his residence, as housing was sorely lacking in the new town. Fr. Radziszewski thought to purchase for himself some sort of inexpensive little house, but inasmuch as he had only a very small amount of personal funds, he was only able to

16 RGIA, f. 822, op. 4, d. 1626, l. 1, 1 ob.

acquire a dilapidated hut, which he right away began to call his little "shack." To fix it up, one would have needed to re-do the walls and roof and to replace the stove—but the priest had neither the time nor the money. Thus it all remained as it was. His next task was to find a place for the chapel. The local authorities allowed him to select any building from a stock of unused buildings. After long inspections and reflection, he settled on the building of the former treasury. Somehow or other they cleaned up and painted this ramshackle building and the first Masses in the first Far East Roman Catholic chapel of Sts. Peter and Paul took place at the end of 1867. Then the twenty-nine-year-old Fr. Kazimierz set about his missionary work throughout all the cities and places of the Far East, a work that lasted more than twenty-five years.[17]

The young missionary from Grodnensk *gubernia*, where there were neither mountains nor powerful rivers nor sea channels nor thick taiga, learned everything. In the Far East Fr. Kazimierz came to know the harsh laws of the sea and the taiga. He learned how to find food in the taiga, the rivers and the sea. Along with other residents of Nikolaevsk, he stocked up on salmon when it was running, then he mastered the art of preparing seafoods—drying, smoking and salting. These skills allowed him to bring to his prisoner parishioners on Sakhalin Island not only the word of God's comfort, but also a little bit of food, which these unfortunate people desperately needed.

Because the majority of Fr. Kazimierz's parishioners were poor, living on the very edge of poverty, none was able to contribute to the offertory collections during Mass. As a result, the priest was also impoverished. It came in handy that he had learned to knit socks and stockings in the seminary. The private sale of knitted goods and salmon allowed Fr. Kazimierz to collect for his unfortunate Sakhalin

17 M. I. Efimova, "Katolicheskii khram Vladivostoka: Istoriia i sovremennost'," *Zapiski Obshchestva izucheniia Amurskogo kraiia* ["The Catholic Church of Vladivostok: Past and Present," Notes of the Society for Study of the Amur Region], v. xxxvi, 2, pp. 67-73.

sheep at least a little money, and, without any exaggeration, this is the picture we have of the missionary life of Fr. Kazimierz....

The official authorities of the Far East treated the Catholic priest with understanding and dutiful respect, but nonetheless he, like all Catholic clergymen, found himself under invisible but insistent control. He had to contend with a vigorous effort on the part of Russian authorities to uproot the Polish language from the Catholic liturgy. In a confidential communication of Lieutenant General Ivan Furguhelm dated December 19, 1876, from Irkutsk, we read the following:

> I enclose with this letter a copy of a Roman Catholic prayer book in the Russian language for your conveyance of same to the priest of the Amur Region, Fr. Radziszewski. I have the honor of requesting, Your Excellency, that the aforementioned prayer book be personally delivered to the aforementioned priest, and that he be given verbal instruction with great care, in order that he be warned to dispel any temptation on his part toward any activity counter to those measures adopted by the government concerning the performance of liturgy in the Russian language, and that under no circumstance should this directive be left unfulfilled.[18]

Unfortunately we do not know how Fr. Kazimierz reacted to this directive. It is not reflected in the documents. One can only suppose that a large part of the Polish Catholics living in the taiga wastelands or in prison barracks continued to pray in their native language and that their religious leader would have attempted not to force his flock to pray in Russian. On the other hand, he would have avoided any aggravation of relations with the Russian authorities in order not to harm his poor congregation.

---

18 RGIA DV, f. 1, d. 305, l. 20-23.

The unflagging industry, the deep spirituality and the moral integrity of the Far East Catholic pastor did not go unnoticed by the highest church authorities. On March 28, 1882, after sixteen years of service, he was granted the highest distinction—the golden pectoral cross. Most likely this award from the Catholic diocese heartened the indefatigable priest, who spent most of the year on the road. No matter how much he tried to arrange his travels such that he would go out to Sakhalin Island in the summer by ship, it never turned out that way. The parish was simply too expansive. Navigation on the Amur was only possible during five months of the year, and during that time he had to visit all the settlements along the Amur and its tributaries. In addition, he had to manage to visit the villages near Lake Khanka, the villages on the shores of the Ussuri and Iman Rivers—in other words, to travel throughout all of the Amur and Primorye regions. Thus it turned out that he was only able to get to northern Sakhalin during the winter, crossing the Tatar Strait on dogsled. The priest very rarely visited southern Sakhalin, which could have been reached by steamship. We know of all these complications from Fr. Kazimierz's extensive accounts in which he requested the religious authorities to transfer the center of the Roman Catholic congregation to Vladivostok.[19]

During twenty years of missionary activity, Fr. Radziszewski apparently became accustomed to all the inconveniences of his nomadic life—even the fact that his rundown little shack and the little chapel were often robbed. He was not able to come to terms, however, with the destruction of the chapel in Nikolaevsk. He often wrote to the Mogilev archdiocese insisting that the archdiocesan bureaucrats show some concern for finding means for repairing the chapel and his humble residence. No concrete actions or even decisions were made on the priest's requests, and the chapel collapsed before one's very eyes. The parish itself fell apart because the status of Nikolaevsk changed when in 1872 the military garrison was moved to Khabarovka and Nikolsk-Ussuriisk and the naval squadron was

19 RGIA, f. 821, op. 125, d. 683, l. 178-183 ob.

moved to Vladivostok. Fr. Kazimierz thus remained in Nikolaevsk practically without a congregation—unless one were to count a few dozen invalids and elderly residents.

Fr. Kazimierz thus concluded that it was time to officially transfer the center of the Roman Catholic parish from Nikolaevsk to Vladivostok and he sent his well-argued recommendations not only to the religious authorities but also to the military and civic authorities as well. On June 24, 1886, he directed to the Amur governor general Baron A. N. Korf an expansive report in which he set forth in great detail his suggestions and his arguments in support of transferring the center of the Roman Catholic parish to Vladivostok. In particular, he wrote that now that most of his soldier-parishioners had been transferred to Khabarovsk, to Vladivostok and its immediate surroundings, it was precisely there that it would be desirable to build the Catholic house of prayer.

During his pastoral visits to Vladivostok, Fr. Radziszewski usually stayed at the house of the Evangelical pastor and said Mass there. This was very uncomfortable inasmuch as most of the Catholic soldiers could not of course fit into the pastor's house and thus stood hearing Mass out on the street. There were approximately 2,000 Catholic soldiers in the garrison. If even only a half or a quarter of them attended Mass, fitting them into the house or on the street was complicated. Thus Fr. Kazimierz clearly realized that the first order of business was to construct a house of prayer and for this he would need to worry about acquiring a plot of land for the construction of both a house of prayer and a rectory.

Thanks be to God! the city council of Vladivostok on June 12, 1886, supported Fr. Kazimierz's official request and set forth as follows: "…place at the disposition and eternal possession a plot of land for the construction of a priest's residence and a house of prayer." In addition, one of Fr. Kazimierz's parishioners, Court Councillor Jan Janowicz Mancewicz, granted to the Roman Catholic parish a parcel of his own land which was adjacent to that which had been granted it by the city.

Unfortunately, Fr. Radziszewski was not able to maintain these parcels of land in good order and manage the building of a church inasmuch as he spent most of the year on pastoral visits throughout all the Far East. Therefore he turned to his own parishioners for their assistance. As he wrote in his report to the archdiocese:

> On the basis of Article 124, Chapter 2, Part 1 of Volume XI, *Code of Laws* [Svod zakonov], and on the basis of the third annex thereto, I have proposed to the parishioners four candidates (selected from among all the parishioners) for an election of trustees and elders of the Catholic parish of the Amur Region, which has been established by Supreme Order—namely, the following people: as elder, Senior State Councillor Ignacyj Osipowicz Makowski; the pharmacist of the Vladivostok Naval Hospital, Court Councillor Stanisław Fiedorowicz; the business manager of the Vladivostok Port, Court Councillor Jan Janowicz Mancewicz; and Capitan of the First East-Siberian Line Battalion Mieczysław Siewierinowicz Wolski. As result of the voting, Ignacyj Makowski and Stanisław Fiedorowicz have been named trustees.

In the same letter he raised the question of the transfer of his parish from Nikolaevsk to Vladivostok. His appeal found the support of the governors and the Metropolitan of the Mogilev Archdiocese, Alexandr Kazimierz Gintowt. But now the Roman Catholic Collegium, not waiting for a final resolution of the question concerning the transfer of the parish to Vladivostok, ordered that the repair of the priest's residence in Nikolaevsk should be suspended, if it had already been begun, until further disposition of the question.

Simultaneous with his concern about the official transfer of the parish to Vladivostok, Fr. Kazimierz took up the question of raising funds for the building of a brick church. Attempting to enlist both the church and civic authorities in support of his plan, Fr. Radziszewski began to send well-argued requests and found everywhere both understanding and support. It would seem then that in a very short period his plans and dreams would begin to come together. Alas, the very most important institution—the Most Holy Synod of the Russian Orthodox Church—having expressed its sympathy to Fr. Radziszewski, for all practical purposes forbade both the official transfer of the Roman Catholic parish to Vladivostok and the construction there of a Catholic church. Answering the letter of the Minister of Internal Affairs, who supported the request of the Vladivostok Catholics, the *Oberprokuror* of the Synod wrote on December 31, 1886:

> Responding to yours of December 5th, on the petition of the Metropolitan of the Roman Catholic churches concerning permission to transfer to Vladivostok the priest presently in Nikolaevsk and also to transfer to that city the Roman Catholic chapel, I am obliged to inform Your Excellency that in view of facts set forth with respect to said petition, inasmuch as there is no Orthodox church in Vladivostok, and the construction of an Orthodox church has only recently been undertaken, and there is already a Lutheran church in Vladivostok, I cannot allow that a Roman Catholic church be constructed there. The existence of foreign churches, in the absence of an Orthodox church, would not correspond to the dignity of the dominant church and might raise the danger of the proselytizing activities of these foreign churches among the Orthodox population. For this reason, in my opinion, it would be desirable and necessary to forestall consent to the above-mentioned petition until such time as the construction of the Orthodox church has been completed.

The Synod's decision most likely upset Fr. Kazimierz, especially since the repair of his dilapidated dwelling and the chapel in Nikolaevsk had now been forbidden by the Metropolitan Archbishop. Now he had in Nikolaevsk neither a place to live nor pray. But no one was able to change the Synod's decision and Fr. Radziszewski had to continue to live the life of a wandering preacher. During the twenty years of his missionary activities in the Far East he had completely lost his health and now he was inclined to seek out a more settled mode of life.

A year later an associate of the Minister of Internal Affairs, Prince Gagarin, repeated the request concerning the transfer of Fr. Radziszewski and his chapel from Nikolaevsk to Vladivostok, but the Synod stood its ground. "Until such time as the Orthodox church is completed and open for services, it would not be appropriate to allow the transfer of the Roman Catholic parish from Nikolaevsk to Vladivostok in view of those dangers which were set forth in my response to Your Highness dated December 31, 1886."[20]

But the construction of the Orthodox cathedral in Vladivostok took a long time and therefore Fr. Radziszewski had to remain in Nikolaevsk and live in the completely run-down house, the repair of which had now been forbidden. He continued his missionary activity in the Far East, regularly visiting his parishioners who were dispersed over this huge territory. Archival documents written in a style that is strange to a present-day reader show how his journeys through the region were arranged and made. In a letter of the military general of the Amur District to the military governor of the Primorye District dated February 7, 1886, we find:

> The curate of the Roman Catholic Church of the Amur Region, Fr. Radziszewski, referring to his obligation to complete in the present year a journey through the Amur District for tending to his congregation's spiritual needs, by report dated January 14

20 RGIA, f. 821, op. 125, d. 683, l. 189-199 ob.

> of this year asks that we send him travel expenses from Blagoveshchensk to Pokrovskaia Station and back, both for himself and for his assistant. He is also asking to be issued a travel permit and an open order. Acknowledging the possibility of issuing to Fr. Radziszewski and his assistant the travel expenses (for the time being only from Khabarovsk to Blagoveshchenk—to the priest for three horses, and to his assistant for two horses) and having enclosed with this letter such funds in the amount of 131 rubles 40 kopecks as well as the state travel permit and open order, I have the honor of requesting Your Excellency to issue to the priest Fr. Radziszewski a travel permit and open orders and 78 rubles 84 kopecks and to his assistant the remaining 52 rubles 56 kopecks and to explain that the traveling expenses from Blagoveshchensk to Pokrovskaia Station and back to Khabarovsk will be issued upon his arrival in Blagoveshchensk.[21]

From similar documents the name and surname of Fr. Radziszewski's assistant, with whom he shared all the burdens of his missionary travels, became known to us. In one of the documents Fr. Radziszewski writes: "I have the honor of presenting to you the enclosed Certificate No. 2164 of the Vladivostok City Police dated June 4, 1886, Certificate No. 1216 of the Fifth East Siberian Artillary Battalion dated June 17, 1886, and the receipt of my assistant, Karl Burżyński, for travel expenses received from me for tending with me to the spiritual needs of persons of the Roman Catholic faith."[22] Thanks to documents found in the archives, one can become acquainted with the rules of processing travel permits in Russia at that time, and also to learn the scope of Fr. Radziszewski's mission-

21 RGIA DV, f. 821, op. 1, d. 1939, l. 17.

22 RGIA DV, Ibid.

ary travels. The priest writes: "During the period of open navigation this year, desiring to travel throughout the Amur District to tend to the spiritual needs of persons of the Roman Catholic faith, I most humbly ask Your Excellency for the issuance of travel expenses to the city of Nikolaevsk for me (for three horses), from Nikolaevsk through Khabarovsk to Vladivostok and back. Then through Razdolnaia Station to Novo-kievsk and back to Nikolaevsk and also a travel permit. From Nikolaevsk to Vladivostok, 1,740 versts; from Vladivostok to Novo-kievsk by way of Razdolnaia Station, 219 versts; from Novo-kievsk to Nikolaevsk, 1,869 versts."[23]

Whether he wished it this way or not, he traveled to Sakhalin in the winter, crossing the ice of the Tatar Strait on dogsled. Invitations for this visit came from the governor of the Amur District who addressed his letter to the governor of the Primorye District. "Following upon the petition of the acting leader of Sakhalin, I have the honor of asking Your Excellency concerning the travel assignment to Sakhalin Island of the priest Radziszewski in order that he might tend to the spiritual needs of the Roman Catholic exiles, having supplied him with travel allowances that are to be found credited and under your jurisdiction for such matters."[24]

In addition to the difficult trip, there awaited at Aleksandrov Post another problem—finding a place to celebrate Mass and the other sacraments. While the Orthodox believers on Sakhalin had regular priests, churches and chapels, Catholics lacked even a place to meet with their priest. Fr. Radziszewski understood that the need for the construction of a chapel for Catholics on Sakhalin was crucial. On March 7, 1889, he directed to the head of the Island a report with the following:

> Being this year in northern Sakhalin to conduct worship, I was obliged to do so in barracks occupied by arrested convicts that had been quickly cleaned

23 RGIA DV, Ibid., l. 1

24 RGIA DV, f. 1, op. 1, d. 1039, l. 1 ob.

for this purpose. This place was very unsuitable and small. Meanwhile, the number of Catholics grows each year and in Aleksandrov district alone has now reached approximately 500 people. The difficulties of finding a suitable place for services have now been repeated every year for several years, and I consider it my duty to turn to Your Excellency with a petition for permission to construct a chapel at Aleksandrov Post. I would consider it entirely appropriate to erect such a chapel in accordance with the proposed plan, in a location near the new bathhouse—to the right or the left of it—according to Your Excellency's discretion. Such a building would be built primarily with the voluntary contributions of the congregation, who have already expressed their readiness to contribute materials, once the permission of the administration is forthcoming.

In addition, I consider it not superfluous to point out to Your Excellency that the number of Catholics on Sakhalin Island has already reached 1,000 and that it would be very useful, in light of the moral effects of religion, if Your Excellency should acknowledge the necessity of petitioning for the assignment to Sakhalin Island of a separate Roman Catholic priest with a fixed place of residence at Aleksandrov Post, the main location of the exiles. I can only add that the above-mentioned number of Catholics would already constitute a parish, and there is a legal basis for having a separate priest.

Signed by the curate of the Roman Catholic Church of the Amur Region, Fr. Kazimierz Radziszewski.[25]

25 RGIA, DV, f. 702, op. 3, d. 63, l. 8–8 ob.

To the letter was attached a plan of the location upon which it was proposed that the chapel be constructed. Having reviewed the proposal, the head of Sakhalin Island inserted into the letter to the governor general of the Amur Region his own opinion on this question. He supported the proposed project and he refined the numbers of Catholics of the Aleksandrov district—according to his data, there were 349 Catholics (264 men, 84 women) in the Aleksandrov district; in addition, there were 202 Catholics (164 men, 38 women) in the Korsakov district. As for the plot of land for the proposed construction, that land belonged to the peasant Skorodumov, and he had willingly granted this land for the construction of a chapel. As for the appointment of a separate priest for Sakhalin Island, he opposed the idea, as he proposed instead that Fr. Radziszewski himself be permanently transferred to Sakhalin Island.

In accordance with the laws of the Russian Empire, the construction of a church for a foreign confession had to be approved by the Orthodox bishop of the territory where the construction was proposed. Bishop Kamchatski Guriy was considered the Orthodox trustee of Sakhalin Island at that time. Having received on January 10, 1890, the request of the Amur Region governor general, the bishop answered that he had "no objection to the construction of a Roman Catholic chapel at Aleksandrov Post on Sakhalin Island for religious services there."[26]

Thus there remained no bureaucratic obstacles to the construction of a chapel—there remained only the need to find the means for its construction. There was announced on the island that there would be a collection of contributions for the construction of a very modest, small chapel at Aleksandrov Post. But Catholics of any financial means on the island were few and far between and alas, it would be impossible to construct the chapel on the funds that could be collected from Catholics on the island. There was at that time, living in Warsaw, a well-known Polish magnate who was close to the Russian court, Prince Ivan Liubomirski, who advised the military general of

26 Ibid., l. 7–7 ob.

Sakhalin that he would pay the stipend of any Catholic priest who would tend to the spiritual needs of the Polish prisoners residing on Sakhalin.[27] Commenting on this proposal, the governor general of Sakhalin, V. D. Merkazin, wrote:

> There was recently an effort to gather the means for the construction of a Catholic chapel, relying on individual contributions—but it all came to nothing, given the insignificance of the contributions received. Neither can one expect favorable results from local contributions, in spite of the rather significant percentage of persons of the Roman Catholic faith among the population of the island entrusted to me, since most of them belong to the exile population and they do not have adequate means for even their basic necessities. In the given situation, the administration is not able to provide any assistance, on account of a shortage of staff and available housing for any staff.
>
> In light of the aforementioned, I consider it appropriate to turn the attention of Prince Liubomirski to that fact of first importance—namely that on Sakhalin Island there is no building appropriate for the gathering of the faithful where even with some discomfort it might be possible to solemnly celebrate liturgy on those rare occasions when a priest comes out to the island—and thus the Prince might render the greatest service to his co-religionists by underwriting the construction of even the most modest chapel for them. The staff engineer-architect of Sakhalin estimates that the construction of a suitable

27 Translator's Note: The publication of Chekhov's account of his trip to Sakhalin in the 1890s stirred up much interest in the conditions on the island, leading to gestures of generosity such as that of Prince Liubomirski.

> chapel would come to approximately 2,461 rubles, including both labor and materials.

Prince Ivan Liubomirski contributed the necessary sum. The local contributions of the Sakhalin intelligentsia supplemented that sum and a very modest chapel was erected at Aleksandrov Post in 1896. It was dedicated September 14, 1897, by the new curate, Fr. Adam Szpiganowicz. The church building itself remained standing right up to the end of the twentieth century. For a long time it housed a movie theater. But on account of its aged condition, it has now been torn down.

In the meantime, in 1889, in Vladivostok the construction of the Orthodox church was finally completed. In the center of Vladivostok there appeared a beautiful architectural wonder—the majestic Church of the Dormition. This was the first cross-shaped building with a cupola in Vladivostok. One of the local correspondents of that time wrote: "The church is built along the lines of the Khabarovsk church and it distinctly stands out among the other city buildings, as it gracefully rises above them. When one enters, the eye is pleased with the fine adornment, the spiral *tiagi* and zigzags give a surprising lightness to the church." The inner adornment of the church also evoked the delight of the faithful and curious visitors, especially the massive iconostas with its exquisitely fine carving and gold trim. In 1894, by decree of the Most Holy Synod, this church became officially known as the Cathedral of the Dormition. In 1896, the artist A. F. Sokolov painted the building—on the cupola he depicted the twelve apostles and on the outer walls an icon of the dormition of Mary and the four evangelists. In honor of the fiftieth anniversary of the founding of Vladivostok, the merchant Chistiakov and his wife Iriada donated to the cathedral a bell weighing approximately five tons, which had been cast in Moscow at the Oloviannikov Factory. In 1902, a new Orthodox cemetery church in honor of the Protection of the Most Holy Mother of God was dedicated, and in 1907 there was established a church in honor of St. Nicholas, in memory of the thousands of Russian soldiers killed in the Russian-Japanese War, 1904-1905.

After the completion of the construction of the Orthodox cathedral, the *oberprokuror* of the Most Holy Synod advised the Minister of Internal Affairs that he no longer had any objection to the transfer of the Roman Catholic chapel from Nikolaevsk to Vladivostok. Thanks to this, Fr. Kazimierz Radziszewski, who had managed to transfer his residence to Vladivostok January 22, 1890, finally received permission for the construction of a Roman Catholic church in that city. At that time, the priest had only 1,000 rubles, which had been given him by the Archdiocese of Mogilev from the auxiliary capital fund, and therefore he requested the Archbishop to authorize a universal collection of contributions for the construction of a Catholic church in Vladivostok. The prelate of the Archdiocese, Appolonarius Degialo, responded that such a collection would be permitted and that it would be conducted over the course of two years for the sum of 3,000 rubles.

The first small wooden Catholic church, dedicated to the Nativity of the Most Holy Virgin Mary, was erected in the period 1890-1891. It was a small log cabin church with a bell tower in front. Mrs. Nelli Miż, a well-known regional scholar of Vladivostok, studied and presented to the parish archives a short article about the celebration of Christmas in the Catholic church that had originally been published in the January 1891 issue of *Vladivostok*.

> The attention of the Catholics to their Christmas liturgy is expressed among other things by the composition of a special amateur choir. According to custom, the public gathers at 11:00 p.m. for the Midnight Nativity Mass. Notably present were a large number of members of the intelligentsia. After a short preliminary service, there was a pause in the liturgy. The priest changed into other vestments and once again approached the altar and at exactly midnight intoned the liturgy during which the beloved Mr. P. played the

> majestic Beethoven sonata on the reed organ. When the ecstatic exclamation "Gloria in excelsis Deo!" was proclaimed, the choir repeated these words in a wonderful song and the believers in attendance were deeply moved. Against the background of other voices, one could distinguish the strong voice of Mrs. T., who one might say led the choir. Mass finished at 2:00 a.m. The moon shone and the colored streetlights added to the festive scene of the congregation dispersing from the church...

In the spring of 1891, there occurred in the Far East a very historic event—the construction of the Ussuri Railroad [connecting Vladivostok and Khabarovsk]. Important personages took part in the solemn and very beautiful ceremonies marking the inauguration of this construction: the heir of the Russian Imperial throne, Tsarevich Nicholas II; the Greek Prince George; the first Amur Region governor general, Baron A. N. Korf; the military governor general, Major Unterberger; the military commandant of the Vladivostok Fortress, Major General Ackerman; and a numerous entourage of officials and distinguished guests. First they prayed, then a signal rocket was launched, echoed by the salute of the batteries and squadrons along the shore. After this noisy beginning, the Tsarevich and Prince George, with their entourage, reverently kissed the cross and proceeded into the pavilion, where shovels and a wheelbarrow awaited them. The guests filled the wheelbarrow with soil and wheeled it to the roadbed of the future railroad—the ceremony concluded with the placement of a silver memorial plaque. From this solemn moment in the Russian Empire began the grandiose construction of the Trans-Siberian Railroad and its branch line, the Manchurian Railroad, which introduced changes on a "planetary" scale. Many unemployed Poles from the former Polish *gubernia*s came to work on this construction and they were all Catholics. Thereafter, Catholic churches were constructed in Manchuria by these Polish émigrés.

Meanwhile, the universal collection of funds for the construction of a Catholic church in Vladivostok was now under way, both in the Far East and in all the Roman Catholic churches of the Empire. The collection yielded excellent results, which allowed in very short time the beginning and the completion of the construction of the first brick Catholic church in the Far East.

But to the great disappointment of the Catholics, the curate of the Roman Catholic church, Fr. Kazimierz Radziszewski, so soon after finally getting permission to relocate his parish from Nikolaevsk to Vladivostok, did not live long among his new parishioners. At the beginning of July 1893, he went to Blagoveshchensk on a routine pastoral visit, and there on July 6, at the age of fifty-five, he suddenly died of a severe intestinal illness. The burial of the deceased Catholic priest was conducted July 7, 1893, in the city cemetery of Blagoveshchensk by the local Orthodox priest, Afanasii Shastin, in accordance with the Orthodox ritual.[28] On the grave of Fr. Kazimierz Radziszewski they placed a cross and four pillars, entwined with chains….

The death of Fr. Radziszewski concerned not only the Catholic parishioners but also the local authorities. The military governor general, Major Unterberger, on July 23, 1893, directed a letter to the Metropolitan of the Roman Catholic churches of Russia. He wrote that in light of the expansiveness of the parish, which was composed primarily of lower ranking officials, it seemed that the appointment of a new priest for the support of their moral lives and for the fulfillment of their religious obligations was an urgent necessity. Therefore the governor recommended that another worthy person be appointed as a very prompt replacement for this newly created vacancy.

---

28 RGIA, f. 821, op. 125, d. 751, l. 5.

Irkutsk Catholic Church, completed and dedicated in 1884 (present view)

Fr. Krzystóf Szwermicki, head of the Irkutsk Roman Catholic Church

First trustee of the Roman Catholic parish in Vladivostok, Senior State Councilor Ignatyj Osipowicz Makowski

Fr. Kazimerz Radziszewski, first Catholic priest of the Far East, Russian Empire, with the family of Mr. Piller. Vladivostok, 1868

First wooden Catholic Church, Vladivostok. Destroyed by fire in 1902

Chapel built at Aleksandrov Post on Sakhalin Island in 1896

Orthodox Cathedral of the Dormition, Vladivostok. Completed in 1889, but blown up during the years of Soviet rule.

III

Catholic Churches and Priests of the Far East

"Go ye into the whole world and
preach the Gospel to every creature."
Mark 16:15

1. *Fr. Adam Szpiganowicz*

When the sudden death of Fr. Radziszewski in 1893 left the Catholic Church of the Far East without a leader, the Metropolitan Archbishop of Mogilev, Szymon Kozłowski, selected as his replacement Fr. Adam Szpiganowicz, the vicar of the Riga church and a graduate of St. Petersburg Theological Academy. He submitted the required petition to the Department of Religious Affairs with a request for its consent to the appointment of the proposed candidate. The Metropolitan soon received a response that "in the files of the Department there is no unfavorable evidence concerning the moral qualities and the political trustworthiness of Fr. Adam Szpiganowicz." The Department thereupon gave its approval to the appointment of the young priest to Vladivostok. Thus a successor had been found to the recently deceased first Catholic pastor of the Far East.

Fr. Adam Szpiganowicz came from a family of the Stavropol nobility. He received his early education in the Stavropol classical high school and then enrolled in the Roman Catholic seminary in St. Petersburg. A year later he transferred to the Imperial Petersburg Roman Catholic Theological Academy, which he completed with a Senior Student Degree in theology. Immediately upon his graduation, Fr. Adam was designated the chaplain for the Mogilev Archbishop in St. Petersburg[29] and he served in that position for approximately a year, accompanying the archbishop on his foreign travels. Then Fr. Adam was transferred to Riga where he was assigned to teach religion in the schools and simultaneously serve as vicar for the local Roman Catholic parish.

His unexpected appointment to the Far East was most likely not a favorable turn of events for the young priest, all the more so since "surprises" appeared at the very beginning of his travels and he had to be bothered with many petitions. For example, it turned out that passage by steamship from Odessa to Vladivostok would take not thirty but forty-eight days, and it would cost no less than 800 rubles. Fr. Adam's travel allowance was only 300 rubles.[30] He had to submit a request to the Mogilev archbishop who on July 27, 1893, in his turn petitioned Senator Pleve at the Ministry of Internal Affairs. After a lengthy exchange of correspondence, the necessary sum was paid to Fr. Adam. But his next problem was that of his stipend. From a letter of Archbishop Kozlowski to the Minister of Internal Affairs, under whose jurisdiction lay all "foreign confession churches" in Russia, it appears that Fr. Adam was to have received an annual stipend of 600 rubles. Fr. Adam pointed out that 600 rubles, given the high cost of even the most basic necessities in Vladivostok, would be far from adequate to meet even the most necessary expenses, not to speak of

29 Translator's Note: The offices of the Mogilev Archdiocese were in St. Petersburg.

30 RGIA, f. 821, op. 125, d. 684, l. 18-18 ob.

the monies needed for his regular travels throughout his huge parish. The 600 rubles would indeed be a paltry sum. Furthermore, the experience of the deceased curate, Fr. Kazimierz Radziszewski, had shown that even his skill with knitting and the salting and sale of fish had not saved him from destitution. Therefore, in Fr. Adam's opinion, the stipend for the Roman Catholic priest in the Far East ought to be increased to 1,200 rubles a year.

Acknowledging the fairness of the priest's petition, the Minister considered it nevertheless necessary to consult with the governor general of the Amur Region. Unfortunately we do not find in the archives the response of the governor general and therefore we do not know whether Fr. Adam received a satisfactory increase in his stipend.

From the parish registry books we can see that he more than once visited Sakhalin Island, the cities of Nikolaevsk, Blagoveshchensk, Nikolsk-Ussuriisk, Harbin and numerous small villages where Catholics lived. In the Amur Region, Fr. Adam regularly visited the village of Rogachevka, which had been founded by émigrés from the Mogilev *gubernia* of the Szkuropacki, Gulewicz and Smykowski families. These Catholics asked the priest for his support of their effort to get permission for the construction of a chapel in the little village. Fr. Adam submitted a request to the governor general September 15, 1901, in the following words:

> I have now visited residents of the Roman Catholic faith in the village of Rogachevka in the Amur-Zeisk district for the third time for the purpose of attending to their spiritual needs, and every year I encounter great difficulties in finding a place where we might be able to celebrate the Divine Liturgy and the sacraments. In light of this, the local residents of the aforementioned village, being predominantly Roman Catholic, have asked that I petition Your Excellency for permission for them to use government lumber to

> construct a chapel where they would be able to fulfill their Christian obligations.

Inasmuch as there were no obstacles to the construction of the chapel, it was constructed from logs in 1907, five years after Fr. Szpiganowicz had left the Far East. Its roof was covered with sheets of iron.[31] Inside the chapel there were an amphon, a confessional and two pairs of benches. The altar, the gift of the Blagoveshchensk parishioner, Stanisław Gartung, was constructed later. Soon the chapel had a reed organ and valuable church vessels—a tabernacle, a silver cross, chalices, lamps, banners, and vestments for the priests—all of this was acquired by the faithful. According to present-day Vladivostok parishioners of the Gulewicz family, this chapel has been preserved in Rogachevka right down to the present time.

One of the most important events during the ministry of Fr. Adam Szpiganowicz in the Far East was the dedication of the Catholic church in Blagoveshchensk, Transfiguration of Our Lord. This solemnity occurred on the Feast of the Transfiguration, August 6, 1896. The beautiful red brick church was built through the efforts of parishioner Dr. Jurgielis, the parish trustees Macejewski and Gartung and the voluntary contributions of many people of Blagoveshchensk. The church was situated in the center of the city on the corner of Irkutsk and Sadovaia Streets. Title to the land was given to the parish by Blagoveshchensk City Decree No. 995, dated April 14, 1893. Along with the title the parish also received approval of the drawings for the construction of the church and permission for the construction, confirmed by the Ministry of Internal Affairs April 26, 1896, No. 2435. The church had a two-gable roof and a 5-foot stone foundation. A bell tower in the shape of a cross, 63 feet long and 42 feet wide, was built onto the church. There were ten windows in the worship space, a stone altar with columns and a wooden altar balcony. This beautiful sacred edifice has been pre-

31 TsGIA, f. 826, op. 1, d. 1342, l. 1-1 ob. TsGIA is the Central State Historical Archive (St. Petersburg).

served right down to the present day. But despite all governmental and human laws, this Catholic sanctuary, which was temporarily occupied by the Orthodox community while awaiting the completion of the construction of the Orthodox church, has not yet been returned by the Orthodox to the Catholics, the rightful owners of this historic church.

The Catholic community in Khabarovsk was also growing during the time of Fr. Szpiganowicz's ministry in the Far East. "Khabarovka" [approximately 400 miles upstream from Nikolaevsk] was at first only a tiny village, but after the transfer of the military contingent from Nikolaevsk in 1872, in a very short time it turned into a quickly developed city, Khabarovsk, with a rather motley population, which was characteristic for all the cities of the Far East. The following table shows the composition of the population in the Far East by religious faith.

	Transbaikalia	**Amur**	**Priamur**	**Sakhalin**
Orthodox	64.50	63.0	72.0	69.00
Old Believers	06.30	10.0	01.0	00.13
Roman Catholics	00.10	00.2	01.5	00.60
Protestants	00.03	00.8	00.4	00.20
Jews	00.95	00.2	00.7	00.05
Muslims	00.30	00.4	00.4	00.60
Buddhists	25.30	16.0	11.0	00.00

From the table it can be seen that in terms of numbers, there were clearly fewer Catholics in the Far East than either Orthodox or Old Believers, but nonetheless the city council of Khabarovsk after long discussions and arguments set aside a plot of land in the city for the construction of a Roman Catholic chapel. The plot of land was 600 square sazhens. Immediately after this important decision, a Building Committee was created and the president of the committee, commander of the Third East Siberian Battalion, Colonel A. D. Szmejko, and members of the committee J. S. Guszcza, K. I. Dubicki, and J. Z. Kolmaczewski began collecting funds. The local paper, *Priamurskie vedomisti* [Amur Region Register], dated April 16, 1899, carried the following announcement: "The residents of Khabarovsk are hereby notified that it has been granted that a Catholic chapel may be constructed in Khabarovsk. A 600-sq.-sazhen plot of land has been set aside for this construction. Contributions will be necessary and accepted with gratitude by members of the Building Committee, Commander of the Third East Siberian Line Battalion, Colonel A. D. Szylewski." In an issue dated December 21, 1900, *Vedomosti* [Register] announced that the collection of funds for the construction of the Catholic church was proceeding well and that already very fine contributions had been received from several people. It seems surprising to us, but even Chinese made contributions to the construction of the Catholic church. For example, a Mr. Ye Haolin contributed 3,000 puds of lime! In spite of these generous contributions, construction of the Catholic church in Khabarovsk progessed slowly and by the appointed deadline, 1903, the construction had not been completed. The reason was simple and clear—the majority of the parishioners were hopelessly poor military and therefore they simply were not able to raise the funds for the inner furnishing and adornment of the church.

Meanwhile Vladivostok Catholics continued to pray in the small wooden churched that had been completed in 1891, before Fr. Radziszewski's untimely death. Unfortunately during a fire the night of February 2, 1902, this first Catholic church burned to the ground. The fire squadron did not have enough water. When they came with the second tank of water, it was too late to save the church. In a very short period, the Catholic community built from logs a temporary church on the foundation of the first, and dedicated it to Immaculate Mary. They maintained their hope for the quick construction of a brick church. Alas this hope was not fulfilled. For twenty years Catholics in Vladivostok continued to pray in their little log church.

On February 10, 1902, in the absence of Fr. Szpiganowicz, a Special Committee was created at a General Council of parishioners. This committee had complex problems before it. First of all it was to verify all the church's property, both real estate and other, and then to begin to petition both governmental and church authorities concerning the means for the construction of a new brick church; to work out the design of a church that would meet the needs of the parish; and to obtain from the authorities permission for the collection of voluntary contributions. Later this committee became known as the Building Committee.

Despite the huge scope of the work, both in Vladivostok and in the outlying areas, the young priest continued to work alone, without an assistant, constantly finding himself traveling throughout his unembraceable parish where he served from 1893 until 1902, when upon a directive of the Archbishop of Mogilev, he was transferred to Omsk. In his last letter to the military governor of the Amur District, Fr. Szpiganowicz wrote:

> I consider it my duty to advise Your Excellency that by directive of my religious superior I have been named head of the Omsk Roman Catholic church. All the property of the Vladivostok church, as described on the parish inventory, as well as the parish documents and other business that was given to me, has been given to the new priest who will be taking my place. Having advised you of this, I have the honor of most humbly requesting Your Excellency for remission to me of a foreign passport for my travel to the place of my new assignment. I plan to depart by the first steamship to Odessa.

By the end of 1902 Fr. Szpiganowicz was in Omsk, where he spent three years ministering in western Siberia as curate of the Omsk Roman Catholic church. In 1905 he was transferred to Tambov—and this was a rather complex, one might even say dramatic, period of his life. The main event occurred during the time of Bishop Cieplak's visit to Tambov for an inspection of the local Roman Catholic parish. Having heard various complaints of some of the members of the local Polish colony who were unhappy with

Fr. Szpiganowicz, Bishop Cieplak most likely had passed on to the priest some of their comments. The priest's reaction was completely unexpected. He immediately submitted a request for his removal from Tambov and a transfer to the Diocese of Tiraspol [in present-day Moldava]. This immediately became known to the whole parish, and dozens of letters from parishioners in defense of the priest flew in to both the church and the civil authorities. Here, for example, is what the governor of Tambov, in his secret missive to the Department of Religious Affairs, wrote:

> The departure of this priest from the Tambov parish is occasioned by the schemes and intrigues of members of the Polish colony in Tambov, to whom the strict, correct ministry and life of Fr. Szpiganowicz are far from pleasing. Upon the arrival of Bishop Cieplak, local Poles hurried to him and began to whisper to him about something or other. The head of this party of those hostile to Fr. Szpiganowicz is the engineer Kłossowski, who works on the Riazan-Ural Railroad. He is a person absolutely indifferent to religious questions, and the activity of Fr. Szpiganowicz as a priest could not possibly have interested him as he has never set foot in a church.[32]

The "Fr. Szpiganowicz Affair" became well known in the highest circles of authority in Russia and the Governor of Tambov found it necessary to dispatch explanatory letters. Here is what he communicated to the Department of Religious Affairs:

> Not daring to judge beforehand the question of the future fate of Fr. Szpiganowicz, and not delving into an evaluation of those accusations made against him, with this letter I am only asking Your Excellency

32 RGIA, f. 821, op. 128, d. 628, l. 46.

> for the respect of the fate of a person who is honorable and humble and has constantly led an exemplary life and has never given reason for rumors or speculations. Having known Fr. Szpiganowicz six years, I cannot without pain think that as a consequence of schemes and intrigues that are hostile to our government, a person who is guilty only in that he never shared the "mindless dreams" of his co-religionists is departing the city.

Despite such warm support, Fr. Szpiganowicz nevertheless left Tambov and was transferred to the Diocese of Tiraspol. It would seem that here the story would have ended. However the priest's stature was so well respected that his fate had interested the *Goffmeister* of the Supreme Court, who demanded of the Archbishop of Mogilev, Metropolitan Kluczyński, an answer to the question, "Did the transfer of above-named Roman Catholic priest to the Diocese of Tiraspol occur upon his personal request or by directive of the Archbishop of Mogilev or was it possibly for other reasons, and if so, we ask that we be informed of those reasons." The Archbishop of Mogilev on October 31, 1911, hastened to respond that Fr. Szpiganowicz had been transferred to the Diocese of Tiraspol October 10, 1911, upon his personal petition, and was assigned to the post of curate of the Taganrog Roman Catholic church.

In the revolutionary years, Fr. Szpiganowicz was killed....

2. *Fr. Peter Paul Bulwicz and Fr. Peter Silowicz*

To replace Fr. Szpiganowicz, Fr. Peter Paul Bulwicz was transferred to Vladivostok from Blagoveshchensk. Fr. Bulwicz was born in 1874 in the village of Bartinki, in the Suvalsk *gubernia*, in a family of petty landowning nobility. After completing middle school, Peter Bulwicz entered the Seinsk seminary where in 1898 he was ordained a priest. But at precisely this moment Fr. Bulwicz was arrested and summoned to a criminal inquiry for his membership in some sort of political circle. In fact the young priest had belonged to no such political circle. He had only been a member of a group of seminarians who had jointly subscribed to Lithuanian newspapers, including some that published anti-government articles.[33] For his participation in such a group, Fr. Bulwicz was sentenced to six months' imprisonment, but on March 30, 1899, by directive of the highest authority he, as a member of the clergy, was freed from prison, but subjected to two years of secret supervision by the police. In addition, he was forbidden to live in the Courland *gubernia*, or to minister in the Vitebsk, Minsk and Mogilev *gubernia*s. Thanks to a petition of the Archbishop of Mogilev, Karl Niedzialkowski, Fr. Bulwicz was transferred from the Seinsk Diocese to the Far East, where he began to serve in the Roman Catholic parish of Blagoveshchensk in 1899 or 1900. Upon his arrival in Vladivostok, the priest fell into a difficult situation. He had been assigned a stipend of 600 rubles a year, but he was unable to obtain these funds since a part of the stipend proposed for him had already been allotted to Fr. Szpiganowicz and the accounting for the year 1902 had already been closed. Fortunately, the situation was resolved through the intervention of the Department of Religious Affairs, and the priest was granted the money from the account of the Ministry of Internal Affairs.

Judging by the parish registry book, Fr. Bulwicz right away set about missionary travels throughout the populated points of the Far East where Catholics lived. Here is an excerpt of his report to the Archbishop of Mogilev, which shows how seriously and responsibly he attended to his pastoral work:

> Yesterday, September 13, I returned from a circuit of the Zeisk Region of the Amur District, during which I visited the little village of Zeisk Wharf (657 versts from Blagoveshchensk) and the villages of Ust-Gerbichek (50 versts further up the Selenga River), Rogachevka (150 versts further up the Zeya River

---

33 RGIA, f. 821, op. 1, d. 118, l. 2.

and 25 versts from its right bank), and Serebrianka (10 versts from Rogachevka). In the little village of Zeisk Wharf, there are no more than fifteen souls, but in the upper reaches of the Zeya River, in the gold mines, the number of inhabitants according to indications of knowledgeable people exceeds a hundred souls. However, the expansiveness of the region throughout which the mines are scattered and a lack of time did not allow me to visit the individual mines, which for the same reasons none of my predecessors has ever visited either. I hope that these mine-workers will come to Blagoveshchensk during the winter, where they will be able to fulfill their spiritual obligations of five to ten years.

At the mouth of the Gerbichek River, at the point of its confluence with the Selenga (a tributary of the Zeya), on the left shore there are fourteen families (fifty-six souls) who settled there in 1903—émigrés from the Kamenetsk-Podolsk *gubernia*. With the end of the [Russian-Japanese] war here they are expecting the arrival of a large number of families. In the valley of the Serebrianka River twenty-four families (211 souls), émigrés from the Mogilev *gubernia*, arrived in the autumn of 1903 and settled. Each "soldier"[34] was allotted from the public lands fifteen desiatins of agrable lands and hayfields, not counting grazing lands. For the time being they are all living very poorly in mud huts, but with the hope of a better future. By their industry and diligence they serve as an example to neighboring émigrés. It is strange that the Catholics of these two villages were not included on the list of Roman Catholic parishioners

34 These peasants would have been considered "Cossacks"—i.e., responsible for defense in exchange for land and certain privileges.

of the Amur District attached to the petition for the separation of the Amur District from the Vladivostok parish, because the total number of Catholics could possibly have reached 750 souls.

The village of Rogachevka was formed back in 1888 by émigrés from the Mogilev *gubernia.* Here each family received 100 desiatins of agrable land and therefore they live relatively well. Only one family has not yet managed to build a house and temporarily still lives in a mud hut. In all three villages gardened plots have been allotted for the church, a social hall, and school. The dimensions of the plots are 3,600, 3,200 and 200 square sazhens, respectively. In Rogachevka permission has been granted for the construction of a chapel but the Forest District has not yet released the lumber.

Fr. Bulwicz describes in great detail the activities of these émigrés—their problems and their successes. Reading these notes one could imagine that their author is not a priest but a scholarly ethnographer. At the end of his letter, Fr. Bulwicz asked permission of the Archbishop of Mogilev to spend his winter in Blagoveshchensk as Fr. Francisk Janulajtis would willingly substitute for him in Vladivostok and Khabarovsk. (Fr. Janulajtis was a chaplain of the Warsaw Red Cross Medical Train Battalion of Captain Wasilczykow, which was stationed in Nikolsk-Ussuriisk.) Unfortunately we do not know whether Fr. Bulwicz received permission to pass the winter in the Amur District, but most likely he did not because there were problems in Vladivostok that could not be postponed, the most important of which was the construction of the new church.

Historical documents inform us that Fr. Bulwicz was expecting additional assistance from the Archdiocese of Mogilev. On April 25, 1902, while Fr. Szpiganowicz was still in Vladivostok, Fr. Peter Silowicz was transferred from Riga to Vladivostok to serve as vicar of the Vladivostok church. When they learned of his transfer, the

Catholics of Riga rose up in defense of their pastor and letters were quickly dispatched to the Archbishop of Mogilev, especially from the local Latvians. They wrote: "He is the only Catholic priest who knows Latvian—and we do not need to rely on the services of a translator at his Masses." But all the tearful requests of the Latvian parishioners went unanswered and Fr. Peter Silowicz departed for Vladivostok where he was to serve for only a short time: from June 7, 1902 until November 11, 1903. His return to Riga, however, was not an easy matter because he was not able to return to his former post. On February 23, 1904, Fr. Silowicz was assigned as the acting curate of Marienburg church during the absence of Fr. Stefan Bermanius, but Fr. Silowicz remained at that assignment significantly longer than had been expected—until September 15, 1907. All the same, it was not until October 2, 1907, that Fr. Peter Silowicz managed to return to his post as vicar of the Riga church. One can only imagine the rejoicing of his Latvian parishioners!

But apparently Fr. Silowicz had enemies because someone wrote several "nasty" denouncements against him and in the end he was removed from Riga. In despair that all his plans had been ruined and perhaps from other injustices, he fell ill and he was sent on a three-month medical leave for recovery of his nervous system. All this time his parishioners continued to struggle for the fate of their beloved priest and he received finally the post of chaplain in the church of Balderaa, not far from Riga. After long efforts, Fr. Silowicz was allowed to live near the Riga church of the Sorrowful Mother of God under the condition that he would attend also to the needs of the Balderaa church. In addition, Fr. Peter was entrusted with the teaching of religion in various educational institutions in Riga and all of these obligations Fr. Silowicz fulfilled very conscientiously. Such favorable activity on the priest's part was very highly valued—on April 8, 1913, he was awarded the highest distinction—the pectoral cross. Judging by notes in the archival documents from 1916, Fr. Silowicz continued to serve in the parish of Balderaa and to teach religion in the educational institutions of Riga until 1917.

Meanwhile in Vladivostok the efforts on the organization of the new church continued. All the parishioners helped the head of the Vladivostok parish, Fr. Peter Paul Bulwicz, and a general council first of all confirmed the authority of the committee for the building of the church that had been selected February 10, 1902, and it gave the committee a concrete directive: to build a brick church. After the lengthy procedures required for various approvals, the committee began to be known as the Building Committee, to which the parish entrusted the future conduct of its affairs. The first order of business was the creation of a design for a church that would meet the needs of the parish and then approval of that design by the parishioners. In addition, the Building Committee was given authority for the supervision of not only the church properties but also for the funds collected for the building of the church. These funds were put on deposit in the Russian-Chinese Bank, where they were converted to government bonds. The parishioners were regularly advised by the newspapers as to who was authorized for the collection of funds and how to make a deposit into the church's account.

The first major activity of the Committee was the expenditure of the 8,500 rubles received as the insurance payment for the wooden church that had burned down in 1902. Of these monies, 4,349 rubles, 40 kopecks were used for the construction of a temporary church resembling a barracks, with dimensions of 12 sazhens by 4 sazhens by 1 2/3 sazhen [84 feet by 28 feet by 11.5 feet]. This wooden building was erected on the foundation of the destroyed church. A well-known city contractor, Jan Skidelski, placed the new structure on the southwest portion of the land allotted by the City Duma on Third Portovaia Street (now known as Shkipper Gek Street). The church was built from 6-inch logs, with an iron roof and a wooden floor. Two wooden structures were built onto the building—one served as the portico and the other led into the sacristy. Inside the building a wooden wall divided the space into two parts: the sacristy (2 sazhens by 4 sazhens [14 feet by 28 feet]) and the nave (10 sazhens by 4 sazhens [70 feet by 28 feet]). Part of the nave was separated from the *presbyterium*, where there were pews for approximately 350 to 400 people.

Despite the fact that the building was like a barracks, photographs show that it was very cozy. Near the eastern wall in the *presbyterium* stood an oaken temporary altar on two steps. There was an oil painting of the Immaculate Conception of Mary. To the right of the altar was a large marble crucifix. In the archive of the Vladivostok Roman Catholic parish there is a note: "The heiress Żukliewicz at her expense constructed the base under the marble crucifix that stands in the church." To the left of the altar at a slight elevation was the old reed organ. On the altar itself stood a small crucifix of overlaid silver and silver candlesticks. There was a five-arshin-long bureau in the sacristy. At both ends of the bureau were small cupboards for liturgical vestments and a small writing desk with three drawers. The sacred vessels that had been rescued at the time of the fire were also kept there, as well as various ciboria, chalices, tabernacle, censors, a pyx, a cross for processions, a bell and several other artifacts for church rituals. The worship space was adorned with icons of Our Lady of Częstochowa, Our Lady of Ostrabramsk, Our Lady of Mercy, a portrait of Pope Leo XIII, an icon of Our Lord, an icon of Christ in the tomb, and many other church articles.[35]

Unfortunately, of all the church's prior possessions, the parish has, with great effort—with tears—managed to obtain the return of only the beautiful two-meter marble crucifix which, after the liquidation of the Catholic parish in the 1930s, was not destroyed only so that it might be transferred to the Vladivostok Art Institute to be used as a "visual aid." Some have surmised that the crucifix might be the work of the well-known sculptor Klodt, but the enigma of its origin

35 "Visitation Excerpts for 1907 from the Book of Engineer's Description of Real Estate and Other Property of the Roman Catholic Church," Collection of the Roman Catholic Parish of the Most Holy Mother of God, Vladivostok.

remains unsolved.[36] The crucifix sustained damages—the fingers of Our Lord were broken off and the face and body damaged.

Other parish buildings were also built using the insurance refund. The coziest of them was the rectory, a beautiful wooden construction on a high stone foundation, with an iron roof, a veranda and a second story added on. It was plastered both inside and out. On the first floor there were seven rooms: an entry way, a reception area, the hall, a bedroom, dining room, a large parish hall and a kitchen. On the second floor there were three rooms: an entry way, a bedroom, and a hall as well as a small pantry. Judging by the inventory, this house was well furnished. There were sofas, couches, armchairs, Viennese chairs, various tables, cupboards and other furniture. In the large parish hall there was a reed organ that was used for choir rehearsals and a parish library with 800 volumes of books on a wide variety of subjects. The priests' residence was heated by stove heat. The courtyard was paved with large flagstones and in the courtyard there was a root cellar. They built two other parish buildings using the insurance money. One of them (6 sazhens by 2 sazhens) was built of boards and from within lined with bricks. It had two rooms—one for the night watchman and one for the sacristan, and also a kitchen and a wooden lean-to. The second building was wooden on the inside and stuccoed on the outside. It was for the organist. It was 3 sazhens by 4 sazhens and was built on the slope of the hill. It seems to us amazing that after the completion of such expansive construction the Building Committee still had 2,575 rubles, 46 kopecks!

After the construction of these parish buildings, all the attention of the Committee was concentrated on the preparation of the documents needed for the construction of a brick church that would accommodate 1,000 parishioners. Local architects proposed several designs to the parish, but preference was given to the concepts of Aleksandr Gwoździjewski. He proposed a beautiful plan for a 1,000

36 Peter Clodt von Jürgensburg (1805-1867), known in Russian as Piotr Karlovich Klodt, is perhaps best known to Westerners for his horse sculptures on Anichkov Bridge in St. Petersburg.

cubic meter church. As a conservative estimate, given that construction costs in Vladivostok at that time were running approximately 120 rubles per cubic meter, it would have taken 120,000 rubles to construct such a church. The parishioners, of course, had no such money, nor could they be expected to have such money. In their letter to the Archbishop of Mogilev, Fr. Bulwicz and members of the Building Committee wrote:

> The expenditure is completely beyond the means of the local Catholic community, who number no more than 200 families who would be able to participate in the expenses for the construction. Further, the contributions would not exceed on average twelve rubles a year per family—which would come to 2,400 rubles. The offertory collections barely meet the parish's running expenses and payment of salaries. One-time donations and other donations could not exceed 1,500 rubles a year which would bring the total to 3,900 rubles. There are no "capitalists" among the local Catholics—there are only a few well-to-do families.

The make-up of the 3,500 parishioners of those years can be described as follows: (1) military ranks from units of the local garrison: fortress regiments, the fortress artillery, sappers and the mine company of the railroad battalion—1,500 people; (2) Eastern Siberian naval flotilla and Pacific squadron—500 people; and (3) civilian population—1,500 people.

This list of potential members of the Roman Catholic parish shows that 2,000 parishioners from the military and a large part of the civilian population would of course not be able to make anything more than very small financial contributions. Furthermore, it was brought to the attention of the authorities that Vladivostok, as a port and the terminus of the Trans-Siberian Railway, served as a transportation hub for many people who were thus temporarily in the city. Approximately 3,450 commercial steamships carrying 80,000 passengers visited the city each year, and traffic at the railroad station was even greater: 250,000 arrivals and departures per year. On an average, among these there could be 5,000 Catholics. In addition, every year foreign squadrons visited the local harbor and thus more and more often there were Chinese, Korean and Japanese Catholics in Vladivostok. It always amazed these temporary guests of Vladivostok that there was not a decent Catholic church in such an important port city. They always placed a modest contribution "for the church" in the parish money box.

Having brought forward all these arguments, Fr. Bulwicz emphasized as well the important moral side of the question. Inasmuch as a large part of the Catholics of Vladivostok and its surroundings were either voluntary or involuntary exiles from their faraway homeland, Poland, this meant they had all been torn from the family hearth, from the traditions of Faith and morality. In a port city, where there were unavoidably customs and vices corruptive to morality—where there was a merciless struggle for survival—it was necessary for a Christian to attend church, where his soul in communion with God might be purified and uplifted.

The local civic authorities shared the Catholics' concerns and supported the efforts of the head of the Catholic community. In fact even the military governor of the Amur District wrote to high-ranking authorities that "on important Catholic feast days, they are not able to fit into the little barracks church and a large number of them pray outside—even squeezing people into the church it is not possible that more than 600 would fit, leaving the faithful, most of whom are soldiers, outside." There was only one conclusion: it was necessary to construct a spacious new church. But the Building Committee saw no way to do so relying solely on locally collected funds and therefore it began to seek financial assistance from the Archbishop of Mogilev. There was talk of the assignation of a 10,000-ruble subsidy from the interest of the auxiliary capital fund of the Roman Catholic clergy. In addition, the Building Committee sought permission for a universal collection of contributions for the construction of the church, in the amount of 90,000 rubles. Both the parishioners and the head of the parish proposed that even small contributions of whatever one might give to the construction of so necessary a church, which found itself in such exceptional circumstances, was the moral obligation of the entire Catholic population of the Empire—not only in accordance with an obligation of Christian charity, but also out of Christian spiritual concern for the soldiers who had been sent forth from their homeland. It was hard for these dressed in soldiers' cloaks to preserve the Faith of their fathers in a foreign land where there was no church. Therefore, for the preservation of the spiritual connection with their homeland, for the preservation in these people in all of its purity and inviolability the Faith and morals, the construction of God's church was necessary, and serious financial assistance was needed by the parish.

The Archbishop of Mogilev, Metropolitan Apollinaryj Wnukowski, taking into account both the moral and the material sides of the question, wrote to the Department of Religious Affairs of Foreign Confessions that in his opinion the Catholics of the Vladivostok parish, the majority of whom were materially needy—they were unskilled laborers, the lower ranks of the military units—would not be able to raise the funds necessary for the construction of the church, and therefore he asked for the release to the Committee for the construction of the Vladivostok church a one-time subsidy in the amount of 10,000 rubles. The next link in the bureaucratic chain regarding the resolution of these requests was the Roman Catholic Theology Collegium of the Ministry of Internal Affairs. A letter written in 1906 by Bishop Jan Cieplak bears evidence of the fact that this echelon also supported the Catholics of Vladivostok.

3. *Formation of the Dobrochinnost' Charitable Aid Society*

Even prior to the outbreak of the Russian-Japanese War (1904-1905), many families were experiencing financial hardship as the cost of living in Vladivostok rose sharply. In January 1903 Fr. Bulwicz and a group of his parishioners submitted a petition to the military governor of the Amur District, General Lieutenant Chichagov for permission to establish a charitable "Aid Society" associated with the local Roman Catholic parish. Inasmuch as there was no response, a second petition was submitted in July 1903 to the new governor general. In part it said:

> A significant number of the parishioners of the Roman Catholic faith living in Vladivostok are persons who are materially needy, who earn their daily existence by hard labor, as unskilled workers or craftsmen. The unfavorable economic turns experienced in recent years in Vladivostok have increased the numbers of those who are homeless or without shelter to such an extent that the absence of properly organized material and moral support can place them in a hopeless situation, conducive to the sad necessity of turning to criminal behavior.
>
> Considering it our moral obligation to meet the needs of our co-religionists, and proposing that the need for the organization of such aid on a strictly legal foundation is extremely urgent, we ask permission of Your Excellency to establish in Vladivostok a parish charitable "Aid Society" for assistance to the most impoverished members of the Roman Catholic parish.[37]

This letter was signed by Fr. Bulwicz, parishioners and members of the Parish Council: Collegiate Councillor Stanisław Fiedorowicz; director of the city bank, Kazimierz Wysocki; associate public prosecutor, Stanisław Zalesski; and Polish noblemen Franz Szczawinski and Jan Kostecki. After many such petitions permission was finally received for establishing this charitable society, which later became known as "*Dobrochinnost'*." The aid of *Dobrochinnost'* was ex-

37 RGIA, DV, f. 1, op. 2, d. 1610, l. 18.

pressed in real actions: they provided the poor with food, clothing, monetary assistance, and a place to sleep; they ensured that the sick were able to see a doctor and obtain free medicines; and they placed the very elderly and solitary Catholics in an almshouse, and when they died they had them buried at the expense of *Dobrochinnost'*.

They found work for many of the poor parishioners, they helped them acquire tools needed for work, and they helped purchase tickets for those who wanted to return to the homeland. Such a huge spectrum of aid required as well huge amounts of money. *Dobrochinnost'* therefore had the right to open cafeterias and tea houses; to acquire inexpensive apartments and sleeping rooms, shelters and dormitories. But in each instance, it needed to obtain permission from the authorities. It was not easy to become an active member of *Dobrochinnost'*. The active members paid annual dues of no less than three rubles or they paid a one-time membership fee of 100 rubles. The funds of *Dobrochinnost'* were put on deposit as government bonds in branches of the State Bank in savings accounts and the Treasury. They were also deposited into the open running account for the expenses of the society. One could become an active member of *Dobrochinnost'* only upon the decision of the general membership, and here doctors and teachers were favored, as they tended to or taught poor children and orphans free of charge. Strict paragraphs of the charter of *Dobrochinnost'* foresaw all possible variants of the development of the society's activities. For example, in order to embrace the greatest number of needy people with their charitable activity, Vladivostok was divided into "guardianship districts," each of which was headed up by a district guardian chosen by the director of *Dobrochinnost'*. In the larger districts there could be created district councils to assist the district guardian. Assistants would work on these district councils seeking out the especially needy people and informing either the district guardian or the central office of *Dobrochinnost'* of them.

Despite his active participation in the activities of *Dobrochinnost'*, Fr. Bulwicz was not able to withdraw from his spiritual obligations as the head of the most expansive Roman Catholic parish of the Far

East. He continued to serve all Catholics in those parts. At this time there occurred significant changes in the distribution of Catholics in Primorye. A large group of Catholic soldiers was transferred from Nikolaevsk to Khabarovsk and Nikolsk-Ussuriisk. Naturally, to meet their spiritual obligations, they needed to attend a Catholic church, but there was no Catholic church in Nikolsk-Ussuriisk. Therefore the Catholic soldiers, officers and residents of the city collected voluntary contributions of 4,000 rubles and built a very small chapel. Such a chapel was built on the edge of the city on land belonging to the Military Department and in those times called "the Fortress." This chapel was a simple square log cabin made of logs 4 sazhens by 6 sazhens. In its shape it was not at all in accordance with church canons, nor was it suitable for worship for a large number of parishioners, but nonetheless a large number of Catholic soldiers came to this homely little chapel.

4. Fr. Stanisław Kajetan Dombrowski

In April 1907 the little chapel built by the soldiers in Nikolsk-Ussuriisk was consecrated in honor of St. Nicholas the Wonderworker, the patron saint of soldiers. Judging by archival documents, the staff priest of the Amur Military District, Fr. Stanisław Kajetan Dombrowski, consecrated the little chapel without permission (for which he received a dressing down by his Catholic superior). The dedication was attended by the curate of the Vladivostok church, Fr. Peter Bulwicz, and another priest who was at that time in the Far East, Fr. Stanisław Lawrinowicz.

The biography of Fr. Dombrowski is, one might say, very unusual. He was born into a noble family in 1870 in the Telzhevsk district of the Kovensk *gubernia*. In 1886 he finished the parish school in the little town of Vorniakh and he continued his education in the city of Nezhenia, Chernigovsk *gubernia*, in the historical philological institute of Prince Bezborodko where he passed his examination in the program of the four-year high school. Then from 1895 to 1902 he studied in the archdiocesan seminary in St. Petersburg and was ordained a priest in 1902.

Fr. Stanisław's first assignment was that of vicar at St. Catherine's church in St. Petersburg.[38] Soon the young priest was sent to Siberia as vicar of the Irkutsk church. There is a letter in the archives from the parishioners of St. Catherine's, who with great difficulty endured the transfer of their beloved Fr. Dombrowski to Siberia. They wrote:

> You have sent Fr. Dombrowski to Siberia. Why? He gives all his meager stipend to the poor. He visits our poor homes. Beyond the Nevsky Gate there are 5,000 Catholics who work in the factories, supporting that many families. For four years we have sought to create a Catholic chapel in that district as well as a shelter for the education of children and a refuge for the elderly. There is also a need there for the organization of consumer shops. Fr. Dombrowski supported all our plans. We invited him to be part of the organizational committee and we named him prefect of the chapel and the shelter.

This letter was signed by many parishioners and sent to the Archbishop of Mogilev. Moreover they sent telegrams requesting that Fr. Stanisław be allowed to remain at his post.

But it was all in vain, as on November 9, 1905, Fr. Stanisław Dombrowski was transferred to the post of chaplain of the Amur Military District where he was to travel and visit all the military encampments spread out on the lands of the Far East. Upon his arrival in Khabarovsk Fr. Stanisław with great zeal oversaw the construction of the Khabarovsk Catholic Church but was not to see its completion, as on November 20, 1907, he was sent to the Roman Catholic parish of the city of Marinsk, Tomsk *gubernia*, as head

38 RGIA, f. 826, op. 1, d. 1383, l. 6-7.

of the parish. After some time he was once again transferred—this time he was named vicar of the Catholic church in the village of Birma, Irkutsk district. On December 10 of the same year he was transferred to the city of Dvinsk.

It was very difficult for us to understand this whole kaleidoscope of assignments and transfers from one parish to another. But in one of the archival documents, which contained the priest's personnel file, there was found a letter of the head of St. Catherine's parish in St. Petersburg, Fr. Budkewicz, addressed to the Archbishop of Mogilev. The substance of the letter was this: that Fr. Stanisław Dombrowski, who had served in the parish of St. Catherine as the head sacristan, had an outstanding debt of 1,576 rubles 79 kopecks. He was obligated to repay the debt, which in those times was a very large sum of money. On April 29, 1911, he was arrested in Dvinsk and taken to St. Petersburg for trial.

The documents from the judicial proceedings that are found in Fr. Stanisław's file are astounding! They give evidence of the fact that apparently this priest, with the goal of personal enrichment, had regularly occupied himself with various shady financial operations. When he was searched, they found a receipt from a Mr. Ippolit Mankiewicz for his acceptance from Fr. Stanisław Dombrowski of a promissory note in the sum of 70,000 rubles. There was also an account book, No. 743, of the Khabarovsk branch of the Russian Bank, and in that account was the sum of 1,800 rubles. These of course could have been the priest's personal savings, but the investigation confirmed that these were "borrowed" or "appropriated" monies. At the same period of time, several merchants and owners of various shops pled to the court. These were people from whom the priest had regularly obtained merchandise on credit, but he had not been willing to repay these debts. Also complaining to the judge was a parishioner, Agneszka Żukowska, who, trusting Fr. Dombrowski with all her heart, had on October 6, 1903, given him for safekeeping 400 rubles, all that she had. And now he refused to return these monies to her.[39] Not satisfied with the widow's mite, Fr. Stanisław had also encroached upon even greater sums, having managed the forgery of the last will and testament of Prince Bogdan Ireenevich Oginskii on July 9, 1903.[40]

In addition to his various financial machinations, Fr. Stanisław manifested a deep disdain toward his parishioners. In the complaint of Anna Bielawska it is noted that Fr. Stanisław kept in his service an entire family who lived in his little house—a husband, wife, their daughter, a 17-year-old girl and several younger girls. They all stole from the church, they hid the stolen goods in the priest's house, and they behaved arrogantly toward and argued with the parishioners. Then they complained to the priest about the parishioners! But the priest, not making any effort to justly resolve the problem, immediately began swearing at the parishioners. Such it happened with Anna, at whom the priest had first shouted rather crudely, then had threatened to beat her. Thereupon Anna sought the defense of the secular court, but the judge had refused the lawsuit, saying that she had no right to bring a lawsuit against a member of the clergy. Then on Palm Sunday the brazen Fr. Stanisław publicly called all the parishioners dishonorable people who had been exiled for thievery.

Outraged beyond the limit, the parishioners complained to the Archbishop and finally the priest was sternly punished for all these activities. By verdict of the St. Petersburg district court dated May 22, 1911, for crimes under Articles 1690 and 1691 of the Penal Code, Fr. Dombrowski was sentenced to prison for one year, four months, and deprived of all rights and properties, both personal and those acquired by virtue of his office. But by ruling of the very same judge June 5, 1912, Fr. Dombrowski was released early from prison and submitted to police surveillance under Articles 58-1 and 58-2 of the Penal Code. He slipped out from this surveillance June 30, 1912, in Novovilesk.

---

39 RGIA, f. 826, op. 1, d. 1383, l. 33.

40 Ibid., l. 35.

Regardless, in accordance with evidence on hand, he was brought up on charges under Article 354 of the Penal Code, but this affair was dismissed by ruling of the St. Petersburg Judicial Chamber September 20, 1913, as having been beyond the statute of limitations.

In 1913 the Metropolitan of the Archdiocese of Mogilev, Stefan Denisiewicz, informed the Department of Religious Affairs of the following resolution: "The priest Stanisław Kajetan Dombrowski is forever deprived of his clerical status, forbidden to appear in clerical garb, and excluded from the roster of the clergy of the Archdiocese of Mogilev."[41] Having received such a severe sentence and having been completely forbidden to act as a priest, the former Fr. Stanisław Dombrowski petitioned His Imperial Highness, the Supreme Commander-in-Chief, to assign him to the post of military chaplain in one of the military units. These efforts were in vain. The *Egermeister* of the Supreme Court stated that the petition of the former priest "deserved no consideration."

5. Fr. Peter Janukowicz

Meanwhile in the Far East, the shortage of Catholic priests continued. In 1904, by resolution of the Metropolitan of the Archdiocese of Mogilev, Stefan Denisiewicz, Fr. Peter Janukowicz was sent to the post of staff Roman Catholic priest for the Amur Military District and the Kwantung District. Biographical information notes that Fr. Janukowicz was born October 18, 1863, in a peasant family of the Disiunsk district of the Vilensk *gubernia*. He received his early education in Vilnius and then studied in the Mogilev Roman Catholic seminary. Upon completion in 1891 he was ordained by Metropolitan Walentin Baranowski in the city of Kovno.

Prior to his assignment to the Far East the young priest served in various parishes of the Novgorodsk *gubernia*, but his most significant assignment was as administrator of the Kamensk Roman Catholic

41 RGIA, f. 826, op. 1, d. 1383, l. 74.

church which had approximately 10,000 parishioners—all of whom were very fond of the priest. Nonetheless the suffragan bishop of the Mogilev Archdiocese Karol Niedzialkowski transferred him to Penza as chaplain of the chapel there inasmuch as there hung over Fr. Janukowicz the accusation that he had incited hatred toward the Orthodox population. Naturally the parishioners sent many requests to the Mogilev Archbishop that the priest be allowed to remain in the parish, but they were unable to be of any assistance. On the day of his departure crowds of weeping parishioners came to see him off.[42]

A serious turn in the priest's fate occurred August 13, 1904, when he was transferred to the Far East, to the city of Khabarovsk, to serve as staff Roman Catholic priest for the Amur Military District and the Kwantung District. A report of Fr. Janukowicz indicates that he was not able to begin his ministry in the Far East because on December 7, 1904, he was in Harbin, at the rear of the Manchurian Army.[43] He was not long in Harbin either because he fell ill with a serious form of hemorrhoids. In his rather wordy missive to Stefan Denisiewicz, he explained that:

> In the Kwantung Army, there are 6,000 Catholics for a single priest. All these Catholics are in need of fulfilling their religious obligations. At the same time, the priest is able to serve only 2,000 to 3,000 of the lower ranks—i.e., those serving one or two corps of the army guard stationed along all the lines of the Chinese Eastern Railroad. This allotment is in fact the official legal norm for one military chaplain.[44]

The heavy conditions and such a huge burden knocked the military chaplain off his feet. After recovering, Fr. Peter Janukowicz

42 RGIA, f. 826, op. 1, d. 1065, l. 83.

43 Ibid., l. 98.

44 RGIA, f. 821, op. 125, d. 684, l. 137.

never returned to the Far East. Later on he served as priest in the Orshansk deanery, then he was transferred to St. Petersburg where he finished his career in the role of head of the Roman Catholic parish of the Most Holy Virgin Mary at the Vyborg Cemetery in St. Petersburg.

After the departure of Fr. Janukowicz, all the clerical activity within the bounds of Manchuria once again lay upon the shoulders of Fr. Bulwicz. In addition to the Amur and Primorye districts, the priest with his assistant was to make annual trips within the boundaries of Manchuria to tend to the religious needs of persons of the Roman Catholic faith.

During the period of military activity with Japan, the city-fortress of Vladivostok was considered under siege from February 1, 1904 until October 31, 1905, because on February 22, 1904, the Japanese cruiser naval squadron of Admiral Kamimu had shelled Vladivostok and its port. This attack was launched from behind Cape Basargin, and therefore in very quick order the construction of Seventh Fort was begun. It was located fourteen kilometers from the city, to the north, between Second River and Sedanka stations, on the shore of Ussuri Bay. One of the members of the construction crew was Andrzej Usas, a Vladivostok parishioner who, along with other construction workers, had come to Vladivostok from Kovno.

In connection with the seige of the city, on the basis of the second part of a Supreme Memorandum affirmed March 13, 1905, the priest was also allotted an increased per diem of 1 ruble, 50 kopeks, for a total of 950 rubles, 50 kopeks. Hassling over the payment of this per diem, the priest submitted a petition to the Mogilev Metropolitan, Jerzy Szembek, for an increase of his stipend from 600 to 1200 rubles a year during the time of military activities.[45]

Expecting to receive these monies, Fr. Bulwicz went on leave to the Suvalsk *gubernia*. But as evidenced by archival documents, the curate was mistaken in his expectations. In a letter of December 21, 1905, written from the village of Bartinki, Suvalsk *gubernia*, to the

45 RGIA, f. 821, op. 125, d. 684, l. 153.

Department of General Affairs, the priest writes that he is wishing to be informed as to which address the promised credit of 958 rubles 50 kopeks had been sent. Instead of money, Fr. Bulwicz received on May 18, 1906, a letter from the Vice-Director of the Department of Religious Affairs advising him that there was under way an attempt "to determine exactly which account of the Ministry of Internal Affairs was to be debited for this disbursement." Fr. Bulwicz sent another letter to the Department of Religious Affairs May 24, 1906, writing that work awaited him out in the Far East—first of all, work with respect to meeting the spiritual needs of Catholics of a huge region, and also work on two committees for the construction of churches in Vladivostok and Harbin. He was unable to return to the Far East because he lacked the money for the return trip.

Unfortunately we do not know when Fr. Bulwicz received the money allotted to him, because there are papers in the archives which suggest that not only the money had been lost, but also a package with warm clothing. The package had been mailed by the priest himself, from Bartinki to Vladivostok, as he expected to arrive in Vladivostok during the winter.

Upon his return to Vladivostok, Fr. Bulwicz served there until 1909 and then he was transferred to Irkutsk as head of the local parish. It was in Irkutsk that a very unusual event occurred that evoked numerous rumors among both the clergy and the parishioners. Here is what happened. On November 1, 1911, he was celebrating the Mass in honor of the feast of All Saints in the Irkutsk church. During the Mass at a moment when all the faithful were on their knees, several military cadets from the Irkutsk Military Institute remained standing. Fr. Bulwicz found their behavior inappropriate. In his homily, he compared the military cadets to empty ears of grain in the field: "For a full ear of grain bends down, while an empty ear of grain juts out—like the heads of military cadets." Naturally all those who were present in the church began to look at the cadets and they, having been shamed, left the church.

This incident was blown up to the level of a political scandal. The Minister of Internal Affairs in a letter of January 21, 1912, to the Archbishop of Mogilev demanded first of all that Fr. Bulwicz be ordered to present a written explanation and second that he be disciplined. The church authorities, however, stood behind the priest. The Metropolitan of the Mogilev Archdiocese, Aleksandr Kluczyński, upon having familiarized himself in great detail with the pastor's report, wrote on March 2, 1912, to the Department of Religious Affairs. He communicated that in his opinion Fr. Bulwicz had acted properly. In accordance with his clerical role and his obligations he was deserving recognition and commendation.

Fr. Bulwicz wrote the following in his report of the incident:

> On the Feast of All Saints, the believers in the church were praying on their knees and only a few military cadets were standing. The gentlemen officers were behind them, on their knees. Had I kept silent, these cadets would have acted in the same way in the future. It is possible that such behavior takes place because while in St. Petersburg and the Pazheski Institute and the Naval Corps there is religious instruction, in the Irkutsk Institute they do not teach religion even though there are twenty Catholic cadets studying there.

This unpleasantness in Irkutsk was not the last. For example, in a letter of the Irkutsk governor to the Department of Religious Affairs dated July 27, 1912, we find: "The Irkutsk curate, Fr. Peter Bulwicz, baptized according to the Roman Catholic ritual an underage Jewish boy, the son of the Balagansk merchant Anatol Jakowlewicz Fluks, without observing the requirements of Part 4 of Article 71 of the *Ustavnaia Instruktsiia*." However, the public prosecutor of the District Court of Irkutsk, after investigating the matter, concluded that Fr. Bulwicz's action did not come under the jurisdiction of the criminal code, but by virtue of Statute 107 of the Code, was to be referred to the religious court as a disciplinary matter.

6. *Fr. Stanisław Agapit Lawrinowicz*

After the transfer of Fr. Peter Paul Bulwicz from Blagoveshchensk to Vladivostok in early 1903, the Blagoveshchensk parish was in need of an immediate replacement. The head of the Archdiocese of Mogilev, Stefan Denisiewicz, submitted a request to the Department of Religious Affairs that he be allowed to send a new priest to the Far East. His request was favorably reviewed by the Department and on December 13, 1903, by Order No. 3212, the vicar of the Neuteransk Roman Catholic church of the Vitebsk *gubernia*, Fr. Stanisław Lawrinowicz, was designated the vicar of the Vladivostok Roman Catholic church.

Stanisław Lawrinowicz was born October 8, 1866, on the Palishka Estate, Kovensk *gubernia*, to the family of the nobleman Feliks Agapit Lawrinowicz and Barbara Lawrinowicz nee Krzyżanowska. The child was baptized Stanisław Agapit in the Krakówsk Roman Catholic church.[46] He was schooled at home and then he enrolled in the seminary of the Archdiocese of Mogilev, where his younger brother was also a student. After completion of the seminary and ordination, the young priest was assigned the post of vicar in the Roman Catholic parish of the little town of Neuteransk. His brother, Fr. Julian, was assigned to the Pisinsk parish of the Vitebsk *gubernia.* His ministry in the Neuteransk parish was very difficult for the young priest since he always felt himself superfluous. For this reason he petitioned the Archbishop to be transferred to any other place. When they learned of this, the parishioners of the Neuteransk parish quickly wrote two very touching letters to the head of the Archdiocese. They wrote of Fr. Lawrinowicz as a fine, empathetic and hard-working priest. Since there was a plan for the building of a new church in the little town of Neuteransk, the parishioners requested that Fr. Stanisław be named the head of that parish. This request was signed by a hundred parishioners of the village of Rogovka,

46 RGIA, f. 826, op. 1, d. 118, l. 15.

where the Neuteransk church was located. A different assignment awaited Fr. Lawrinowicz—the Far East.

At the beginning of March 1904, the young priest set off on his journey—and he got lost! From Vladivostok came a telegram from Fr. Peter Paul Bulwicz stating "He has not arrived!" The priest's relatives responded, "He has already left!" Everyone was very upset—a priest had been lost. Then suddenly came some very disturbing news from the head of the Orenburg parish, who communicated that Fr. Lawrinowicz had fallen ill with typhus and was taken from the train in an unconscious condition at Kinel station. He was transported to the hospital in the city of Orenburg on March 12, 1904. After several weeks in a deep coma, Fr. Stanisław, thanks be to God, came to. He immediately wrote the Archbishop that typhus had unexpectedly thrown him off his path. He was now gradually recovering and once again learning to walk, but unfortunately he had developed pleurisy and he would need to drink kumiss in order to avoid tuberculosis. Under these circumstances he was not yet able to set off to his assignment.

While he was unconscious, his assignment document to Vladivostok satisfied the local police, but as he began to recover, the police demanded a "residence permit."[47] On the one hand, Fr. Stanisław had no such document and on the other hand, his health would not permit him to depart yet for Vladivostok. He had no idea what he was to do in this predicament. Fortunately, on September 7, 1904, Fr. Lawrinowicz received a communiqué from the Archbishop that he was to set off immediately for Samara, where he would fill in for Fr. Lapszis, who had fallen ill. Once Fr. Lapszis had recovered, Fr. Lawrinowicz would then without delay depart for Khabarovsk in order to tend to the needs of local Catholics there and also to teach religion in the city high schools. All the same, it was not until November 4, 1904, that Fr. Lawrinowicz finally managed to leave for the Far East.

47 RGIA, f. 826, op. 1, d. 118, l. 58.

Having arrived in Vladivostok, Fr. Lawrinowicz received from the Archbishop on January 22, 1905, a telegram advising him "Superseding my directive of September 7, 1904, No. 2285, I propose that Your Reverence remain in residence in Vladivostok to tend to the spiritual needs of the Catholics in Vladivostok."[48] But then on the following day, January 23, 1905, he received another directive, that he was to quickly set off for Blagoveshchensk to fill the post of chaplain in the local chapel.[49] One may suppose that this reversal came about because of numerous letters from the parishioners in Blagoveshchensk to the Archbishop, pointing out that in the Amur Region there were already 1,500 Catholics, but Fr. Bulwicz had been transferred from Blagoveshchensk to Vladivostok and no other priest had been sent to the Amur Region. On the other hand, they pointed out, Vladivostok already had a priest (Fr. Bulwicz), and there were chaplains in nearby Nikolsk-Ussuriisk, and the local vicar served the needs of Catholics of the cities of Nikolaevsk and Khabarovsk. After lengthy negotiations, Fr. Lawrinowicz was formally placed in Vladivostok but his obligations were to include visitation of all the parishes of the Far East. Then on August 23, 1905, Fr. Lawrinowicz was directed to relocate to Blagoveshchenk, where he then remained until 1909.[50]

On March 4, 1909, Fr. Lawrinowicz received his next directive from the Archbishop: "as the result of the transfer of Fr. Bulwicz to other responsibilities in the Archdiocese, I propose that Your Reverence relocate to Vladivostok to serve as curate of the Vladivostok church." This assignment was supported by the Department of Religious Affairs and Fr. Lawrinowicz finally departed from Blagoveshchensk to Vladivostok where a very important process was already under way: preparation for the construction of

48 RGIA, f. 826, op. 1, d. 118, l. 70.

49 RGIA, f. 826, op. 1, d. 118, l. 71.

50 Translator's Note: By 1900 the population of Blagoveshchensk (50,000) exceeded that of Vladivostok and Khabarovsk combined. (John J. Stephen, *The Russian Far East*, p. 83)

the brick church. The temporary wooden barracks church named in honor of Immaculate Virgin Mary for a long time had not been able to accommodate all the Catholics who at that time numbered more than 4,000. In the fortifications section of the city there were significantly more—approximately 10,000.

7. *Visitation of the Far East by Bishop Jan Cieplak*

In the summer of 1909 Bishop Jan Cieplak traveled by a special train to make a missionary visitation of many Roman Catholic churches in Russia, including the Far East. While he was in Vladivostok he presided over solemn liturgy in the "barracks church" and then led a procession of the faithful to the place where the cornerstone of the future brick church had been laid in 1908. The bishop blessed the cornerstone, and after the solemn ceremony he was photographed with a group of parishioners on the hillside. Happily this photograph has been preserved in the local archives and it allows us to see the bishop and Fr. Stanisław Lawrinowicz and other clergy who accompanied the bishop on his visitation.

Among Roman Catholic clergy of Imperial Russia at the beginning of the twentieth century, the suffragan bishop Jan Feliks Cieplak was a distinguished figure. He was widely known in the Catholic world as a zealous Catholic, a highly educated clergyman, and a fighter for justice.[51] His biography is full of extraordinary events which more than once threatened his life. But no matter what the circumstances, Bishop Cieplak never lost his own self-respect, nor did he ever disparage that of any other.

He was born August 17, 1857, in the little town of Denbrov Gornich of the Keletz *voevodstvo*, Poland, in a miner's family. After graduation from high school in Keletz in 1873, he enrolled in the local theological academy. Upon his completion of studies, he received a master's degree in theology and he was ordained July 24, 1881. In 1904 Fr. Cieplak, first as chaplain and later as canon, served

51 *Encyklopedia Katolicka*, v. 3, p. 471.

in the chapel of the Good Shepherd Orphanage. On November 7, 1908, he was elevated to the rank of bishop in the St. Petersburg church of St. Catherine where he served as suffragan bishop.

After defending his doctoral dissertation, Fr. Cieplak, now as professor, began teaching Biblical archeology and dogmatic and moral theology at the St. Petersburg Theological Academy. At the same time the young professor was assisting the preparation for printing of Nowodworski's *Church Encyclopedia.* In June 1908 Professor Cieplak was designated auxilliary bishop of the Archdiocese of Mogilev. He immediately took up its practical work, which primarily involved a study of the situation of the very furthest Roman Catholic parishes of the Empire. In the summer of 1909 he undertook a large-scale inspection of his archdiocese. Traveling with a group of clergy in a special train and by naval transport, he made a visitation of all the Roman Catholic parishes in Siberia, the Far East, Manchuria and Sakhalin. This visitation enabled him to make a thorough investigation of many Roman Catholic parishes in both the European and Asian parts of the Empire and to acquire a clear understanding of the state of affairs in these far-flung communities of Catholics.

Bishop Cieplak and his entourage arrived in Khabarovsk on June 20, 1909, on the postal steamship *Korf* after having visited Nikolaevsk. By the time of his visit Khabarovsk had already been designated the capital of the Far East. In 1888 a preparatory school of the Siberian Cadet Corps had been established in Khabarovsk and in May of 1890 the school had graduated twelve cadets who had been sent on assignment to Omsk. The city also boasted a women's high school. Long before his death, the first governor general, Baron A. N. Korf, had entertained the dream of establishing in Khabarovsk if not a scholarly society at least a small regional museum. His successor, General Lieutenant S. M. Dukhovskoi, carried out the dream of his predecessor. Thanks be to God, he managed to create in the Amur Region a special scholarly entity, the Amur Branch of the Imperial Russian Geographical Society. General Lieutenant N. I. Grodekov on April 10, 1899, was named its president. It was he who, thanks to the support of the Emperor and members of the royal family, was able to create in Khabarovsk in association with the Geographical Society a marvelous scholarly library.

The construction of the Catholic church in Khabarovsk was moving along well, and the *Priamurskie vedomosti* [Amur Region Register] informed its readers of the progress of construction. In one of the issues an author writing under the initials V.S. wrote: "Very likely the altar will soon gleam with candlelight and we will see Christians on bended knee." And in fact, the altar was soon gleaming on the occasion of the arrival of Bishop Cieplak and his entourage. The local paper in Issue No. 1422 of 1909 published a short notice of this event:

> For the arrival of the bishop the humble wooden chapel from early morning was adorned with garlands of green branches. At the entrance into the church courtyard was a solemn arch crowned with flowers. Catholic soldiers brought from the shores of the Amur several bags of pure white sand and sprinkled it along the path to the church, which was bordered with young saplings. The clergy, parishioners with a cross and banners, and the local Catholic priest and military chaplain, Fr. Bolesław Janowicz, met the bishop at the church courtyard.[52]

Leading the bishop into the church were children dressed in white with crowns, strewing beautiful flowers along the path. The Divine Liturgy was celebrated after the Bishop's homily.

This most distinguished guest stayed three days in Khabarovsk. He presided over the Divine Liturgy, he preached, and he performed anointings and other church rituals. The presence of this high-ranking churchman was the cause for many of the rank and file Catholic members of the Amur garrison to take leave so that they would be able to attend morning Mass and participate in the evening ceremo-

52 RGIA, f. 826, op. 1, d. 2208, l. 22.

ny of anointing. The joy and sincerity of the Khabarovsk parishioners made such an impression on Bishop Cieplak that he decided to remain in Khabarovsk for another day in order that each Catholic would have the opportunity to go to confession and receive Holy Communion. The church was full from morning until late in the evening. It was not only the Bishop and the local priest, Fr. Janowicz, who participated in the liturgies, but also those priests who were accompanying the Bishop on his journey. But naturally most of the tasks fell on the shoulders of Fr. Janowicz, who successfully managed them. During the Bishop's visit to Sakhalin Island, Fr. Janowicz was able to help the Bishop deal with a complicated and very difficult situation that prevailed on the prison island.

The oppressive need of the Catholic Poles exiled on Sakhalin, the complete absence of any charitable organizations or services for them shook Bishop Cieplak and those accompanying him. When the Bishop learned that there was not, nor had there ever been, a Catholic church or a regular priest assigned to Sakhalin, and that priests from Khabarovsk or Vladivostok visited Sakhalin only once a year, he decided to leave behind on the island someone from his entourage. He was able to convince Fr. Władysław Mieżwinski to stay. He agreed to one year of service on the prison island, which in its turn, freed up the military chaplain of the Amur Region, Fr. Bolesław Janowicz, to extend his visits throughout the territory of the Far East.

As a result of Bishop Cieplak's visitation, three new deaneries were established in Siberia: Omsk (38,000 Catholics) and Tomsk (35,770 Catholics) in western Siberia and Irkutsk (30,000 Catholics) in eastern Siberia. But in these geographically expansive deaneries there were only thirty priests.

The later fate of Bishop Cieplak was difficult—one could even say that it was tragic. After Wincentij Kluczyński, Archbishop of Mogilev, resigned, Bishop Cieplak was appointed Apostolic Administrator and he served in that capacity from August 6, 1914, until December 1917, when Eduard Baron von Ropp was appointed Archbishop. After the arrest of Archbishop Ropp in 1919, Bishop Cieplak became the Vicar General.

After the February (1917) Revolution, the Provisional Government created a Commission on Religious Denominations and selected Bishop Cieplak to serve on the Commission. At the same time, the Provisional Government was considering the appointment of Bishop Cieplak as Bishop of Vilnius, but the erupting October Revolution swept away all these plans and set the bishop's life upon a harsh and thorny path. Although he was appointed Titular Archbishop of Achrida, his freedom was very limited as he was now on the list of those considered "unreliable." But no threats or fears were able to change the bishop's character. He organized an "underground" seminary where "disgraced" priests taught. The ring of suspicion tightened around him and he was arrested in 1920 and then again in 1922 for anti-Soviet activity, and he found himself in the Petersburg prison on Shpalernaia Street. In March 1923, Bishop Cieplak, Monsignor Konstantin Romuald Budkewicz (pastor at St. Catherine's church and dean of the St. Petersburg Deanery), Leonid Ivanovich Fyodorov (exarch of the Eastern Rite Catholics) and fourteen priests were sent to Lubianka Prison in Moscow.

The judicial proceeding was officially considered "open," but those present in the courtroom were actually a specially selected group of people. *New York Herald* correspondent Francis McCullagh described what was seen and heard in the courtroom:

> The prosecutor Krylenko tried with all his might to give the proceedings a political character, but the Catholic priests and Bishop Cieplak denied all the accusations, stating that they did not engage in agitation against Soviet power. Thus this trial in the eyes of the world was turned into a campaign for the annihilation of Christianity in Russia… I once again regained my faith in people, when in those days of disappointments and spiritual oppression I saw

> how high these people could rise. Quite possibly no Christian martyrs had achieved this...[53]

Bishop Cieplak and Monsignor Budkewicz both received the death penalty. The bishop's sentence was commuted to ten years' imprisonment, but Monsignor Budkewicz was shot.

The Vatican and English diplomats intervened on behalf of Bishop Cieplak. As a result, he was released from prison and expelled from Russia. Upon arriving in Poland he was met by thousands who turned out to welcome him. He then went to the Vatican where he took part in the canonization process for Andrzej Bobola. Soon he was invited to America, where he visited several Catholic parishes. It was while he was in America that he learned that he had been named Archbishop of Vilnius. However, despite his ardent desire to set off quickly for Poland, he was unable to do so: he developed pneumonia and suffered complications that led to his death.

Bishop Jan Cieplak died February 17, 1926, in St. Mary's Hospital in Passaic, New Jersey, at age sixty-eight. The coffin with the body of the deceased bishop was taken to Europe, where he was buried in an underground crypt of the cathedral in Vilnius.

Stanisław Wojciechowski, president of Poland (1922-1926), posthumously awarded the bishop the Grand Cross of the Rebirth of Poland. The process for his beatification has been under way since 1952.

8. Fr. Bolesław Janowicz

The head of the Khabarovsk parish, Fr. Bolesław Janowicz, came from a bourgeois family of Vilnius, where he was born June 24,

---

53 Francis McCullagh was a British officer who was retained as a correspondent for the *New York Herald* to attend the trial. He dispatched his reports to the *Herald* throughout the course of the trial. The author was unable to provide the source for her Russian citation, but the interested reader can find a full description of the trial in McCullagh's full-length book, *Bolshevik Persecution of Christianity* (New York: E.P. Dutton and Company, 1924).

1869. Upon graduation from the city high school, Bolesław studied from 1886 to 1890 at the seminary and then he continued his education at the St. Petersburg Theological Academy but a serious illness cut short all his plans. In 1892 he was ordained a priest and set out upon his path in service of the Lord. At first Fr. Bolesław worked in Belorussian parishes and then, in 1907, he was transferred to the Far East as staff priest for the Amur Region Military District. As military chaplain his responsibilities included service to the Amur Region Military District, but in addition he also had to teach religion in the Cadet Corps as well as in the high school and technical school of Khabarovsk. However, before he had even arrived in Khabarovsk, he had to overcome serious battles with bureaucratic obstacles, since for such a complicated journey the priest needed appropriate documents and sufficient funds. He was unable to reach his destination until April 17, 1908, since the correspondence concerning the payment to him of sufficient travel funds dragged on for almost six months.

Judging by the archival documents, Fr. Bolesław often made pastoral visits throughout the whole region and he was greatly concerned that his service of God should have a beneficial effect upon his whole congregation. In his letter to the Mogilev archbishop dated December 8, 1908, the priest writes: "I have the honor of most respectfully requesting of Your Reverence that in the humble parish of Nikolsk-Ussuriisk I would be allowed to conduct solemn liturgies (with the collection of gifts) on the followings days: (1) the feast of St. Nicholas, (2) the most important feasts of the Blessed Virgin, (3) during Lent, (4) Corpus Christi, and (5) Pentecost."

Fr. Janowicz's ministry went well and he liked his work. But the Sakhalin authorities unexpectedly brought a criminal action against him on account of his having married an Orthodox man to a Catholic woman during one of his pastoral visits to Sakhalin. This was a scandal because performing such a marriage was looked upon as a crime and accordingly it would require a trial at the scene of the crime—i.e., on Sakhalin. The panel of judges, however, would not be able to get out to the island until the water passage would be navigable, which would be during the month of May. The frightened priest petitioned the Mogilev Archbishop to keep him in his assignment as military chaplain for otherwise he would have no means of supporting himself. But he received a negative response as another priest had already taken his place.[54] Fr. Bolesław found himself for all practical purposes without any rights to his ministry and at the same time he had no right to leave. His situation was completely hopeless. He turned to his home diocese, the Diocese of Vilensk, to ask for help and they responded with assistance. In spite of the angry letters of the Director of the Department of Religious Affairs and the Chamberlain of the Supreme Court, Fr. Bolesław upon receipt of the funds from his compatriots departed for his native land and once again took up responsibilities as the head of a parish in the city of Ishchole, in the Lidsk district of the Vitebsk *gubernia*.

9. *Fr. Antonij Żukowski*

The fate of yet another Catholic priest was dramatically played out in the Far East.[55] Fr. Antonij Żukowski came from a bourgeois family of the city of Borisov, Minsk *gubernia*, where he was born February 24, 1885. In 1903 the young man completed the Borisov city four-year school and received a certificate as pharmacy apprentice. In 1904 he entered the Mogilev Archdiocesan Seminary which he completed in 1908. On January 25, 1908, Antonij Żukowski was ordained a priest and on April 21, 1909, we find him appointed vicar of the Roman Catholic parish of the city of Tomsk.[56] An unpleasant surprise awaited him upon his arrival. The governor of Tomsk summoned the priest and explained that, in violation of Article 42 of the *Rules Concerning the Appointment of Catholic Priests to New Assignments*, the appointment of Fr. Żukowski to the city of Tomsk had not received the governor's approval. The governor gave

54 RGIA, f. 826, op. 1, d. 2298.

55 Ibid., l. 5.

56 RGIA, f. 826, op. 1, d. 1839, l. 121.

Fr. Żukowski a month to clarify the situation, after which he would have to leave Tomsk.

Naturally, Fr. Żukowski turned to the Mogilev archbishop for direction. He received in turn notification of a new transfer "to the Far East, to the city of Blagoveshchensk, as military chaplain." The letter was supplemented with a money order in the amount of 100 rubles for travel expenses. For Fr. Żukowski this was a real catastrophe, since from Tomsk to Sretensk (2,922 versts) one would need to travel six days by rail and it would cost 45 rubles. Then from Sretensk one could travel only by horse, and that segment of the journey would take ten days and cost 300 rubles. As a result, in spite of the governor's stern order, Fr. Żukowski was not able to leave Tomsk for some time inasmuch as sufficient monies for his travels were not received until March 23rd. Thus he was unable to reach his destination, Blagoveshchensk, until May 18, 1910.

In Blagoveshchensk, where 250 to 300 Catholics were living in 1910, Fr. Antonij undertook his pastoral obligations and right away began visitation of the villages of the Amur Region Catholics—of whom approximately 800 were newly arrived. In the Blagoveshchensk parish the young priest's obligations included meeting the parish's needs, maintaining the parish registry and also teaching religion in the city high schools. Fr. Antonij paid great attention to the minor administrative details of the parish, but he also strove to resolve larger, more complicated problems. Having received permission of the Ministry of Internal Affairs, he was able to find the means to complete alongside the church the construction of a beautiful brick 48-arshin bell tower. The roof of the bell tower was covered with zinc-clad iron and the cross upon the bell tower was also of iron, covered with black lacquer. It weighed 7.5 puds (270 pounds). Four bells were hung in the bell tower—the three smaller bells were donated by the parishioner Francysk Ożdżenski, and the fourth bell, which weighed 25 puds, 19 funts [close to a half ton], was donated by Stanisław Gartung in 1912. On this bell was an inscription showing St. Stanisław with the words "St. Stanisław—Gift of Stanisław Gartung."

Despite the conscientious ministry of Fr. Żukowski, many serious complaints were made to the Mogilev archbishop that Fr. Żukowski was attempting to convert Orthodox to Catholicism. In an explanatory report to the archbishop, Fr. Żukowski wrote the following:

> I have been accused of attempting to convert to Catholicism certain Orthodox who are married to Catholics and that I am generally intolerant in my relations with Orthodox. It has been said that during a visit in February 1911 to the little town of Ozernoe I refused to hear the confessions of Catholics who are married to Orthodox and that I denied them Holy Communion until such time as they should cease living with their Orthodox spouses. But I have never taken upon myself the propagation of the Catholic faith among the Orthodox and I do not intend to do so, for such an undertaking in the first place is not part of my responsibilities and in the second place I have not the time for it. The villages where the Catholics live are 150 to 300 kilometers from Blagoveshchensk and possibly even further, in the higher reaches of the Amur River. Thus I can visit them no more often than twice year. When I visit them, I marry the couples, I baptize the infants, I hear confessions and I give communion to the parishioners. I make it no secret that I give moral instruction to the parishioners—but that comes within my responsibilities as a priest. I insist that my parishioners live morally and peacefully. I tell them also that they should avoid mixed marriages, for these are often the source of familial complications. But to confession I always accept all Catholics. I never turn Catholics away from confession.

But Fr. Antonij Żukowski was not destined to continue his pastoral ministry either in Blagoveshchensk or in the District, since an Orthodox priest, Fr. Andronik Liubovich, had submitted a complaint against him. This priest wrote to the Orthodox bishop that the Catholic priest of the Blagoveshchenk Roman Catholic parish, Fr. Żukowski, criticized the Orthodox church for its activities and he referred to a short note that Fr. Żukowski had left on his visiting card once, not finding Fr. Andronik at home. He had written the following: "In order to avoid any familial misunderstandings, it would be better if you, Fr. Andronik, would not marry Catholics and Orthodox." Naturally this "scandal" was exaggerated. They firmly demanded explanations from Fr. Żukowski as to why he was interfering in the affairs of the Orthodox. They complained that he wanted to marry Catholics and Orthodox only according to the Catholic rite. To this Fr. Żukowski responded that "Fr. Andronik did not understand my thought." Later on, Fr. Żukowski wrote, "I am certain that marriages of Catholics and Orthodox, with very few exceptions, are unsuccessful. But I never, and to no one, have ever said that the bishop orders that we not hear the confessions of those married to Orthodox." They also found fault with Fr. Żukowski in the following event. On January 10, 1911, Maria Pegasovna Goldobina submitted to the governor a petition to be allowed to accept the Catholic faith. The document was sent by post; she had a receipt. But a long period of time passed and there was no response. Fr. Żukowski, taking into account the complicated circumstances, baptized Maria into the Catholic faith and then, on February 13, 1912, married her to the Catholic Stanisław Krzyliński.

But the most egregious fault of Fr. Żukowski was the fact that in 1911 he accepted into the Catholic faith the Jew Naum Minski "without the preliminary request to the Ministry of Internal Affairs and without the permission of said minister." This was a violation of Article 17 of the Statutes of the Ministry of Foreign Confessions. For this violation, Naum Minski was exiled from the Amur Region, and upon Fr. Żukowski came crashing down a whole heap of accusations. In defending himself, Fr. Żukowski wrote that he had not converted any Orthodox to the Catholic faith, nor had he any wish to do so, for each person ought to decide such questions in accordance with his own conscience. Naturally, the metropolitan archbishop Wincentij Kluczyński was unwillingly drawn into this scandal. On February 21, 1912, he wrote the following to the Department of Religious Affairs:

> I have the honor of proposing an explanation. However, knowing and understanding to the fullest the universal hostility of the administrative authorities toward the Roman Catholic clergy, I am sure that no explanations, no justifications of Fr. Żukowski would be able to help him. His situation is incomparably worse than that of a criminal for he is deprived of a lawyer's defense. It is not within the power of the head of the archdiocese to render him assistance, since his opinion would be considered impartial and one-sided. In order to somehow rescue Fr. Żukowski I am freeing him from his responsibilities as head of the parish and transferring him to the German colonies of the Turgansk district to serve as chaplain. I hereby inform the Department of Religious Affairs of this transfer.

And thus Fr. Żukowski was transferred February 22, 1912, to Tugai, but his ministry there did not go well because most of his parishioners were German and did not know Russian and he on the other hand did not know German. The Mogilev archbishop then transferred Fr. Żukowski to Barnaul where he served as the head of the parish and in addition taught religion in the city high school. In Barnaul there were also German prisoners of war, Catholics with whom he had reason to associate by virtue of his position as the local priest. Unexpectedly, on September 23, 1914, the Barnaul *ispravnik* received a secret order from Tomsk in which he was advised that he was to place Fr. Żukowski on notice that he was to cut off any "close association" with the German and Austrian prisoners of war. If he would not do so, then he would be prosecuted and expelled beyond the bounds of the Tomsk *gubernia*. In his letter of explanation, Fr. Żukowski wrote to the metropolitan of the Mogilev archdiocese that Catholic prisoners of war came to him in his capacity as a Catholic priest for confession. Being a pastor, he did not have the right to refuse Catholics confession and to remove them from his apartment. Therefore, as a subject of the Russian government, he considered the accusations lodged against him insulting.

After the October Revolution, Siberia for a full two years was broken off from Russia. In Barnaul things were relatively peaceful although the new Soviet authority had removed the Barnaul registry books. Fr. Żukowski therefore had no choice but to violate several church canons, for example, marrying couples without taking into account various church regulations. He was also unsure as to which language to use for maintaining the parish registry—Polish or Latin. He was unexpectedly arrested as a Polish spy—war had broken out between Poland and Russia. He spent fifty days in a prison cell. After a long sorting out of who was who, he was released from prison—but now he was numbered among the Polish prisoners of war. It was only the intervention of Bishop Jan Cieplak that allowed Fr. Żukowski to extricate himself from this difficult situation and to accept a transfer to Novo-Nikolaevsk (now Novosibirsk).

Soon thereafter, at the request of Bishop Cieplak, Fr. Żukowski traveled to Omsk and other cities of western Siberia and then reported back to Bishop Cieplak in great detail on the fate of Catholic parishes and Catholic pastors in Siberia. Fr. Żukowski identified as the most serious hardship the shortage of Catholic priests in Siberia and wrote "if the number of priests is not increased, the people will simply go to seed and forget their religious obligations." In 1924 Fr. Żukowski was transferred to Irkutsk to the position of acting dean and then somewhere in Siberia during the time of the revolutionary upheavals … Fr. Antonij Żukowski was shot.

10. Fr. Stanisław Agapit Lawrinowicz – Continued

Meanwhile in Vladivostok Fr. Stanisław Lawrinowicz continued his ministry, which required him to serve practically the entire Far East. His ministry progressed not without various complications and from the archival documents we relate one of those. This was a complaint sent to the Mogilev archbishop from the headquarters of the Amur Military District against Fr. Lawrinowicz, who had been invited to perform the funeral service for Iwan Zaginczak, a clerk of the Tenth East Siberian Rifle Regiment. Fr. Lawrinowicz said the funeral service for the deceased, but he declined to accompany the body to the cemetery. The chancellor of the Archdiocese of Mogilev requested an explanation from Fr. Lawrinowicz. He prepared a detailed report in which he set forth the facts of the matter. He explained that he always performed the funeral services for the lower rank and file and other military personnel even though he was not the military chaplain and such funerals would not be included in his staff responsibilities. He said "for five years I have served in the Far East and I have never refused anyone anything. But in this case, it would have been necessary to go approximately five kilometers by foot to the cemetery, and I had to decline." The Archbishop defended the priest's action, explaining that Fr. Lawrinowicz had many responsibilities throughout the whole expansive parish and therefore the military ought to request a special military chaplain to serve the military contingent.

On August 14, 1910, a new place of service was proposed to Fr. Lawrinowicz: the post of military chaplain of the newly established St. Petersburg Marinsk Chapel. In his place as the head of the Vladivostok parish would be Fr. Jósef Skokowski. But on August 25th, the Archbishop noted that Fr. Skokowski had already been named the curate of the Tashkent parish and therefore Fr. Lawrinowicz would need to remain in Vladivostok.

On October 12, 1911, there was a new directive concerning the transfer of Fr. Lawrinowicz to the post of curate of the Tambov parish. One might suppose that this assignment would be of interest to

Fr. Lawrinowicz, since he would now be relocating to the western part of Russia, nearer to his homeland. During the time of his service in the Far East his mother had died and he had not been able to accompany her in her last days. Now his father was often ill and in letters to his son begged him to return to the west. Therefore, upon receiving the notice of his transfer, Fr. Lawrinowicz wasted no time and by January 24, 1912, he was able to advise the Archbishop that he had assumed his new post in Tambov. His service in his new parish went along peacefully without any complications. In February of 1912 he was notified that he would be admitted to teaching religion in the city high school and the private girls school. In June of 1912 came sorrowful news about the death of his father and he set off for the funeral.

Having returned to his own parish, Fr. Lawrinowicz fell ill—most likely the result of typhus and the difficulties of missionary work in the Far East. In the summer of 1917, Fr. Lawrinowicz was transferred to the post of head of the Radom parish, Chausovsk district, where he served five years. This was a very difficult time—economic ruin, the horrors of civil war and the complete impoverishment of the parishioners. But the head of the parish needed to be concerned about his flock and to take whatever means necessary to save the church and church property.

It is difficult today to understand how it would be possible to manage the church and save church properties in such a difficult time for the Faith, for there had now begun the epoch of so-called "War Socialism," and from the churches, both Orthodox and Catholic, they took absolutely all religious items and destroyed parish libraries—and therefore to preserve church objects could have been possible only for a person who was fanatically dedicated to the Church. And indeed such a person was Fr. Stanisław Lawrinowicz. His strength, however, quickly dissipated and by September 21, 1924, he had died.

11. Fr. Bolesław Wolyniec

In 1912, Fr. Bolesław Wolyniec was transferred from Samara to Blagoveshchensk. This priest was born to the peasant family of Jósef Wolyniec and his wife Anna Wojszes, in Sedlisk *volost*, Oshmiansk district, Vilensk *gubernia*. He was baptized in the Germanisk Roman Catholic parish. He graduated from high school in St. Petersburg, where he received a certificate as a pharmacy apprentice, and then he completed the Mogilev archdiocesan seminary and received his clerical title. His first assignment began in 1909 in Vitebsk, the parish of St. Anthony, where he landed upon the request of the Vitebsk dean, Fr. Andruszkiewicz. The arrival of the new priest had been approved by the governor of Vitebsk. The dean wrote to the archbishop: "The parish of St. Anthony is vast—and in addition to serving parishioners in two parts of the city, the priest must often go beyond the city limits to tend to the spiritual needs of the people. In addition the priest is required to appear in district court to administer the oath to Catholics on trial." In addition to his service as a priest, Fr. Bolesław was permitted to teach religion in the city's Second and Third Boys' High School as well as in the city's two-year girls school.

Fr. Bolesław worked in Vitebsk only until April 1911, then upon the directive of Bishop Cieplak he was transferred to Samara. What was the cause of this transfer? In the priest's personnel file, it is recorded that the head of the Vitebsk parish, Fr. Benedict Andruszkiewicz, complained about the unbearable vulgarity and arrogance of Fr. Bolesław—who responded to Fr. Andruszkiewicz's observations with profanity and a threat "I'm outta here!" He in fact did leave, having been transferred to Samara. But he wasn't able to make a go of it in Samara either for the very same reasons and therefore the archbishop, on February 21, 1912, transferred him to the Far East, to Blagoveshchensk, to serve as the acting head of the Blagoveshchensk parish. The archives contain documents evidencing a lengthy correspondence between Fr. Bolesław and the chancery concerning payment to Fr. Bolesław for his journey from Samara to Blagoveshchensk. The priest proposed the following accounting:

1. Railway passage from Samara to Khabarovsk, second class—93 rubles, 70 kopecks
2. From Khabarovsk to Blagoveshchensk by steamship up the Amur River, first class—24 rubles, 23 kopecks
3. Per diem for food on the steamship—2 rubles, 50 kopecks.

Altogether, Fr. Bolesław was requesting 120 rubles, 43 kopecks. The documents show that after much red tape, he received 200 rubles for his journey and he was satisfied.

His arrival is recorded in a report dated June 11, 1912, "I received from Fr. Antonij Żukowski the Blagoveshchensk church with all its accoutrements as noted on the inventory list." In the same archival material concerning Fr. Bolesław there is a very interesting historical document, a peculiar oath of a Catholic priest to the Emperor. Set forth below is the text of this oath, which was obligatory for all priests.[57]

> I, the undersigned, do hereby promise and swear to Almighty God, upon His Holy Gospel, that I desire to serve His Imperial Majesty, my true and natural sovereign, the all-merciful Emperor Nicholas Aleksandrovich, the Ruler of all Russia, and the lawful Heir of his Imperial Majesty to the Throne of all Russia, faithfully and without hypocrisy; and to obey him in all things, without sparing my life, to the last drop of my blood; and to protect and defend, in accordance with my utmost understanding, strength and ability, the rights and advantages belonging to the great autocracy, power and authority of His Imperial Majesty, both those that are now legally in force and

57 RGIA, f. 826, op. 1, d. 1968, l. 4.

> those that in the future shall become legally in force, and in so doing to try at the very least to give my allegiance to everything that is concerned with faithful service of His Imperial Majesty and benefit to the state in all cases; and as soon as I should learn of any damage or harm to, or loss of, His Majesty's interest, I will not only expeditiously make this knowledge known, but I will endeavor by all means to ward off and prevent any such damage, harm or loss; and I will firmly keep any secret entrusted to me; and I will be faithful to His Majesty's will; I will not act for any profit, possession, friendship or enmity that is opposed to my duty and my oath; and thus I will act as befits a true subject of His Imperial Majesty and in a way that before God at that Last Judgment I will always be able to give an answer; so may the Lord God judge me in body and soul. In concluding my oath, I kiss the words and the cross of my Savior! Amen

Fr. Bolesław Wolyniec took this sworn oath February 1, 1910. The oath was administered by the Vitebsk dean, Fr. Andruszkewicz.

Despite having taken such an important government oath, even in Blagoveshchensk Fr. Wolyniec was not able to establish normal contact with his flock, as one can tell from the content of a letter sent September 2, 1914, to Archbishop Jan Cieplak: "In view of the hostile attitude of Catholics in Blagoveshchensk to religion and toward me personally, it is not possible to support myself on voluntary contributions, which have almost stopped completely. In addition, my health is not good and the majority of parishioners are unhappy with me on account of "medieval fanaticism" and my frank demands that they fulfill their religious obligations. All this makes my existence at this post impossible. I ask that you release me from this position and call me back to St. Petersburg."

Upon receiving such a serious communiqué, Bishop Cieplak transferred this priest, who was so hard to get along with, to the post of vicar at the Krasnoyarsk parish. It was not until the 1920s that Fr. Boleslaw Wolyniec turned up in the European part of Russia.

12. Beginning of the Ministry of Fr. Karol Sliwowski

After the departure of Fr. Stanisław Lawrinowicz to western Russia at the end of 1911, the metropolitan of the Mogilev archdiocese, Wincentij Kluczyński, sent to Vladivostok a very experienced priest, a distinguished canon of the Mogilev Archdiocese, a bearer of the Order of St. Stanisław, Third Degree—Fr. Karol Sliwowski.[58] Naturally this very experienced priest, having raised up and made famous the Roman Catholic parish of Kazan, had completely other plans. Referring to his venerable age, he asked the Mogilev archbishop to send him somewhere closer to a warm sea. Alas they sent the sixty-six-year-old priest to the not very warm Pacific Ocean....[59]

In Vladivostok there awaited the priest the very same barracks-like chapel dedicated to the Immaculate Virgin Mary and thousands of concerns of a different character. Even though there was a Building Committee in the parish, the construction of the brick church had for all practical purposes come to a complete halt because of the lack of funds. To the amazement of all the Catholics, the new pastor began his transformations in the parish with the renewal of the trustees and the composition of the Building Committee, proposing an open system of election of the trustees. These innovations called forth a storm of indignation on the part of those personages who had up to that time been able to "boss around" both the parish and the Building Committee.

---

58 M. I. Efimova, *Episkop Vladivostokskii - Karol Slivovskii*, Vladivostok, 2003.

59 The details of Karol Sliwowski's early life are not known—his family, his education, his early assignments. There is no information in the parish records or archives in Kazan, where he served prior to his assignment to Vladivostok. Presumably he was born in Belorus, where the devastation of World War II possibly accounts for the loss of the historical record.

The local magnate Bartolomej Karlowicz Borowiks was most indignant of all. He brought complaints to the new curate against the open balloting for the trustees, then he dashed off a complaint against the priest, addressing this so-called document directly to the metropolitan of the Mogilev archdiocese. In this complaint Mr. Borowiks demanded the immediate transfer of Fr. Sliwowski to another parish.[60] In the complaint of this petty whiner, the metropolitan saw the evil intention and so he asked that all complainers sign the complaint with their own hand and have their signatures officially notarized. But very few of those persons listed by Mr. Borowiks wanted to place their officially notarized signatures on the document—and there it all ended. They stopped interfering with the work of the new pastor and he began to stubbornly move forward on the construction of the brick church, the cornerstone of which had been dedicated by Bishop Jan Cieplak back in 1909. The building had practically been completed—it stood surrounded by scaffolding, without bell towers, a roof or the interior wall paintings. The head of the parish did not have the means for these.

Simultaneous with the business of the construction, the priest had to deal with a number of other concerns, the most serious of which were the affairs of the Roman Catholic parish in Nikolsk-Ussuriisk. There was a rather large parish in this city, largely made up of the lower ranks of the military contingents. Among the civilian members of the parish, a large number were railroad workers, the local intelligentsia and businessmen. Back in September 1908, during the period of the ministry of Fr. Stanisław Lawrinowicz, there were serious changes in the parish. At a general meeting of the parishioners, two trustees were selected: Dr. Jósef Tripolski and the homeowner Franc Mialkowski. Fr. Lawrinowicz then sent a letter to the governor general in which he advised that in the garrisons of Nikolsk-Ussuriisk and its surroundings there were already approximately 3,000 Catholic soldiers and approximately 500 *raznochintsy*. All these Catholics needed to attend Mass and it was now necessary

60 RGIA, f. 826, op. 1, d. 1419, l. 106-106 ob.

to transfer the wooden chapel of St. Nicholas the Wonderworker to the center of the town—or to build a new church on a plot of land that had been allotted to the Catholics by the city council. The Mogilev archbishop supported these concerns of Fr. Lawrinowicz, affirming by letter that from his side there were no obstacles to the relocation of the chapel. The question as to payment for the relocation of the old chapel or the construction of a new chapel—in the opinion of the archbishop—ought to be decided by local authorities.

After these clarifications, the Catholics of Nikolsk turned to the local authorities with a proposal that the city convey to them for the transfer of the chapel or construction of a new church a parcel of land in the center of the city. In short order, the city council allotted such a plot of land, suggesting land that was part of a former cemetery. Alas the Catholics were not to rejoice for long. It turned out that according to Article 701 of the Health Regulations of the Code of Law of the Russian Empire dated 1892 and the decision of the Criminal Appellate Department of February 8, 1890, it was forbidden to erect a structure on former cemeteries. Thus the Catholics did not have the right to build a church on the parcel of land granted to them by the city. The question of the allotment of another parcel of land to the Roman Catholic parish for the church simply hung in the air for a long time.

At a special meeting in March 1913, authorized representatives of the Catholic parishioners once again returned to the discussion of this disturbing question. Speaking at the meeting was the head of the postal telegraph office of the city, N. K. Marcynowski, who introduced a proposal to request of the city authorities permission for the sale of Parcel No. 1 in Block 142 that had been allotted to them, in order that they might use the money obtained from the sale to acquire another parcel of land for the church. To the great joy of the Catholics, their proposal was supported by the city council.

In addition to these questions, it fell upon Karol Sliwowski to resolve dozens of other complicated questions which are laid out in the following sections of this work.

13. Fr. Jan Dyrijallo

Fr. Jan Dyrijallo, a military chaplain transferred to the Far East from the western *gubernia*s of Russia, provided great assistance at this time to the parishioners of Nikolsk-Ussuriisk. His biography is very similar to those of other Polish priests—he was born November 5, 1884, to a peasant family in the village of Liaigakh, Kovensk *gubernia*. At first the young boy studied in the Kronstadt gymnasium and then he enrolled in the St. Petersburg Seminary. After graduation from the seminary, he was ordained a priest January 9, 1908, and soon thereafter was named vicar of the Rezhetsk Roman Catholic parish. A year later the young priest was transferred to the post of vicar for the Warsaw Military District and on March 28, 1912, the Mogilev archbishop transferred him to the Far East, to the post of staff priest for the Amur Military District.[61]

Having arrived in Khabarovsk and having become acquainted with the situation, Fr. Dyrijallo clearly realized the difficulties that lay before him. His first journey from Khabarovsk through the surrounding areas where the military contingents were dispersed showed him that the harsh climatic conditions of the Far East did not suit him, and that the most acceptable place for him would be in Nikolsk-Ussuriisk, where the climate was significantly milder than in Khabarovsk. As in a mirror, the frame of mind and the concerns of the young priest were reflected in his report to the Mogilev archbishop dated February 9, 1913:

> In his free time, a residence in Nikolsk would be useful to the military chaplain since there are more than 3,000 Catholics in the military there and several hundred Polish *raznochintsy*. In the absence of a priest, there is no one to celebrate liturgies on the feast days or to tend to their spiritual needs. Nikolsk is located in the center of the Military District and from

61 RGIA, f. 826, op. 1, d. 1782, l. 16.

> there it is easier to travel to the other garrisons to tend to the spiritual needs of Catholic military personnel. A residence in the headquarters in Khabarovsk is not at all useful, given that the spiritual needs of persons there can easily be met by the chaplain of the local church. In view of all the foregoing, I most humbly ask Your Excellency to petition that the main headquarters permit me to select Nikolsk-Ussuriisk as my place of residence.
>
> Fr. Jan Dyrijallo
> Chaplain of the Amur Military District

The priest's request was not acted upon. They answered him that up to this time he had not complained about the climate and that he was therefore obligated to continue his regular visitations of all parts of the Military District, and he was required to live in Khabarovsk. The priest submitted but nevertheless Fr. Dyrijallo allocated to the Catholics of Nikolsk-Ussuriisk more time than to his other parishioners. Soon Fr. Dyrijallo wrote another letter—this time addressing himself to the Amur District Governor General on the question of the transfer of the chapel of St. Nicholas the Wonderworker to a new plot in the center of the city. It was not meant that he should be involved with this question as he was soon transferred to Harbin.

14. Fr. Dominik Mikszys

A new priest, Fr. Dominik Mikszys, now began to tend the flock in Nikolsk-Ussuriisk, and it was he who managed to revive the activity of the parishioners with respect to the construction of the Catholic church. First of all, on March 19, 1915, at a general meeting of the parish, a new Building Committee was created, the president of which was Fr. Dominik. Soon thereafter news of this event and a request for material support were sent to the Collegium of the Mogilev archdiocese. The reaction of the Mogilev archdiocese was positive, and on June 25, 1915, the Mogilev archdiocese sent 500 rubles to Fr. Dominik for the construction of the chapel from the interest of the Maintenance Fund.[62]

By this time in the parish of Nikolsk-Ussuriisk there began to arise certain serious circumstances affecting the "inner climate" of the Catholic parish. It all began with a resident of Nikolsk-Ussuriisk who was among the number of very wealthy citizens—a Mr. Feliks Steckiewicz, who proposed to have prayer services in his spacious home and to have the Catholic church constructed on his land, inasmuch as construction of the church on the land of the former cemetery had been forbidden. Not suspecting anything foul, Fr. Dominik supported these proposals. Gradually Mr. Steckiewicz became the "main figure" in the Nikolsk parish—which was all right with Fr. Dominik. But not everything was all right to the chancellor of the archdiocese in the financial accounting of Fr. Dominik. On May 10, 1916, Mr. W. Pluskiewicz of the archdiocesan chancery sent Fr. Dominik an inquiry and a request that he submit supporting documents regarding expenditures of certain sums. It was not Fr. Dominik who submitted the answer, but the secretary of the Building Committee, who advised that the sum of money in question had been placed in the bank by Fr. Mikszys in his own name, and now the money had been transferred to the savings bank of Nikolsk-Ussuriisk in the name of the Building Committee.

Instead of Fr. Dominik, the response was signed by all the leading figures of the clique of Mr. Feliks Steckiewicz. Apparently the response did not at all satisfy the chancery. On this basis, Bishop Jan Cieplak notified the Military Governor of the Amur District that Fr. Dominik Mikszys had been released from his responsibilities as chaplain of the Roman Catholic chapel of Nikolsk-Ussuriisk. He would remain at his post as chaplain of the Amur Military District, with permission to live temporarily in the city of Nikolaevsk. Fr. Mikszys never did serve in Nikolaevsk, however, since without permission he departed for Harbin.

---

62 RGIA, f. 826, op. 1, d. 169, l. 39.

15. Fr. Stanisław Kolodzejczyk

Fr. Stanisław Kolodzejczyk, a refugee from the enemy invasion, the vicar of the Laskarzhevsk parish, Lublinsk *gubernia*, was sent to the vacated post of chaplain of the Roman Catholic chapel in Nikolsk-Ussuriisk in the summer of 1915.[63] Fr. Stanisław undertook his ministry in the new parish with great willingness, but very soon he became interested in the amazing fate of the church under construction and therefore he expressed an insistent interest in the work of the Building Committee. Here the priest ran up against the strange (to his fresh view) activities of the head of the Committee, Mr. Steckiewicz. This very wealthy man was the owner of the parcel of land on which the church was being built, and he for some reason conducted all the meetings of the Building Committee and all the prayer services in his residence.

The appearance of a new priest was met by Mr. Steckiewicz with undisguised displeasure. At first Fr. Stanisław was not able to correctly evaluate the situation. In a rather harsh way, they gave him to understand who was in charge of the construction of the church on the parcel of land belonging to Mr. Steckiewicz. Inasmuch as even the Masses were said in the personal home of Mr. Steckiewicz, the priest was always having to come to terms with the ways of this household. Naturally, Fr. Kolodzejczyk became fed up with the situation and he turned for help to Fr. Karol Sliwowski, inviting him to come to Nikolsk in order, as he wrote, "to investigate the malicious affairs of the Steckiewicz gang."[64] Bishop Jan Cieplak also asked Fr. Sliwowski about this investigation. But apparently Fr. Sliwowski tried not to interfere in this foul and complicated affair—thus Fr. Kolodzejczyk had to go one on one with the very well-organized so-called Building Committee, the members of which declared a real war against the priest. For example, they wrote a long-winded letter to Bishop Jan Cieplak in which they rather unceremoniously

63 RGIA, f. 826, op. 12, d. 1646, l. 27.

64 RGIA, f. 826, op. 1, d. 1646, l. 46.

announced that the presence of Fr. Kolodzejczyk in Nikolsk was unacceptable and that it would be necessary to transfer him to some other parish. Although in the future it became known that none of the members of the Building Committee had ever seen or signed the letter, the letter nevertheless was not able to change the course of events for Fr. Kolodzejczyk.

What could he do? He once again sent to the archbishop a lengthy letter in which he informed the archbishop of the completely unacceptable activities of Mr. Steckiewicz and the Building Committee. All the liturgies, all the parish meetings were conducted in the personal home of Mr. Steckiewicz. The church itself was built on land owned by Mr. Steckiewicz and with his money. Apparently the previous priest, Fr. Mikszys, had been "tamed" and Mr. Steckiewicz expected the same of Fr. Kolodzejczyk. When he did not achieve the desired result, a real war was declared against the priest—and the priest not having received support from the Catholic Church, after only two and a half months left the employ of the parish, taking up a teaching post in one of the city's educational institutions.

Reading the long-winded, eleven-page letter of Fr. Kolodzejczyk to the Mogilev archbishop, one is struck by how cleverly Mr. Steckiewicz and his domesticated Building Committee had completely subverted the authority of the head of the Roman Catholic parish of Nikolsk-Ussuriisk! For example, in an announcement published in the newspaper that there would be a meeting of the Building Committee in his apartment on May 22, 1917, Mr. Steckiewicz stated that important questions related to the construction would be discussed. Upon their arrival the parishioners encountered something completely unexpected—they were asked to participate in the composition of a formal Complaint against Fr. Kolodzejczyk. The parishioners in attendance, however, refused to sign the letter of complaint. All the far-fetched rumors and slanders and endless arguments simply wore out Fr. Kolodzejczyk so that he could not endure it any longer—on August 9, 1917, he wrote to the archbishop and Dean Karol Sliwowskii a report concerning his departure from the post of head of the Nikolsk-Ussuriisk parish.

9 August 1917
To His Excellency, Bishop Jan Cieplak

> I humbly ask you to release me from the post of acting chaplain at the Nikolsk-Ussuriisk chapel and to allow me to live in Nikolsk-Ussuriisk in residence without duties. If possible, I humbly request to be allowed to say Mass in my apartment.

With utter respect and dedication,
Fr. Stanisław Kolodzejczyk[65]

In addition, Fr. Kolodzejczyk sent Mr. Steckiewicz an open letter which was published in the local newspaper, *Ussuriiskii Krai*, June 6, 1917:

Mr. Steckiewicz!

> By an announcement in the newspaper, you invited the members of the Building Committee and all parishioners to attend a meeting on May 22 for the discussion of very important and urgent questions of the parish. When the parishioners arrived, instead of important and urgent questions connected with the construction of the church, you asked them to sign a Complaint against me. None of the parishioners agreed to sign the Complaint. Then you, Mr. Steckiewicz, proposed to elect from among those parishioners in attendance so-called delegates from the meeting who were to read to "judges" elected from the parishioners. It turned out that none of these

65 RGIA, f. 826, op. 1, d. 1646, l. 54.

judges were elected—you simply designated them. These people read the Complaint but they refused to sign it.

Why was this "Complaint" so secretly kept from me? Most likely you, Mr. Steckiewicz, feared the responsibility of your slander against a priest. All the parishioners advised me of all your intrigues. Therefore I accuse you, Mr. Steckiewicz, of the following crimes:

1. By false newspaper announcements, you misused the title of president of the Building Committee and having thus deceived the parishioners, you wanted to affirm this scurrilous piece of writing against me.
2. No one of those who arrived at your apartment signed the Complaint.
3. You would not even let the parishioners touch this Complaint - you understood that the law could charge you with forgery.
4. You dragged even under-aged parishioners into your slanders.
5. For your indecent pranks and tasteless behavior, you have been permanently forbidden entry to the local chapter of the Polish Union.

To all that has been said above, I would add that in light of the great expenses for the construction of the church, back in 1916 I turned down my own salary and financial subsidies for the church expenses and without these subsidies (225 rubles a month) during the construction on the Steckiewicz land, there could be no liturgies. With the departure of Fr. Gurnicki worship services altogether came to an end. I earn money as a teacher in the girls high school—250 ru-

> bles a month—and at my own expense I support the sacristan. And when there was not enough money for the chapel's expenses, I paid 40 rubles. I also pay for my own apartment from my own pocket 50 rubles a month from my teacher's salary.

In sending a copy of this letter to the archbishop, Fr. Kolodzejczyk attached to his letter an expansive eleven-page report in which with great detail he exposed Mr. Steckiewicz. Having left the parish, Fr. Kolodzejczyk accepted an invitation to teach religion in the city's girls high school and the boys school.

Upon learning about what had happened, Archbishop Cieplak on August 16, 1917, issued a directive that Fr. Aleksandr Ejsymontt, then serving in Harbin, should serve as the head of the chapel in Nikolsk-Ussuriisk. But Fr. Ejsymontt turned down this directive. On October 21, 1917, Fr. Władysław Mieżwinski was sent to the parish in Nikolsk-Ussuriisk.

***

The historical material herein shows us the difficult circumstances in which the Catholic church in Nikolsk-Ussuriisk was constructed. By truths and by lies, the clever and deceitful entrepreneur Mr. Feliks Steckiewicz grabbed into his hands the building affairs of the future church. As historian O. V. Kovalenko points out, in the spring of 1918, Mr. Steckiewicz, without the concurrence of the Polish Society or the Building Committee very energetically set about moving forward the construction of the church which had previously been closed down. What called forth all this activity? Kovalenko suggests that the activity became necessary because Soviet power, which had been established in Primorye, could nationalize any "bourgeoise property." In November of 1918 the "Supreme Ruler of Russia," Admiral A. V. Kolchak, arrived in Siberia and then came even to the Far East. He announced elections to the organs of local self-government and Mikhail Steckiewicz, Felix's brother, very quickly took advantage of this opportunity, becoming a candidate for the Narodnaia Svoboda [People's Freedom] Party. On September 8, 1921, the local newspaper, *Primorskaia mysl* [Primorye Thought], announced that "the sensational and notorious affair between the Polish Society and the builder of the Catholic church, F. I. Steckiewicz, which has dragged on for more than two years, has finally been resolved." The Vladivostock court determined that inasmuch as F. I. Steckiewicz was the owner of the parcel of land on the corner of Nikolaevskaia and Korfovskaia Streets, the Ussuriisk Polish Society and the Roman Catholic parish were obliged to release the premises located on that parcel of land. In addition the society of Catholics was obligated to pay Mr. Steckiewicz 480 rubles in court costs.

But Mr. Steckiewicz was not to celebrate for long—in 1922 General M. K. Dieterich[66] was elected ruler of the Priamursk Zemskii Krai. He did not believe the "self-excusing petitions" of Mr. Steckiewicz and by Decree No. 48 dated September 22, 1922, he returned the chapel to the Catholics, since he believed that the chapel had been "nakedly and shamelessly seized from the Catholics by Mr. Steckiewicz." In addition, General Dieterich ordered Mr. Steckiewicz to pay the Catholics fifty thousand rubles. A commission created under the direction of General Dieterich had begun an inventory of the property of Mr. Steckiewicz for the purpose of finding the resources needed for the payment of the fine. General Dieterich "deeply believed in the miracle" of the realization of his plan of overthrowing Soviet power. But there was no miracle. Instead, the Fifth Red Army came to Vladivostok and on October 25, 1922, Soviet power was established in Primorye. General Dieterich emigrated to Manchuria and most likely the Steckiewicz brothers also went to Manchuria.[67]

66 Translator's Note: Mikhail Konstantinovich Dieterich was chief of staff of the Czech Legion.

67 O. V. Kovalenko, "Ussuriiskii kostel," *Ussuriiskii kraevedcheskii vestnik* ["The Ussuriisk Church," Ussuriisk Regional Studies Bulletin], No. 4, 2005.

16. Scouting Among the Children of the Vladivostok and Nikolsk-Ussuriisk Roman Catholic Parishes

It is fully possible that the constant scandalous stories arising in Nikolsk and drawn out complaints connected with them annoyed the pastor of the Vladivostok Roman Catholic parish, Fr. Karol Sliwowski, since he had a large number of his own serious problems, the resolution of which could not be put aside. Above all, the pastor was worried about the fate of the very smallest of his parishioners, since the First World War had swallowed up huge resources of the Empire and many families were very impoverished. In 1917, with Fr. Sliwowski's blessing, a Scout troop named in honor of Tadeusz Kościuszko was created in Vladivostok. A hundred young boys and girls from Catholic families joined the troop. The troop's organizer was Zygmund Jankowski, who was assisted by Antonij Gregorkiewicz. Later the 26-year-old medical doctor, Jósef Jakubkiewicz, who had much experience in the Scout movement, became the leader of the Vladivostok Scouts. He strove to familiarize the Scouts with naval traditions. In the first year of the troop's existence, the Scouts had tents, camping equipment, naval uniforms and three lifeboats. All these supplies had been donated to the Scouts by sailors from the vessels of the Intervention squadrons which at that time were based in the Vladivostok harbor of the Golden Horn.

As is known, Scouting, as a system of educating children that had been founded in England at the beginning of the twentieth century, proposed a well-rounded formation, which would hopefully lead to the development of the "ideal man." In Scouting there are no such concepts as child-beating, humiliating punishments and threats and thus the members of the first Vladivostok Scout troop felt themselves "free sailors." They sailed along the Amur Gulf and made small training stops on Russian Island—then in the evening they all went to their own homes. Of special pride for the Scouts was the national flag of independent Poland.

Maria Ayewska, the mother of Eugeniusz Ayewski, one of the Scouts, later brought this flag to Poland and donated it to a museum.

We were able to establish written contact with the former Scout, today a very well-known Warsaw architect. The author was a guest of Mr. Ayewski in Warsaw, thanks to which the parish archive has been supplemented with very valuable historic information provided by the former Vladivostok Scout. He told us that in 1918, when the Scout troop was based on Russian Island, there were activities for Boy Scouts and Girl Scouts in various groups that studied crafts, boating and swimming. Great attention was given to the study of the history of Poland. Despite the difficult situation with bread and food products in Vladivostok, the Scouts received three meals a day, which were provided by the foreign sailors. The main medical doctor of Vladivostok, Jósef Jakubkiewicz, concerned himself with the health of the children.[68]

The Vladivostok Scouts had friendly relations with the Scouts in Harbin and in the middle of the summer of 1918 the Harbin Scouts visited the Vladivostok Scout camp. A return visit of the Vladivostok Scouts to Harbin was intended but they could not do so due to the complicated political situation in the Far East. In the camp on Russian Island, a lot of time was allocated to studies of the geography and history of Poland, but formation drill was not overlooked nor was the study of the various rules of behavior and nature. They also studied gymnastics and they learned songs and various games. The main rule of the Scouts was "to faithfully serve God and the Homeland, to be a knight, and to fulfill all one's obligations."

In December 1918, a Scout troop named in honor of Adam Mickiewicz was formed in Nikolsk-Ussuriisk. Its organizer and leader was Eugeniusz Kozicki. Edward Mincer, a professor at a local school, was selected as honorary Boy Scout, and Jadwiga Budzińska, the leader of the Polish Military Alliance, was chosen the honorary Girl Scout. The shared activities of all the Scouts of the troop took place on Saturdays and Sundays; in addition the instructors and their assistants conducted supplemental activities on Mondays. Among

68 M. I. Efimova, "Dvizhenie skautov na Dalnem vostoke," *Sibirskaia katolicheskaia gazeta* ["Scouting in the Far East," SCN], No. 7-8, 2000.

the Scouts there were Polish children who were completely unfamiliar with the native language of their homeland, so free Polish lessons were organized for them, taught by the teacher of the local Polish school, Władisław Rappe. Each member of the Polish Scout troop contributed 50 kopecks monthly to the Scouts. All the basic expenses were paid by the local Polish House. Although they gave a lot of attention to sporting activities, the Scouts constantly remembered their main goal: preparation for exams for their four-year school.

In February 1919, the Scouts of Nikolsk-Ussuriisk put on their own "festival evening" in the hall of the National Building. They sang, they marched, they read poetry—and the concert on the whole was very successfully received, bringing in approximately 300 rubles. There was a Scout troop in Nikolsk-Ussuriisk until approximately the beginning of the 1920s when, in the local Roman Catholic parish, there were disputes between the head of the parish and several parishioners. These arguments and petty lies forced the young priest, Stanisław Kolodzejczyk, to abandon the parish and in the end they brought about the curtailment of worship services and the interruption of the construction of the church.

17. Creation of the Rescue Committee and Its Activities

During World War I, when war was being waged on the western territories of the Russian Empire (the former Polish *gubernias*), Nicholas II ordered that there was not to remain standing a single dwelling on any lands from which the Russian armies had retreated. All the homes and other structures at the time of the retreat of the Russian armies were to be scorched. Huge crowds of impoverished, completely dispossessed refugees, primarily Poles, were sent deep into Russia, into Siberia, and some of them made it even as far as the Far East. All these people needed a roof over their heads, food and clothing, which they expected to receive from their co-religionists. It was only natural that the head of the Vladivostok parish, Fr. Sliwowski, the parish council, and practically all the parishioners took a lively interest in the fate of the refugees. They sought out dwellings and they contributed food and whatever clothing they could.

It was completely understandable that in such conditions, the construction of the brick church in Vladivostok came to a halt. The Building Committee lacked the necessary funds for acquiring building materials and paying the work force. From the fragments of the bricks the parish did manage to construct two parish buildings. One of these was a two-story building, and Fr. Sliwowski resided on its upper floor, while the parish offices were located on the lower floor. In the second brick building, the two upper floors were occupied by the parish school, and the third floor, which was a quasi-basement floor, had a kitchen, a dining area and living quarters for the parish workers.

At this very difficult time, the activity of the *Dobrochinnost'* charitable society that had been organized during the Russo-Japanese War was significantly expanded. In the parish school, which at first had only two grades, and then later four grades, the children not only studied but also received free meals. Then the Polish orphanage was established and members of *Dobrochinnost'* continued to collect from among the parishioners items of clothing, footwear and food. The most frightening of all was the fate of the children whose parents at the time of evacuation had either died of illness or had been murdered at the hands of bandits. These orphans flitted along the rail lines, suffering and dying from hunger and disease.

All these tragic events deeply disturbed the Poles living in Siberia, nor did they leave those Poles of the large Far East colony indifferent, inasmuch as they had come to believe in the rebirth of the Polish government. On September 16, 1916, a Rescue Committee was established in Vladivostok. This committee enlisted such Polish organizations as the following: the Polish People's Committee (led by Jan Wyżykowski), the Committee of the Polish Army (led by Lt. Alozij Piotrowski), Polish House (led by Wilgelm Miller), the Society for Aid to Invalids (led by Ludwig Champel), and the Cooperative Society of Transport and Trade. Anna Belkiewicz, a Polish patriot and a parishioner of the Catholic parish of Vladivostok, was chosen president of the Rescue Committee. Anna had considerable experience with humanitarian causes. On her recommendation the chief military medical doctor of Vladivostok, Dr. Jósef Jakubkiewicz, was named vice-president of the committee; its secretary was Michal Belecki.

The Rescue Committee issued the following appeal:

> Now that Poland has been resurrected, we need working hands in order that from the fragments we can build new buildings—in order to sow grain in the empty earth. We need an army to defend the boundaries of the Polish government. We need people! And Polish children are dying from hunger in the Far East. Save the children! This is not a request, not a prayer. To ask, to beseech, one can only do with respect to foreigners. Anyone who considers himself a Pole, having read these words, will grasp his obligation. Poles! Save the future of our homeland! Save the children!

The words of this fiery appeal were heard and affiliates of the Rescue Committee were formed in the settlements at all the large railway stations. As soon as it became known that trains were bringing Siberian children, representatives of the local Rescue Committee, carrying hot food, clothing and shoes, set out for the railway stations, because the little wanderers were hungry, shoeless and half-dressed. Naturally for all these charitable activities they needed funds, and therefore they held meetings of activists and even in the very first few months they managed to collect 500,000 rubles! Nor did the Vladivostok Catholic parish stand to the side of this patriotic activity, being a true oasis of salvation for the Catholic refugees and the orphan children. Thanks to the impassioned sermons and appeals of Fr. Sliwowski, the Vladivostok parishioners contributed 10,000 rubles in a single day. In addition, the faithful brought to the church the most necessary items for the refugees—underwear, clothing, shoes, medicines. The children of the refugees could attend the parish Polish school, where they studied and also played and ate.

The Rescue Committee expanded its work in October 1919, when the largest groups of refugees reached the Transbaikal region, and then from there came eastward to Vladivostok. Their situation was horrifying. They needed medical assistance. They needed blankets, clothing and money as well as shelter. But the Rescue Committee at that time only had a small office in Polish House, at 50 Svetlanskaia Street, and the very modest, at that time, sum of 14,000 rubles. Russians, Americans, English and Japanese, as well as Poles, responded to the committee's efforts to raise funds. Contributions were received from firms as well as from private individuals. It was the Vladivostok Roman Catholic parish, however, that showed the broadest and most touching concern for its co-religionists who found themselves refugees. From among the parishioners the following significant contributions were received: Bronisław Sienkiewicz, 100,000 rubles; Maksimilian Zalewski, 50,000 rubles; Messers. Bolesław Arct, Babincew, Konstantin Krynski, Mlynarski-Czekanski, Skidelski, Zygmund Tokarzewski, and Lucian Arct each contributed 10,000 rubles; and Mr. Arct also contributed a wagon of coal. Even the Polish children collected money in other towns and villages of the area. For example, in Novo-Kievsk the children of the well-known Kaczanowski family—Milia, Helenka and Janna—collected 1,053 rubles. Only the Kolchak supporters refused to give donations to benefit the Polish children. They announced that they would collect money only for White Guard refugees, and in 1919 they handed over to the Kolchak leaders 120,000,000 rubles!

It was the children of the refugees who suffered most in this situation, especially the orphans whose parents at the time of their evacuation had either died of disease or had been shot by bandits. Such orphan children wandered close by the railway stations. They slept in empty train cars, in hay sheds and in abandoned homes, dying from cold, hunger, typhus and cholera. Only a few of these managed to survive under these conditions. As soon as news about this catastrophe reached independent Poland, a committee for the rescue of Siberian children was immediately formed. When in Vladivostok there arose the question, where to place these rescued children, the city granted to the Rescue Committee a shelter for the children suitable for forty children. It was located on Staraia Morskaia Street, and Elena Bocheńska was placed in charge, followed by Teodozia Marecka. Kazimierz Zaleski also served there as a teacher. Naturally such a shelter was very necessary for the city, as many homeless children roamed the streets. The situation of the orphans was especially dangerous because in Vladivostok and in Harbin there were instances of the sale of young children. Nevertheless this shelter was too small and wretched. Taking all these circumstances into account, the Rescue Committee sought out a more suitable place. Finding available space in Vladivostok, which was overflowing with refugees, was practically impossible.

At first the American Red Cross promised Anna Belkiewicz assistance. Inasmuch as the road to Poland by way of Russia was now closed, the American Red Cross proposed to send the rescued children to the United States. Representatives of the American Red Cross set up their base on Russian Island. In 1918 American specialists created a colony of Petrograd children, numbering approximately 800 children. They had sought out these homeless children in the European part of Russia and sent them to the Far East. On Russian Island the children received medical treatment, they rested up and recovered their strength. In the first half of 1920, the Americans transported the children along a complicated itinerary: from Vladivostok, to San Francisco, via the Panama Canal to New York, then to London, Gdańsk, Finland and then Poland.

After the appropriate preparation, on December 23, 1919, the Rescue Committee undertook a new activity—the evacuation of children from Siberia and Manchuria. For this effort, Dr. Jakubkiewicz traveled by the American Red Cross military train in the direction of Irkutsk, along the route Vladivostok—Harbin—Chita. In Chita, they gathered up orphans and children from the poorest families. Recalling that period, Dr. Jakubkiewicz wrote that they found children in Russian and Chinese orphanages; they gathered them up from abandoned railroad cars and barracks; they found them in the fields and on the forest roadways. They took these orphan children, whose parents had died of disease and hunger, and in their dying moments had only asked that at least their children be saved. When all these children had been gathered, it remained only to transport them to the American base on Russian Island. But the unexpected and unforeseen occurred: the American Red Cross quickly abandoned Siberia, Vladivostok and its base on the island. This was a cruel and unexpected blow for Rescue Committee, for now where would it take these gathered children?

But obviously the Lord was looking out for these poor orphans because in Vladivostok the brothers Genrich and Władisław Sienkiewicz, the owners of bookstores and large forest concessions, came to their aid. They laid at the disposal of the Rescue Committee their beautiful villa on the Sedanka River, and it was there that a temporary shelter was established for the children, where they could be treated and taught.[69] This "Oasis of Salvation" began to function in March 1920 and Polish children from the city shelter organized by Anna Belkiewicz were sent there.

How much joy this luxurious mansion afforded these Polish children! Having experienced all the horrors of their long wanderings through hay sheds and ditches along the Trans-Siberian Railway, these Polish orphans were now able to live in a spacious, well-appointed villa in a beautiful forest, on the shores of the crystal clear Sedanka River, under the care of their kind headmistress, Maria Miecznikowska. They divided the orphans by age into three groups. The children studied, they had gym class, they sang, they set up small concerts, and they were taken on hikes into the forest. While the little girls mastered the domestic sciences of embroidery, sewing, knitting and other skills, the little boys cleaned house, cut wood, carried water and washed laundry. In addition, all the children took part in gymnastics, music and singing. On the holidays all the

69 "Ochronka na Sedance," *Echo Dalekiego Wschodu*, 1992, No. 10, pp. 15-17.

children could go on excursions to Vladivostok and its surroundings. Often games were organized for them in the forested fields of Sedanka. On Sundays the children were sometimes taken to the Catholic church in Vladivostok where they attended Mass and received Holy Communion from the hands of Fr. Sliwowski.

In 1920 the Mogilev archdiocese organized some new deaneries on the territory of Russia: Kharkov, Turkestan, and Vladivostok. The latter included the following parishes: Vladivostok, Blagoveshchensk, Khabarovsk, Nikolsk-Ussuriisk, and Alexandrovsk on Sakhalin. The Vladivostok deanery also included the Harbin churches of St. Stanisław and St. Josaphat and also a small village church at the Manchur railway station. The Vladivostok deanery included 11,000 Catholics, but it was served by only five priests. The head of the Vladivostok deanery, Fr. Karol Sliwowski, now came to be called the Vladivostok Dean. In spite of his busyness and new responsibilities, Dean Sliwowski found the time to visit the orphans at Sedanka, inasmuch as these children came from Catholic families and consequently also belonged to the Vladivostok Roman Catholic parish.

Soon still another group of Polish orphans brought from Siberia made it to Vladivostok. Thanks to the assistance of the Japanese Red Cross, they settled these children together with their caretakers in a suburb of Vladivostok, Okeanskaia Station. They placed the children in a warm, well-constructed barracks that had been given to the children by the Japanese military. A little later a group of orphans brought from Khabarovsk was added to these children. The Japanese military not only allotted for the Polish orphanage a warm dwelling, but they also began to supply the shelter with food. The Japanese Major Oto often visited the little ones and they liked him a lot. Most likely Major Oto was grieving for his own children and his paternal love extended to the little Poles. He taught them to sing Japanese songs and the Japanese anthem, and he was also concerned that Japanese watchmen protect the barracks at night because in those frightening years hungry and angry people wandered about and thus robberies were a common nighttime event. In all there were 113

Polish children at Okeanskaia Station. In the middle of September 1920, all these children were sent to Japan.

18. Assistance of the Japanese Red Cross to the Polish Orphans

In her memoirs, Anna Belkiewicz has described how she managed to reach those persons who then organized assistance for the Polish orphans. Upon her arrival in Tokyo, as a Catholic woman, she first counted on the assistance of the French Catholic mission. They very politely received her but refused her any aid. Then this wise woman decided that since in all the troubles of the children it was the military that was to blame, it followed that one should seek assistance from the military ministry. Overcome by doubts and the hopelessness of the situation, Anna went to the highest Japanese military officials. But her fears and doubts had been misplaced, because the emotional story of this strange Polish lady was very attentively heard. It was then explained to her that assistance to the Polish children would definitely be granted—but it was necessary for her to go to the ministry of foreign affairs. Once again a very favorable reception awaited her at the secretary of foreign affairs, Mr. T. Morishime. This Japanese official, dressed in a kimono, was extremely polite and courteous. Knowing French very well, he listened with great attention to the emotional story of this unexpected visitor, not once interrupting her with questions. Then Mr. Morishime asked her to set forth her story in writing and to bring her notes to the ministry and then wait two days.

Taking heart, Anna spent the whole night writing this document that was so important for her, praying and asking the Almighty for assistance. Then at ten o'clock the following morning, the document was conveyed to Mr. Morishime. Exactly two days later they invited her to the ministry of foreign affairs where very joyful news awaited her: the Japanese Red Cross was very seriously concerned with the Polish children.

They gathered all these unfortunate young homeless wanderers in Vladivostok, then they transported them on Japanese ships to the Japanese port of Tsuruga. The first group of Polish children departed from Vladivostok for Japan on July 20, 1920. They settled them in a beautiful park in Tokyo, in small cottages of an orphanage for Japanese orphans run by the Buddhist society "Fukudenkai." The Polish and Japanese children at the orphanage quickly became friends, and games, concerts and excursions were arranged for all the children. The children especially liked the musical activities, where they learned both Polish and Japanese songs, especially the Japanese anthem "Ki-mi-ga-yo" and the Polish anthem "Poland Yet Lives!" Recognizing that all the Polish children were Catholic, their caretakers periodically took them to the Catholic church in Tokyo. But most of all the Japanese caregivers were concerned with the health and nourishment of the small Poles. When an epidemic of typhus broke out among the Polish children in Tokyo and several small children fell ill, the doctors and nurses were determined that not one Polish child should die on Japanese soil. The Japanese doctors were indeed successful. They cured the children of typhus—but one of the caregivers, the young nurse Matsuda, succumbed....

Each day spent in Japan brought the little Poles pleasant surprises. But the most stunning event for them was a reception held by Her Majesty, the Empress Nagako, which occurred April 6, 1921. This very solemn ceremony took place in Tokyo on the grounds of the Japanese Red Cross. Observing all the protocols of a court ceremonial, the President of the Japanese Red Cross, Baron S. Hirayama, and other high-ranking officials stood at the main entrance, and to their side stood Dr. Jósef Jakubkiewicz and Anna Belkiewicz. Then there were the hospital doctors and rows of nurses. Not far from the main entry stood motionless rows of ladies of high Japanese aristocracy and representatives of Japanese social organizations. The path along which the Empress was to pass was laid with a white cloth.

On her arrival, the Empress at first secluded herself in the salon, then she went out to those assembled, and Baron S. Omori, her personal secretary, presented her with an essay by Anna Belkiewicz about the work of the Committee to Save Polish Children and about the assistance that the Japanese Red Cross and the Japanese people had rendered to the Polish children. At the same time, they presented to the Empress a Letter of Gratitude for the assistance to and care of the Polish children. The Empress then ascended the pavilion, surrounded by her retinue and representatives of the highest circles of Japan.

One hundred one Polish children and fifty Japanese orphans who lived in the same orphanage stood in rows by height. The solemn mood had taken hold of the children and they stood motionless in deep silence, turning their little heads toward the pavilion where the Empress of Japan, as though stepping out of a fairy tale, stood in light blue attire against a background of a light blue sky and flowering sakura. At a signal from the senator, Anna Belkiewicz led a row of little girls toward the pavilion, and Dr. Jakubkiewicz led a row of little boys. They all stood at previously designated places. According to court etiquette, the Empress never spoke, and one was not to go closer to her than thirty or forty meters. But unexpectedly the Empress gestured with her hand, inviting a row of Polish children to come closer. The children moved forward a little. Then Her Majesty said, "Come closer!" But they all stood frozen in their places, afraid to violate court etiquette. The Empress insisted: "I want to see the children more closely!" The children again moved forward—now they were separated from Her Majesty by not more than ten steps. All the children bowed, as they had been taught. A minute later the children were singing with great enthusiasm the Japanese anthem "Ki-mi-ga-yo" and the Polish "Poland Yet Lives!" The Empress listened to the children's singing with a smile, then she said, "I want to see the youngest child—bring the youngest one to the pavilion!" A deep silence fell on those gathered—the retinue was astounded, and Baron Hirayama helplessly looked now at Anna Belkiewicz, now at the child. This was unheard of! It was an impermissible violation of the strict court etiquette! But Her Majesty smiled and gestured to Madame Belkiewicz, who did not believe her own eyes and stood helplessly looking around, afraid to do anything that was forbidden. (The night before they had spent a long time explaining to her the strict rules of Japanese court etiquette.) A minute of bewilderment on the part of the whole court dragged on! And then something happened that is recorded as a historic fact of the Japanese Court of Her Majesty: The Empress came down from the pavilion, approached the row of Polish children, and asked Mme. Belkiewicz to point out the youngest child. They brought to Her Majesty a little girl of three and a half years who had been found half dead in the autumn woods. The Empress asked about the age of the little girl and where she had been found. Mme. Belkiewicz began to respond in French, and Baron Hirayama attempted to translate, but the Empress indicated that she understood French, and she placed her hand lovingly on the little girl's head. It was such an unexpected and touching scene that the ladies of the court began to cry. Her Majesty turned to Mme. Belkiewicz, wished her success in her work, and expressed the hope that the children would be happy. In response, Mme. Belkiewicz thanked the Empress for her assistance and said that thanks to Her Majesty's kindness and goodness these Polish children would certainly be happy. All the ladies of the court, overcome by delight and joy, kept crying, and all that happened seemed like a fairy tale, because *never before in the Japanese Empire had foreign children seen the Empress!*

When 370 healthy Polish children set sail for America, the Japanese Red Cross proposed to send the remaining 400 children directly to Poland by sea. The itinerary of the young voyagers took them by way of the Indian Ocean, the Red Sea, Gibralter, the Baltic Sea and from there directly to Gdańsk. The young Poles traveled uneventfully sixty-two days by sea and arrived in their homeland strong, healthy and happy—not a single child had fallen ill en route.[70]

They placed the newly arrived children in Wejherowo, Pomerania, where, thanks to the care and support of Minister Sion and the Director of the Department Shubartowicz from the Ministry of Work on Social Guardianship, the children received a beautiful residence for their dormitory. In addition, in spite of the difficult period of the

70 *Echo Dalekiego Wschodu*, 1924, 1 (11, p. 8).

reestablishment of order and well-being in Poland, the officials saw to it that the dormitory would have adequate financial security.

19. Assistance of the American Red Cross to the Polish Children

The stay of a group of Polish children in America, which had been arranged by Dr. Jósef Jakubkiewicz, was very interesting and unusual. At first the doctor was unsuccessful in reaching the hearts of Americans with his plea for help for the Polish children. In order to arouse the interest of American society in the problem, Dr. Jakubkiewicz presented papers and reports, he met with well-known Polish figures and he placed publications in journals on this theme. He contacted famous compatriots—Helen and Ignacy Paderewski—who soon became enthusiastically involved in the cause. Thanks to the help of compatriots, Jósef Jakubkiewicz appeared at a special session of a council that represented the main Polish organizations in Chicago, and he asked for help to bring 300 Polish orphans to Chicago. The council listened attentively to his presentation, they took a vote, and they approved a contribution of $35,000, the amount estimated as needed for the effort. The chairman of the section, Jan Smulski, and Fr. Kazimierz Liubomirski, the plenipotentiary chairman of Poland in Washington, were especially attentive to the issue. Finally, there was an agreement that the Siberian children from Japan would be sent to the United States, and thence directly to Poland.

Begun in the fall of 1920, this activity took a whole year. The largest group—132 children—arrived in Seattle at the end of December 1920. A photograph of the event shows young, needy travelers against the background of the Polish Home Assocation. And from that time to their return to Poland, the Polish children found themselves under diligent care, surrounded by the touching sincerity of various Polish-American organizations. The role of the main governmental organization was filled by the Polish National Department, to which the orphanages and schools in several cities near Chicago and Pittsburg that had been given to the Polish children belonged. All the Polish children taken there were included in systematic schooling, and the older boys were provided with practical study of various trades.

Jósef Jakubkiewicz, in whose hands lay the organization of Polish assistance, showed tremendous energy and inventiveness in his efforts to interest broad social circles in the plight of the children. It was he who founded the Polish-American Association for Aid to Children, which unfortunately was not long in existence. In addition, Jakubkiewicz traveled extensively, he organized personal meetings with members of various Polish organizations and he published numerous reports about the activity of various societies of assistance for the Siberian children. Thanks to his efforts, "Siberian news" was published in all the large Polish journals in Chicago, New York and Pittsburg. In these publications he described the fate of the Polish brethren in Siberia and appealed for aid on their behalf. One should note that it was not just the Polish diaspora who responded to his appeals, but Americans of all backgrounds.

Unfortunately, there was some opposition to his activities. Amazingly, it came from those Poles who had arrived in the United States together with the repatriated children. Officials of the Polish Embassy in Tokyo, who tried to "torpedo" the success of Anna Belkiewicz's activities in Japan, also put up obstacles. Toward the end of his work in the United States, Jósef Jakubkiewicz wrote to the Paderewskis in a letter dated September 7, 1921: "In the affairs of the mission assigned to me, I have done all that a person could do. I plucked all the strings I could, and I did this by all means available to me. Unfortunately, I see that the results, for reasons beyond my control, are not what was expected."

The last stage of the transport of the Siberian children began at the end of January 1922. The USS Princess Matoika set sail from New York, carrying 310 children; fifty-seven remained in the United States and two others had departed earlier. After their three-week voyage to the port of Bremen, the children traveled by train to Poznań. At the station in Zbonszyn, the children were received by representatives of the Polish Caritas society. The newly arrived children, who brought with them a "dowry" of $25,000, were placed in children's homes in Melzin and Broniszewicz.

The arrival of the children did not bring to an end the work to rescue Polish orphans. In July 1922 the Japanese Red Cross offered to help conduct an immediate "Rescue Operation" in Siberia. Anna Belkiewicz promptly agreed, since time was running out—the Japanese forces were abandoning Siberia and the Far East. This time Anna set up the center of operations in Harbin and she herself set off to look for children, first in Sretensk, then further down the Shilka and Amur Rivers, as far as Blagoveshchensk. She returned to Harbin via the Sungari River. Later she wrote: "Success always accompanied me through fortunate events." A group of 391 children was gathered, and they were taken by steamer to Osaka. Japanese hospitality had not changed and, as before, the Siberian children were treated with great affection. The 11-year-old Genrich Sadowski, who was part of that group, later in his adult life would recall: "Our month stay in Osaka could be described as life in paradise because life for us poor and frightened children seemed like a fairy tale."

And again the Polish children experienced the warm, sincere regard that the Japanese had toward them. They felt this touching concern and warm regard the whole way—sailing to Poland via the Indian Ocean, Suez Canal, the Mediterranean Sea, to London. The voyage was like a cruise, lasting more than two months, thanks to which the children had unforgettable impressions from their stops in such port cities as Singapore, Shanghai, Hong Kong and Colombo. In London they were met by Anna Belkiewicz who quickly took them under her care. When the children reached the Polish port of Gdańsk, it was already a cold Polish autumn that greeted them. This group of children was dispersed throughout Poland—many of them ending up in very poor children's homes where there was a shortage of food and the staff had not the slightest idea of how to raise children. Soon Dr. Jósef Jakubkiewicz also arrived in Poland, so that together with Anna Belkiewicz they could look after the children that had been returned to their Homeland. Thus concluded the beautiful and noble effort to rescue Polish children.

20. Fr. Julian Bryllik

Back in 1918, Fr. Julian Bryllik, a refugee priest from the western lands, came to the head of the Vladivostok parish and Fr. Sliwowski sent him to serve in Nikolsk-Ussuriisk. The First World War had found the ailing Fr. Julian in a small Polish village of the Piotrowski district that had been invaded by the German army. With great difficulty, he succeeded in being evacuated first to Warsaw, then he ended up in Petrograd. Bishop Cieplak ordered him to serve in the city of Belgorod, near Kharkov. The local Catholics, who had long awaited a pastor for their parish, accepted the refugee priest very kindly. The priest's entire parish consisted of approximately fifty Polish families of Belgorod and its surroundings. They were representatives of the intelligentsia, office workers and railroad workers. The recently constructed church in Belgorod was beautiful, and the parish social hall was spacious enough and very comfortable. After his difficult wanderings in a crowd of refugees, Fr. Julian felt as though he was in heaven.

But after the revolutionary events in Petrograd and the overthrow of Nicholas II, the quiet and peaceful little town of Belgorod in the course of literally a couple days was turned into one huge, constantly raging Communist meeting! A death threat hung over the Polish priest, who had actively assisted Polish children not only in Belgorod but also in Kharkov. He requested of Bishop Cieplak that he be transferred to Nikolaevsk in the Far East, where very wealthy, long-time acquaintances had invited him to join them. The bishop willingly gave his permission and assigned him to the post of military chaplain of the Roman Catholic parish of Nikolaevsk.

Traveling by rail, it took Fr. Bryllik six weeks to go from Moscow to Khabarovsk, since all along the rail line, especially in Siberia, the train would be detained and inspected, now by the White Guards looking for Reds, then by Red Army patrols looking for Whites. They shot many passengers without a judge or evidence, right on the bed on the railroad. Fr. Bryllik, who considered himself neither a Red nor a White, feared that either one or the other would "liquidate" him. The dangerous journey finally came to an end in the capital of the Far East—Khabarovsk—where his friends met him. Together they then traveled by steamer down the Amur River to Nikolaevsk. Having arrived in Nikolaevsk, exhausted and utterly terrified by the events of the Revolution, Fr. Bryllik fell as it were into bygone times: a peaceful and orderly life still prevailed in the city, and one could shop at luxurious stores like Kunst & Albers and Churin and Company and buy whatever one wished.

Local Catholics greeted the news of the arrival of a Catholic priest with great enthusiasm, as they had never had a permanent priest—not counting the rare pastoral visits of Fr. Władisław Mieżwinski when he served a year on Sakhalin Island almost ten years earlier. They promptly set up a chapel in the local high school, which they decorated with antique Florentine altar cards and prayer-books. Catholic children from all the city schools gathered in the small chapel for religious instruction, and the adults willingly came on Sundays for confession, Mass and preaching. With great pleasure the Catholics sang carols and other Christmas songs on Christmas, and the ladies with great delight played the school's reed organ. In addition to preaching in Polish, Fr. Julian also preached in Russian for the Japanese and Lithuanian Catholics.

Seeing the great interest of the local residents in Catholic worship, Fr. Julian thought it might be feasible to construct a Catholic chapel in Nikolaevsk. Bishop Cieplak heartily endorsed the proposal, immediately sending him 500 rubles. He also counseled Fr. Julian to establish a strong cooperative relationship with the local Orthodox church—which Fr. Julian did. But the Orthodox priest explained to Fr. Julian that all church questions—especially the question of building a chapel—now could only be resolved by the Revolutionary Soldiers Committee. Remembering the events in Belgorod and Kharkov, and what the activities of revolutionary soldiers led to, Fr. Bryllik abandoned his beautiful idea. Studying the surroundings of Nikolaevsk, Fr. Julian fulfilled Bishop Cieplak's wishes by visiting a colony of lepers, among whom he found three Catholics, to whom he administered the sacraments.

Despite the rather peaceful "political atmosphere" of Nikolaevsk, people who at that time were considered "wealthy" gradually began to leave the city. Fr. Julian's benefactors sold their beautiful home to the English consul, and after navigation opened up on the Amur in June 1918, they left for Vladivostok with Fr. Julian. Because their dream of returning to St. Petersburg by rail could not be realized (since the fierce Civil War was raging all along the rail line), they decided to go to Europe via Asia. Fr. Bryllik of course did not have the means for such a voyage. So he turned to Fr. Sliwowski and offered his services. Fr. Sliwowski sent him right away to Nikolsk-Ussuriisk. His assignment was to establish and lead the Roman Catholic parish and renew the efforts of building the Catholic church. But this was not easy because there was no peace among the local parishioners. And what most astounded the newly arrived priest was the fact that the "main figure" here was not the military chaplain, but some Mr. Feliks Steckiewicz. By intrigues, squabbles and letters of complaint to the archdiocese, Mr. Steckiewicz had managed to isolate the priests and the most authoritative parishioners from the leadership of the Building Committee, completely usurping the authority of the Building Committee.

Taking into account all these circumstances, and having been apprised of the difficulties that his predecessor, Fr. Kolodzejczyk, had endured, Fr. Bryllik rented a large spacious building where he set up a small chapel as well as his own quarters in order not to fall into dependence on anyone, since the building of the brick church had not been completed. The large Polish community in Nikolsk-Ussuriisk on the one hand had the best of intentions with respect to the restoration of the parish, but on the other hand it was constantly torn apart by disputes between parishioners who supported the new political directions and those who held different political views. Life in those times was full of various stormy events and an endless change of power, and the fighting was not only outside the city, but often right in the city streets. First it was the Social Revolutionaries ("SRs") who held power, then the Communists, then anarchists, and finally power went into the hands of nationalists, whom Japanese military units defended. Large Japanese military units were encamped in the city; their armored trains stood on the tracks; and American military units protected the railroad in Nikolsk-Ussuriisk, the trains running only during the day and accompanied by the armored train.

In this complex situation, Fr. Bryllik had to travel on guarded trains to visit ailing Catholics in far-away villages and bring them the sacraments. While he was away on pastoral visits, his responsibilities in Nikolsk-Ussuriisk were assumed by a French priest, Fr. Cadars, the military chaplain of the colonial forces in Korea. He knew Korean very well and organized a parish of hundreds of Koreans, very diligent Catholics. When the Allied forces reached Krasnoyarsk, they brought from there another 6,000 prisoners of war—Austrians and Hungarians—mostly officers. Although they were Austrian and Hungarian subjects, they were actually Poles. Among the prisoners of war were two Catholic priests—the German Fr. E. Shorr from Munich and the Polish Fr. V. Kotys from Pszemysl. The prisoners were starving—every day tens and even hundreds of them perished. For these deceased a special cemetery was set aside in Nikolsk, where during the course of three years 10,000 prisoners were buried.

Fr. Bryllik helped these unfortunate parishioners as much as he could. He invited the priests to Masses and he performed funeral rites in the cemetery. In return the prisoners formed a beautiful choir for the parish. Former singers of the Vienna and Budapest operas sang in the choir, performing very complex religious choral pieces during the liturgy. And craftsmen among the prisoners made three beautiful altars for Fr. Bryllik's chapel. The authorities allowed one young prisoner—Adam Wetsztejn, a nobleman from Kalocsy—to help Fr. Bryllik and for two years this young man assisted with liturgies and burials—and he cooked, he cleaned the apartment and the chapel, he did laundry. In addition he stood for hours, in the heat and in the cold, in endless lines in order to buy a loaf of bread for the priest and himself.

Thus progressed the ministry of Fr. Bryllik in Nikolsk-Ussuriisk. But he had not abandoned the dream of somehow returning to his homeland. He had no foreign currency and Russian rubles were worthless. He had only a glimmer of hope that he might receive help from American priest friends—and lo! his dream came true! In February 1920 quite unexpectedly he received a letter from the United States and a check in the amount of five hundred dollars with a cordial invitation to come immediately to America! After lengthy hassles and unpleasant misadventures, Fr. Bryllik finally received a foreign passport and visas from five (!) consulates. It was especially difficult to obtain these visas because the Bolsheviks had now come to power in Vladivostok and they were very unwilling to allow anyone to leave the country. Fr. Bryllik went by way of Harbin, Korea and Japan to board an ocean liner for Vancouver.

From Canada Fr. Bryllik traveled by train to Chicago, where he was met by Fr. Grudzinski and several other Polish priests. They invited him to remain in America or at the very least to prolong his stay—but he was firm in his ardent desire: to return to his homeland as quickly as possible. From Washington he traveled with Fr. Muszyński to New York and from there they sailed on the steamship *Finland* across the Atlantic to London, then by way of La Manche to Belgium, then to Berlin. Upon his arrival in Warsaw, Fr. Bryllik was assigned to the little village of Kozminek. Recalling the experiences of his life, Fr. Bryllik wrote that he wanted nothing more—and that nothing could surprise him. He wanted only "to stay in my own land, among my own people, for whom I want to live and among whom I hope to die…."

In spite of the political upheaval and ruin in Russia, the head of the Vladivostok parish, Dean Karol Sliwowski, continued his pastoral work, continuing to hope for the establishment of peace and order in the country. But the priest's hopes, alas, were not realized. After the establishment of Soviet power in Primorye, a significant part of the wealthy parishioners left Vladivostok. Because the rail connection with Manchuria had been destroyed by military activities, one could only emigrate by sea—and this was affordable only to rather well-to-do people. Some refugees tried to make it into China by crossing the Amur, but very few managed to do so. Along with civilian refugees, the remnants of the military divisions of the White Army and the Polish divisions were also rapidly abandoning Vladivostok. Since Poland had become an independent state, a Polish consulate was now functioning in Vladivostok, headed up by Consul Karczewski. Many of Fr. Sliwowski's parishioners hurried to get registered at the consulate and get Polish passports.

Economic ruin in the country and the impoverishment of the population led to the halt of any work on the Catholics' brick church. They simply had not the means to complete the interior painting, or cover the roof, or build the two bell towers. And so the unfinished church stood surrounded by scaffolding....

21. Visitation of the Vicar Apostolic, Bishop de Guébriant, to the Far Eastern Roman Catholic Parishes

In June 1921 the Soviet authorities allowed the Vicar Apostolic, Bishop de Guébriant, to make a visitation of the Far Eastern Roman Catholic parishes.[71] This visitation by such a distinguished guest became possible thanks to the generous humanitarian assistance rendered by the Vatican to the population of the young Soviet government: ships laden with grain and flour, designated for the starving population of southern Ukraine, arrived in Odessa from Italy.

Bishop de Guébriant received permission to visit Catholics in Siberia, in particular in Chita, Vladivostok and Nikolsk-Ussuriisk. Included in the entourage were Bishop Gaspais, the Co-adjutor Vicar Apostolic of Northern Manchuria and head of the French Catholic

71 Jean-Baptiste-Marie de Guébriant (1860-1935) was appointed Superior General of the French missionary order, La Société des Missions Etrangères (MEP) in March 1921. He had served in China at least since 1910 when he was appointed Vicar Apostolic for Kienchang, and then as Vicar Apostolic for Canton from 1916. He was elevated to archbishop in December 1921.

mission in China; Fr. Władisław Ostrowski, the head of the Harbin Catholic parish; his vicar, Fr. Aleksandr Ejsymontt; the Franciscan Fr. Marius Kluge, the Vicar's secretary, working in the Catholic missions of China; and other clergymen. All the details of this visit became available to us thanks to notes in Archbishop de Guébriant's diary, a copy of which we were able to obtain from Paris.

The bishop arrived in Vladivostok at 9:30 a.m. on June 18, 1921. At the train station to greet him were Dean Sliwowski; the Polish consul, Mr. Karczewski; the Lithuanian consul, Mr. Wattekajtis; and several French citizens who were in Vladivostok. When he arrived at the church, he saw that a large crowd of the faithful had gathered to greet him warmly. They asked him to bless them, which he did with great delight. In the afternoon he paid a visit to the three consuls, then he had an excursion through Vladivostok. They showed him the historical points of interest, the beautiful Golden Horn Bay, and the shore of the Amur Gulf.

On the second day, June 19, there was a small Mass at the Catholic church early in the morning, then at a large Mass at noon the bishop confirmed 196 Catholics! Then he held conferences with the faithful and the priests. He held an especially lengthy conference with Fr. Władisław Mieżwinski. The Polish and Lithuanian consuls hosted a dinner in honor of the distinguished guest. In the evening they saw Bishop Gaspais off to China.[72]

On June 20, after studying the affairs of the Vladivostok parish and a lengthy consultation with Dean Sliwowski, the distinguished guest made two decisions: first, he permitted Dean Sliwowski to finish building the church "without bell towers," for which he gave him 3,000 rubles; and second, he approved the organization of a Vladivostok Minor Seminary for boys from devout Polish families. It was decided that the Minor Seminary would be housed in the former wooden "barracks" church and 1,000 rubles were allocated for it. The bishop named Fr. Marius Kluge rector of the future seminary. After a mid-day dinner, the bishop conferred with Consul

72 Archives of Archbishop de Guébriant (Paris), AZ-24, p. 366.

Karczewski and the Polish entrepreneur Tomaszewski, and then together they visited the Polish orphanage. After supper, an evening excursion through Vladivostok was organized for the bishop.

On June 21 at a 9:00 a.m. Mass, approximately 35 Catholics were confirmed. Then there were face-to-face conversations with some parishioners. The bishop returned again to the question of the Minor Seminary, finding out more about the details, its location, etc., and then after mid-day the bishop once again visited the uncompleted brick church and spoke with Dean Sliwowski concerning some technical questions. Then the parish trustees—five Poles and two Lithuanians—came to meet with the bishop and to present him with a letter of gratitude. On that day the dinner for the bishop was hosted by local Polish magnates—the Sienkiewicz brothers and other Polish entrepreneurs. At 8:30 p.m. a large group of Poles accompanied the distinguished guest to the railroad station, from where he departed for Nikolsk-Ussuriisk.

Because the train arrived in Nikolsk-Ussuriisk the following day at 4:00 a.m., there were only five or six local Catholics at the train station to greet the bishop. He was taken right away to the home of the wealthy Feliks Steckiewicz, where a comfortable room awaited him. At precisely 8:00 a.m., he arrived at the Catholic church, the construction of which had come almost completely to a halt. The bishop knew that the church under construction practically belonged to Steckiewicz, since it was being built on his land with his money. In his journal the bishop carefully described the appearance of this Catholic church, noting that the exterior, made from red brick, was of a pseudo-Gothic style, and its interior was decorated with numerous as yet unfinished architectural details.[73] It should be noted that unfortunately this description of St. Nicholas Church in Nikolsk is the only written evidence about this church. During his conversation with the bishop, Mr. Steckiewicz asked permission for the provision of sleeping quarters for his family in the basement of his church—to

73 Ibid., p. 365.

which the bishop answered that it would be possible to do so, if permission were granted by the Mogilev archbishop.

Unfortunately, during the Revolution, the bell tower in front of St. Nicholas Church was destroyed, and on the inside all the architectural adornments were torn from the walls. In the archival documents there is only the architect's sketch of the outer appearance of the church. According to older residents of Ussuriisk, the "remains" of the church were used for some time during the Soviet period as a store for household goods, then even the store was torn down….

After visiting the church and participating in a Mass, the guest was invited to a gala dinner given by Mr. Steckiewicz. At the dinner the most well-known Catholics of the city were presented to the bishop, then after the dinner the bishop, accompanied by Fr. Sawicz Maturin, visited the city's Orthodox church. Bishop de Guébriant's visitation of Primorye concluded June 23, 1921, when he returned to Harbin.

22. *Completion of the Vladivostok Catholic Church and Organization of the Vladivostok Roman Catholic Minor Seminary*

There is no doubt that the visit of the Vatican official brought Dean Sliwowski spiritual comfort. Now he not only knew what he had to do, but he also had the funds for work on the completion of the church. They quickly set about plastering and painting the interior walls, laying down the floor and hanging and painting the doors. Dreams of beautiful stained glass windows, however, remained only dreams, for there was only enough money for stained glass windows on the very highest transoms. But these small details did not bother the priest or the parishioners—all the Catholics were happy. Fr. Sliwowski wrote to Archbishop de Guébriant in Rome:

> …As for the new church, we have moved forward a little—they will soon finish the doors, they have installed the windows, the capitals have already been fastened to the columns, and the floor boards

> have been laid. Soon we will begin to build and decorate the balustrade for the choir and to construct the pulpit. The capitals, the pulpit and the balustrade are all of imitation marble and cost us 770 yen. We would also like to build two side altars. The builders ask another 800 yen for this—which exceeds our financial resources. However, I would like to ask you, Monsignor, when you are in Paris, to let me know the price of two paintings by Murillo (I will send you the dimensions)—the "Immaculate Conception" and "Saint Anthony"—for the side altars. I would like to purchase these myself, but not knowing how much they would cost, I am not certain whether I would have the means to do so."[74]

In spite of numerous difficulties, thanks to the efforts of the Building Committee, the construction of the church was approaching an end, and indeed in the autumn of 1921 it was finally completed. Of course a church without bell towers looked rather sorrowful, but the Catholics were nevertheless happy that they would finally be able to worship in their own beautiful church, under whose lofty arches would resound their prayers and hymns. The solemn dedication of the church took place on October 2, 1921, and the event was reported as follows in the local newspaper, *Slovo* [The Word]:

> The architecture of the building is beautiful. Made of brick, the building is spacious and very majestic. Despite the very difficult time in which we are living and a complete lack of funds, thanks to the efforts of the Building Committee, which included energetic people dedicated to their religion and their national heritage, the church has successfully been

74 Ibid., p. 492.

> completed. The local Catholic community can be proud of its new religious acquisition.

And in fact the church delighted the parishioners with an architectural perfection that is characteristic of basilicas—it had three naves, the middle one much higher than the others and with a separate roof. Groups of snow-white columns, decorated with capitals with a vine pattern, and the very beautiful lancet windows separated by narrow spaces—all lent to the solemnity and fine appearance of the interior. At the center, near the first group of columns was the amphon, and at the altar stood a snow-white marble Crucifix, which was brought to the new church from the wooden church. There were several flags and banners which would be used in processions on feast days—Corpus Christi, the Assumption of the Mother of God and Palm Sunday. The interior walls had been painted with mosaics as well as icons of Our Lady of Częstochowa, Our Lady of Ostrabramsk and the Merciful Mother of God. In the chapel were statues of Christ in the Tomb and the Sorrowful One.

After the church had been completed and all the furnishings had been transferred, Fr. Sliwowski, remembering the archbishop's recommendation, closely inspected the former wooden church that had served the Catholics for approximately twenty years. What he saw was frightening! It turned out that the walls, the floor, the ceiling and even the window frames were completely rotted out and the furnaces and fireplaces were also in a hazardous condition. Distraught and alarmed, Fr. Sliwowski sent Archbishop de Guébriant an immediate report:

> It will be necessary to replace not only the walls and the floor, but also the furnaces. Therefore this week we will begin laying new flooring and building new furnaces, fireplaces and another stove for baking bread.... These enormous expenses have led me to despair, and I am very upset—suddenly there is no money to buy beds, tables and kitchenware. Here is

> my brief accounting: for heating, 30 yen; for lighting, 15 yen; for water, 18 yen; for the services of a cook, 35 yen. And this means that for feeding fourteen or fifteen seminarians I will have only 207 rubles—i.e., 7 yen per month per person. With ten to thirteen pupils, I doubt that we will be able to make ends meet.
>
> But what especially worries me is the question of their education. People ask, what will the seminarians study and who will teach them? Right now I cannot answer them concretely, and therefore I await impatiently the arrival of Fr. Marius Kluge, the director of the seminary, in the hope that he will be better enlightened than I with respect to questions concerning the academic program and financial matters.... He will teach Latin and religious subjects. I have found an engineer, Mr. Rudziński, who knows Polish, history, mathematics and natural sciences very well, but I would need to pay him 100 yen a month for his work (three hours a day). I ask you, Monsignor, to give an affirmative response to these questions, since I am afraid that right from the beginning people will say that they teach poorly in the seminary or that they don't teach them anything—and consequently we will lose the trust of the parents and parishioners. I consider this a very serious and important issue, and if we lose sight of it, we risk all that we have invested. This is the subject of my concerns.

Being a realistic and responsible person, Dean Sliwowski clearly saw how much would have to be invested in the construction of the seminary, and he did not see any real possibility of finding the needed money in his parish. The more affluent parishioners had already left Vladivostok, and those remaining thought only of where they could find the means to get their families out of the country. The parishioners who had no intentions of leaving Russia and emigrating were very poor and would hardly be able to give any money to the construction of a seminary.

But financial problems did not interest Fr. Kluge. Furthermore, he had taken a dislike to Dean Sliwowski and thought only of how he could get him removed from Vladivostok. In his letters to Archbishop de Guébriant this thought appears in almost every paragraph. He was especially angered by a letter of the Vladivostok dean in which he wrote that the director of the seminary, i.e., Fr. Marius, ought to give money for the support of the seminary. But to all Fr. Marius' complaints, Archbishop de Guébriant gave the same response: "One must show greater modesty and tact." But Fr. Marius was a stubborn Bavarian German and therefore made no secret of his dislike of Dean Sliwowski and he continued to bombard Archbishop de Guébriant with various suggestions, trying however he could to have Fr. Sliwowski deposed from his position as head of the Vladivostok deanery. "I am somewhat afraid of remaining without a bishop with an elderly dean—if they can't find a bishop in Poland, perhaps they could send one of those bishops who does not have a diocese? You know that Dean Sliwowski is old, so you need to hurry."[75]

When the parish had finally moved into the new brick church, there was no end to the parishioners' rejoicing—and Dean Sliwowski with great pleasure was photographed near the new altar together with Fr. Władisław Mieżwinski and the parish children who had just received their First Communion in the new church. This photograph was saved by the Brzeziński family and parishioners today look at it joyfully, finding their mothers and fathers, aunts and uncles among the children in the photograph. The tall, sad-looking girl in the white dress standing behind Dean Sliwowski is the venerable Sofia Brzezińska—who in the spring of 2005, at the age of ninety-four, went home to God….

When Fr. Kluge returned from Harbin, he and Fr. Karol once again looked into how they would repair the former wooden church in order to begin the work of the Vladivostok Minor Seminary. The

75 Ibid., p. 367.

roster of future seminarians was not large, but the material security of the seminary was very fragile. Nevertheless the seminarians' studies were begun and they progressed successfully. But the financial security of the seminary still remained very unreliable. Therefore on May 22, 1922, the worried Vladivostok dean once again wrote to de Guébriant:

> We considered keeping the boys at the seminary through the summer vacation, lest in a hostile atmosphere they lose all that we had managed to instill in them. Fr. Marius also wanted to remain through the summer until the arrival of his successor, when he could turn over to him all the seminary business. But unfortunately material affairs have destroyed our hopes for all projects. Now in the face of this reality, I do not know what to do with the seminarians. Who will be able to keep and feed them? I will not be able to, because the situation day by day becomes worse and perhaps I myself very shortly will have nothing to live on. It is not possible to count on the support of our parishioners either, because an all-encompassing poverty has set in. Even those who work receive nothing—or just a "credit" slip. In such a situation it is problematic to find resources here—and so we have decided that the seminary will close July 15 of this year. But I beg you, Monsignor, to pay the seminary's debts, which Fr. Sallu knows in detail. There are people who have waited seven months to receive their salary, and for me this is a torment....[76]

The Seminary's problems were resolved in a completely unexpected fashion: it was closed for an indefinite period by decree of the city authorities on February 13, 1923.... Taking into account

76 Ibid., p. 460.

the complexity of the political milieu, they transferred the seminary to Harbin, where it was named the St. Charles Vladivostok Minor Seminary. But only four of the Vladivostok seminarians went to Harbin: Samojlo, Maculiewicz, Mateuszek and Wolanski; the parents of the rest of the Vladivostok seminarians would not let them go abroad. Fr. Marius thereupon announced that the seminary had opened in Harbin and soon it became the central seminary for all the Far East.

Letters were sent to all parishes of East Asia with a request to seek devout young boys from good Polish families and send them to Harbin. But these ardent appeals could not bear results, since the political situation in the Far East was very complex and sending children abroad was practically impossible. Nonetheless, a group of seminarians was gathered from local boys in Harbin, and the small St. Charles Vladivostok Minor Seminary in fact opened!

But it immediately became necessary to resolve the question of financing the reborn Vladivostok Seminary. Kazimierz Grochowski, one of the organizers of the seminary and a resident of Harbin, wrote:

> Several ideas as to raising money came to me. I tried to borrow money from acquaintances, but I had no luck. People told me to go to the bank (this I could have known without any advisors!)—but the bank was charging 11% interest and furthermore it would mean registering the seminary building in the bank's name, which I found completely unacceptable. Finally I came upon a happy thought—to telegraph one of my bishop acquaintances in China to ask for a loan. This worked—the bishop loaned me twenty-five thousand dollars. But the whole process took a long time.[77]

77 K. Grochowski, *Polacy na Dalekim Wschodzie* [Poles in the Far East], p. 44.

After a difficult period of organization, the St. Charles Vladivostok Minor Seminary was finally opened. At first it was housed in the Harbin Genrich Sienkiewicz High School, then later it was given a beautiful two-story mansion. The seminarians were boys from Polish families, most of whom lived along the line of the Chinese Eastern Railroad.

23. Episcopal Ordination of Dean Karol Sliwowski

On October 30, 1922, a message from Willem Cardinal Van Rossum, Prefect of the Congregation of the Faith, was received in Vladivostok and Harbin, notifying the faithful that the deaneries of Vladivostok, Irkutsk, Omsk, Tomsk and Tashkent were being separated from the archdiocese of Mogilev and that they would now comprise a separate Apostolic Vicariate. A vicariate of such an enormous area—encompassing all of Siberia, the Far East, Turkestan and northern Manchuria—larger than all of Europe—would of course be divided later into smaller deaneries, depending on future increases in the Catholic population. The Catholics of the Far East with anxiety awaited the future development of events—and then on October 23, 1923, the Apostolic Delegate to China, Archbishop Celsius Costantini arrived in Harbin with good news!

The meeting of the distinguished guest at the Harbin train station was very festive. In addition to local clergy, the distinguished guest was welcomed by the Polish consul, Mr. Pidor; the Polish vice-consul, Mr. Simonolewicz; the French consul, Mr. L. Epissiero; a representative of the Lithuanian consul, Mr. Poliszajtis; the director of the Chinese Eastern Railroad, Mr. Stefan Offenberg; the commander-in-chief of the Chinese Army, General Chu; and several others. A Polish scout troop from Harbin formed an honor guard.

After being welcomed in the rail car, the distinguished guest accepted a bouquet of flowers from Galina Zajanczkowska, the best student at the local high school, and upon stepping onto the platform he was literally strewn with flowers by the local high school students. A festive procession headed by Bishop Gaspais went directly by automobile to St. Stanisław church. At the corner of Cicikarsk Street a procession of parishioners with banners and lit candles awaited them. The distinguished guest and his entourage emerged from the automobiles and joined the procession. At the gate to the church the guest was met with bread and salt by Pan Apollon Pomian Brudzewski, a veteran of the Polish Army and a participant in the 1863 Uprising. At the doors of the church the guest was greeted by local Polish priests and then, in accordance with liturgical canons of the Catholic church, they all prayed at the main altar.

After the prayers, His Excellency the Apostolic Delegate Celsius Costantini stood before the faithful and addressed this huge audience in classical Latin. In his sermon, he noted that Poland had always been faithful to the Catholic Church. And he exhorted his listeners to always honor their homeland and by their work and actions to hold high the value of the fatherland. His Excellency named Polish heroes—Sobieski, Mickiewicz, Sienkiewicz—urging the young people to follow their example. And His Excellency expressed his conviction that despite the long distance from the fatherland the local Poles would always love the Church and their homeland.

All in attendance listened with deep emotion to the speech, which was translated from Latin to Polish. The anxiety that was oppressing the souls of many of those present quieted down after they listened to the speech, which was full of deep wisdom and knowledge of Polish feelings and ideals. They brought the distinguished guest a letter that had been placed in a silver folder with an engraved inscription: "To His Excellency the Apostolic Delegate Archbishop Celsius Costantini, from the Roman Catholic Polish parishioners living on the territory of the Concession of the Chinese Eastern Railroad."

The Apostolic Delegate also visited the local Polish high school, Genrich Sienkiewicz High School, and St. Vincent de Paul grade school. The guest first visited all the classes, then all the pupils of the high school and the grade school gathered in the high school hall to hear him speak. He spoke very simply and earnestly to the children, again in pure Latin. The archbishop gave them his view of the position and obligations of Polish children, especially concerning their relation to their homeland and the Catholic Church. He expressed the hope that these ideals would accompany the pupils their whole lives. His Excellency said that he had met many Poles, and these people always were remarkable for their deep patriotism and their deep religious feelings. At the end of his speech he blessed all those in attendance.

But the main purpose of the Apostolic Delegate's visit was the search for a candidate for the position of bishop, and therefore he held meetings and conversations with many representatives of the Polish clergy. They all understood that the Apostolic Delegate would decide who was to be named bishop, and the opinions of the priests were divided. Some asserted that Fr. Władisław Ostrowski should definitely be named bishop, as he was young and energetic—and it was he who had been able to convene a Catholic Congress in Harbin on November 9, 1921, to which were invited not only priests but also numerous honored guests, including the consuls of all the governments accredited in China. The opening of the Congress had been beautiful and unbelievably solemn: all in attendance sang "Ecce Sacerdos," then they prayed together. Bishop Gaspais presented an interesting report in French, then followed Fr. Władisław Ostrowski's presentation on the history and meaning of Catholic Congresses. After the solemn opening of the Congress, there were several sections that set to work, including sections on education, social issues, youth, parenting, Third Orders, the propagation of the faith, and the St. Vincent de Paul Society. The Congress concluded with the singing of the "Te Deum Laudamus."

Naturally the priests who had participated in this Congress were inclined toward the selection of Fr. Ostrowski to the post of bishop—others preferred to see Fr. Sliwowski, a very experienced and highly educated churchman, named bishop. Apparently the Apostolic Delegate himself did not have a definite opinion, and therefore he held conversations with numerous clerics in an effort to make the right decision.

Archbishop Costantini finally named Fr. Karol Sliwowski bishop, with the title of Apostolic Vicar of Eastern Siberia, and the solemn and beautiful ceremony of the ordination of Karol Sliwowski as bishop took place in St. Stanisław Church on October 28, 1923. The magazine *Tygodnik Polski* [Polish Weekly] filed the following comment on this event: "We can be glad that the Apostolic Delegate has chosen Fr. Karol Sliwowski. He is a very active man, a fine priest, and very knowledgeable about life in the Far East."[78]

Bishop Karol Sliwowski did not return to his diocese until November 15, 1923, and at the border station a "surprise" awaited him. It turned out that during those days when the ordination was taking place in Harbin, some of the rules at the border had been changed. Now each person crossing the border had to have an entry visa. Bishop Sliwowski of course had no such document. He rushed about the station trying to get his papers in order, but he was unable to do anything. Suddenly something most unlikely happened: a clerk in uniform came up to the bishop and said: "Dear old man, what are you doing here on the border? Do you recognize me? I am that poor little boy whom you helped during the famine—you gave us bread and vegetables! I am now the head of this station and I can help you." And in fact he helped the bishop get the required document, then seated him on the train bound for Vladivostok.

Upon the return of Bishop Karol Sliwowski to Vladivostok, there awaited him a heartfelt meeting of his parishioners—and many difficult problems which the bishop was not able to resolve. The fact that he had not for a long time visited his congregation in Khabarovsk or the Amur Region bothered him—but he had only two subordinates in Vladivostok—Fr. Władisław Mieżwinski and Fr. Georgij Jurkiewicz.

Bishop Sliwowski did not forget to share his joy and experiences with Archbishop de Guébriant. In a letter to him dated February 18, 1924, Bishop Karol Sliwowski writes:

> Your Excellency cannot imagine what gratification your friendly letter brought me. I was deeply

78 *Tygodnik Polski* [Polish Weekly], 1923, no. 83, p. 2.

touched by such inexhaustible kindness toward me and I am so delighted by Your Excellency's large heart, which among all its various concerns has not forgotten the parishes that you have visited.

As Your Excellency knows, on October 28 I was consecrated bishop by the hands of the Holy Delegate in the presence of Bishop Gaspais. I was touched to the bottom of my heart, and I must acknowledge that it was the most beautiful day of my life. However, I sense my imperfection and my inactivity. And even though these arise not out of my own will, they nevertheless arouse doubts within me.

My solemn *ingress* [into my cathedral] was on November 18. The Good Lord gave us good weather and—what is very rare—a temperature of 12 degrees Réaumur [59° F]. The church was completely full. This winter it has been very cold and there have been fewer faithful in attendance at Mass than usual. But in spite of the weather, when Mass was celebrated on Christmas as well as the Feast of Three Kings, the church was full.

But we are experiencing a dire shortage of priests. In my whole diocese [with the exception of Harbin] there are only two priests: Fr. Georgij Jurkiewicz and Fr. Władisław Mieżwinski. The churches in Nikolsk, Khabarovsk, Aleksandrov on Sakhalin and Blagoveshchensk are without priests. In addition, material conditions have become extremely difficult—the faithful have become so impoverished that for several months now there have been no Mass stipends. It is with such difficulties that my pastoral activity now contends. And only the undying Faith and Hope which I place in the Most Sacred Heart of Jesus support me and keep me from collapsing.

Fr. Marius Kluge will remain in Harbin until June, where he is in charge of the Seminary. The Seminary presently has ten seminarians, including four of our own from Vladivostok: Maculiewicz, Mateuszek, Samojlo and Wolanski. The first two ought, finally, to continue their studies in Europe, but this business proceeds very slowly and not without difficulties. These poor young men have already been three years in complete uncertainty.

Once again I ask Your Excellency to accept my gratitude for all that you have done for us and, finally, for the papal gift. I am happy that I can assure Your Excellency of my deep respect and gratitude.

In unitate orationum
Addictissimus Filiu in Christo
Karol Sliwowski

24. Fr. Władisław Mieżwinski

Fr. Władisław Mieżwinski was selflessly dedicated to the Church and the parishioners. He was very stubborn—an insistent Catholic pastor who never avoided the difficult pastoral visits that took several days of travel in the huge territory of the Vladivostok diocese. In order to present the essence of this priest, we will attempt to become acquainted with his biography.

Władisław was born into a family of the nobility in Minsk *gubernia* in 1880. From 1892 to 1899 he studied in Dvinsk at City School No. 1. In 1898 he enrolled in the seminary of the archdiocese of Mogilev, and upon his completion of studies in 1903 he was ordained to the priesthood by the suffragan bishop Gaspar Cyrtowt. They gave the energetic young priest a temporary assignment as vicar for the Roman Catholic parish of the little village of Rakow in the Minsk district. His assignment as vicar was made permanent by the archdiocesan consistory February 7, 1904.

The ministry of the “violent Catholic” Fr. Mieżwinski was very complicated because no matter where they sent him, there was always a “tail” of complaints of Orthodox priests, who disliked his acutely expressed animosity toward Orthodoxy. For example, on May 12, 1905, a lengthy missive from the Department of Religious Affairs was received by the archdiocese, stating that on January 14, 1905, Fr. Władisław had been in the village of Krylowo, where the residents were predominantly Orthodox, and he began to walk from house to house with holy water, urging the Orthodox to become Catholics. Amazingly, he managed to “seduce” several Orthodox families into the Catholic faith! In another village, on January 16, 1905, Fr. Mieżwinski married the peasants Julia Goladka and Wikientij Dozowski, ignoring the fact that these two were closely related. In the village of Zachariczi on January 21, Fr. Mieżwinski “re-christened” the largest Orthodox family as Catholics. And in the village of Diczki, accompanied by local Catholics, Fr. Mieżwinski went through the streets singing psalms, intruded into the homes of local residents without invitation, and again managed to “seduce” another four families into the Catholic faith. Moreover, during these “excursions,” Fr. Mieżwinski allegedly spoke blasphemously about Orthodox churches and forced peasants to burn Orthodox icons, assuring the peasants that the Emperor and his heir had already accepted the Roman Catholic faith!

It is difficult to judge what actually happened and what arose as popular rumor. But the strict Russian institution, the Department of Religious Affairs, sternly demanded that the priest submit to it a written explanation. But the metropolitan of the Mogilev archdiocese responded that the priest in question had already left the Belorussian parishes and was now serving as vicar in the St. Petersburg church of St. Stanisław. However, Fr. Mieżwinski was soon sent as vicar and religion teacher at the local high school in the city of Bobruisk—but he was not there long, as he was transferred to the post of vicar of the Mogilev cathedral and simultaneously to serve as head of the Catholic church in the little village of Swietlowiczi.

It seemed that this would be the end of Fr. Mieżwinski's wanderings, but on August 7, 1907, he was once again transferred: they appointed him head of the Roman Catholic parish of the Belorussian village of Ulla, and by September 11 he had received all the property of the Ulla Roman Catholic parish according to its inventory and undertaken his pastoral responsibilities. It should be noted that although Ulla had only a very small population, its history went back to 1566, during the reign of the Polish king Sigmund August.

It was in this very old parish that Fr. Mieżwinski began his ministry in 1907. More than once people called him crazy, but he had only one very rare "disease"—more than all else in the world, he loved the Church and the faithful—and he was not at all concerned about personal gain. Being quite proficient in Belorussian, with his preaching Fr. Władisław always found a way into the hearts of his parishioners, and they gave him their allegiance. And so it was in Ulla.

But nonetheless, on April 18, 1908, the Mogilev archdiocese transferred him to the post of vicar in the town of Faszczewka. Upon the death of Fr. Kurowski, the pastor of the church in Faszczewka, Fr. Mieżwinski became the head of that church. In addition, he was offered the opportunity to teach religion in the Faszczew public school, and he gladly accepted the offer.

At the same time, the routine complaints of Orthodox priests continued to arrive at the Department of Religious Affairs. These priests constantly kept watch over the unruly Catholic priest Władisław Mieżwinski and regularly informed the Department of all the (in their view) illegal activities of the Catholic priest. On December 6, 1908, for example, the Mogilev archdiocese received a message advising that

> We have received information that the priest Mieżwinski even in his new place of service continues his pernicious activity. On September 28, 1908, for example, he opened a secret Polish school in the village of Dubowka, in the house of the peas-

> ant Kulbicki, where thirty-four Catholics aged nine to fourteen were discovered; on October 6 the priest Mieżwinski opened the same kind of school in the village of Faszczewka in his own apartment. There he conducts intensive propaganda against Orthodoxy, and he convinces the peasants not to send their Catholic children to the public school. We ask that you relieve Fr. Władisław Mieżwinski of his position and so advise us.

Most likely all these denunciations played their role—on December 11, 1908, by directive of the Mogilev archdiocese, Fr. Mieżwinski was dismissed from the Faszczewka parish and sent to Vyborg to await a special directive. He did not have to wait long: in a letter dated January 17, 1909, he was advised of the following: "The Mogilev archdiocese is concerned for the proper attention to the spiritual needs of Polish, Lithuanian and Latvian Catholics, and thus we propose that Your Reverence from time to time visit Helsingfors [Helsinki] to tend to their spiritual needs."

Studying the numerous archival documents concerning Fr. Mieżwinski, one can conclude that the Mogilev archdiocese had no intention of handing their priest over to the police, and so they kept transferring him from one place to another. In 1909, when Bishop Cieplak undertook his long trip to visit Siberian and Far Eastern parishes, among his entourage was this very Fr. Mieżwinski, who at that time was officially registered at the St. Petersburg church of the Most Holy Virgin Mary at Vyborg Cemetery. During his pastoral visit to the prisoners on Sakhalin Island, Bishop Cieplak was staggered by the condition in which hundreds of Catholic prisoners were living. They begged the bishop to assign them a regular priest, since they only had pastoral visits once a year. Of all the priests accompanying the bishop, only Fr. Mieżwinski agreed to work for a year on the prisoners island. Thus when he received a routine inquiry from the police concerning the priest Mieżwinski, the metropolitan Kluczyński answered "The priest Mieżwinski, formerly serving at the cemetery church of the Most Holy Virgin Mary in St. Petersburg, has been designated chaplain for Catholics living on Sakhalin, in Nikolaevsk, and along the coast of the Tatar Gulf as far as Olga Bay."

One can only imagine the astonishment of the judicial authorities as they looked at a geographical map of the Russian Empire, trying to understand where Fr. Mieżwinski now served and how one could get there!

Although Fr. Mieżwinski agreed in 1909 to a one-year assignment on Sakhalin Island, he was never to leave the Far East. A study of the registry books of the Vladivostok parish shows that from 1914 through 1916 he made pastoral visits not only in Sakhalin but also to all the distant regions of the Far East where Catholic émigrés lived—Dalnegorsk, Olginski, Imanski, Suchanski. In November 1914, Fr. Mieżwinski was arrested in one of the villages of the Imansk region. The priest himself in a letter to the head of the Vladivostok parish, Fr. Karol Sliwowski, described the incident as follows:

> I was arrested completely unexpectedly, since I had lived several months in Vladivostok, and I was registered with the police there. Wanting to make a pastoral visit deeper into the region where many Catholics live, I requested permission for this trip from the governor of the region. He received me very kindly and ordered that I be given an "open pass" so there would be no problems en route and I would be able to get horses. For about two weeks I traveled through the Ussuriisk region, between Nikolsk-Ussuriisk, Khabarovsk and Iman.
>
> When I was getting ready to return for the Christmas holiday to the village of Mitrofanovka (which is 20 versts from the Ussuri railroad station), the village elder informed me that he had received an order from the prosecutor to arrest me. I then showed him my "open pass" and this satisfied him. But on

> that very same day an Orthodox priest arrived in that very same village; he knew of the prosecutor's order for my arrest. He went directly to the elder and informed him that I was to be arrested immediately. He then began to swear at the elder because the elder had allowed me to baptize two infants of a Catholic family. This priest knew that Catholics had children—and that if the Catholic priest was arrested, then all the villagers would have to have the Orthodox priest baptize their children!
>
> They arrested me and then the village elder and several villagers took me to the Ussuri railroad station in the village of Lutkovsk where I sat under arrest until December 28. Then they placed me in the prisoner car of the train and took me to Nikolsk-Ussuriisk station, from where I had to walk under guard 6 versts to the prison. In two days, soldiers armed with rifles took me again to the railroad station and sent me to the prison in Vladivostok, where I spent a whole night, with the convoy soldiers all the while poking me in the back, and at night taunting me, even though they could see I was in clerics… They subjected my Mass kit to careful inspection—they ordered me to give up the chalice and other liturgical items. When the Vladivostok pastor came to visit me, they would not allow him in. In addition, the prosecutor said to the priest: "He deserves it! No use hiding him!"

So why was Fr. Mieżwinski arrested? From historical documents we know that at the beginning of the century they tried to arrest him in the Belorussian *gubernia*s because he actively struggled with Orthodox priests for every Christian soul. Owing to his sincere and vivid preaching, many Belorussian families accepted the Catholic faith, and this was not well received by priests of the Orthodox parishes. The Mogilev archdiocese transferred the disfavored priest from one parish to another and finally, when he accompanied Bishop Cieplak on his visitation of Siberian and Far Eastern Catholics, he agreed to remain on Sakhalin Island for a year. He remained thereafter in the Far East, where he was arrested.

Fr. Mieżwinski explained his arrest by the fact that as far back as 1909, when he served in a Catholic parish in Omsk, he had come across so-called *pochaevski* leaflets, the whole text of which consisted of nothing but vulgar torrents of filth and slander against Catholicism and the Catholic Church. Naturally, this caused Fr. Mieżwinski, as a Catholic priest, considerable pain. He took to writing an "anti-leaflet." In the Polish *gubernia*s such an anti-leaflet was not considered a "political document" and it was not illegal. But in the Russian *gubernia*s these "anti-leaflets" were seen as revolutionary, and thus the authorities sought out their authors and arrested them as "politicals."

When he heard of the arrest of Fr. Mieżwinski, Fr. Karol Sliwowski began to seek ways to free the priest, who was to be indicted under Paragraph 1 of the second part of Article 73 and Article 90 of the Criminal Code. Of course everything could have been smoothed over for a very modest "ransom," but Fr. Sliwowski had no such money. But, as they say, the world is not without good people, and 10,000 rubles for the ransom of Fr. Mieżwinski, sent by Princess Magdalena Radziwillowa, allowed the priest to get out of jail January 15, 1915. However, there is in the archives a letter from Fr. Karol Sliwowski that we found surprising—Fr. Sliwowski was writing to a Lithuanian bishop (whose name is not known), advising him that he, Fr. Sliwowski, was sending the 10,000 rubles from Magdalena Radziwillowa to Lithuania to help those suffering from famine. Did Fr. Sliwowski ransom Fr. Mieżwinski with other money? We will never know.

According to archive documents, it is apparent that Fr. Mieżwinski continued to serve in the Far East up into the 1920s: he is seen in a photograph taken in the summer of 1921 in the new brick church, together with Fr. Sliwowski and parish children on the occasion of their First Holy Communion. The parish registry indicates that he presided at parishioners' funerals as late as 1923. The parish has no further information about Fr. Władisław Mieżwinski.

25. Warsaw Catholic Conference and Its Results

Judging by historical documents, it was well into the 1920s before the Vatican and all Catholic clergy began to understand that Soviet power in Russia was now a serious objective reality and that they had to give up the hope that it would be overthrown. But as early as 1920, the Catholic Church in Poland recognized that there remained in Russia many who were of the Catholic faith, the majority of whom were Polish, who needed the regular care of spiritual pastors. But where could they be found? And how could they be sent into Soviet Russia? All these questions troubled the Catholic hierarchy and there appeared to be no answers. To address these questions, a Catholic Congress under the leadership of the Polish primate and with the permission of the Archbishop of Warsaw was convened on December 14, 1920, at the Polish Catholic Union Hall in Warsaw.

The chief purpose of the Congress was the creation of some sort of organization that would be able to help those Catholics who remained on the territory of Russia. After all, there were whole villages of former exiles and émigrés who did not want to abandon land they had gained by so much suffering and now return to Poland! It was these Catholics who needed spiritual care for the sake of their Faith and their national heritage. Through all the wide expanses of Russia, where Roman Catholic churches had been built thanks to the labors and sacrifices of Poles, the Catholic faith had to survive!

The fulfillment of this spiritual "mandate" would require the effort of Catholic missionaries who had an excellent command of both the Polish and Russian languages. The whole world knows that the spirit of missionary work continues to live in all Catholic countries—and Poland had no right to lag behind. Taking into account historical events and the needs of the times, there was formed as part of the work of the Congress a "Society for the Support of the Faith in the East. The goal of the Society is the material and spiritual support of the Faith." The Society realized it was necessary to quickly prepare young cadres of Catholic preachers and priests, and for that purpose a special educational institution was founded—a missionary seminary. Later this seminary, located in Lublin, would be called the Missionary Institute.

On December 14, 1921, the Alliance of Catholic Women met. The Alliance supported the concept of Catholic mission, but it categorically rejected any political activity on the part of the future Missionary Institute. Edward von der Ropp, metropolitan archbishop of the Mogilev archdiocese, confirmed that the purpose of the future work of the graduates of the Missionary Institute would only be missionary work—any political ideas were completely rejected and the Mission was to carry only the Faith to those Catholics scattered throughout Siberia and the Far East. Fr. Tadeusz Krzyszkowski, editor of the journal *Misiji Katolicki* [Catholic Missions] in his article "The State of Catholic Missions in the World," pointed out that Poland's participation in international missionary activity had until this time been very modest, and the opening of the Missionary Institute or Seminary for Missionaries in Lublin was an important contribution of Polish Catholics to this God-pleasing activity. The Apostolic Delegate also supported the idea of creating an educational institution for the preparation of missionaries. In a letter to the organizers of this educational institution, he wrote: "We thank God for it and we ask that He bless this plan and those who endeavor to carry it out, in particular, the Polish bishops. How wonderful that even Poland, following the example of other civilized people, will now have its own Missionary Seminary!"

The new educational institution was located in the medieval part of Lublin, on Zielona Street, on the grounds of the church of St. Josaphat, Bishop and Martyr, which had been built back in 1786 as an Orthodox church. The Missionary Seminary was housed in a two-story brick building in the courtyard of the church. It was dedicated April 4, 1924, by the canon priest Antonij Songajllo.[79]

In 1923 the Congress of Polish bishops convened in Częstochowa, at which time they confirmed the "Charter" of the Congress. Some of the participants introduced a proposal that 0.5 percent of all funds collected should be allocated for the support of the Missionary Institute, but Cardinal van Rossum, Prefect of the Propagation of the Faith, advised the participants to awaken the sacrificial spirit of the faithful, so that they would be proud of their homeland for having created such an institute, and contribute the means for the formation and support of this new Catholic institution. Archbishop Ropp then designated December 8 as the "Day of Donations" for the Missionary Institute.

26. *Last Period of the Life of Bishop Karol Sliwowski*

From a letter dated July 4, 1926, written by Bishop Sliwowski to Archbishop de Guébriant in Paris, we have learned much of the real state of affairs for the Roman Catholic parishes of the Far East.

> Your Excellency! My very dear and beloved Father!
>
> I ask that you not think that I have not written you for so long out of sloth. The main reason for my silence is the impossibility of writing candidly—given the strict censorship to which all my letters are subjected. Only now has an opportunity arisen to transmit a letter to you.
>
> The general nature of our situation is most likely well known to Your Excellency. We have been robbed—they have taken all church properties. In

79 Archives of the Archdiocese of Lublin, Poland, "Katalogus Soolepianum et cleri Dioiecesis Lublinensis pro Anno Domini 1927," p. 23, Institute for Missions (ad. Tccl. S. Josafat, Lublin).

addition we have to pay various taxes—for example, on the land on which the church stands and another 600 yen for the parish hall, where I live. But thanks to Our Lord, I have complete freedom with respect to our Masses in the church. The greatest misfortune for me and for many parishioners is the fact that with the exception of Vladivostok all the parishes of my diocese are without priests. In Blagoveshchensk the pastor, Fr. Kaminski, was arrested and expelled from the country—he was sent back to Poland. Khabarovsk has been deprived of its priest on account of the fact that Fr. Władisław Mieżwinski, who has given scandal by his refusal to obey his bishop, for three years now has been roaming around, dissolute. This is the sorry end, worthy of pity, that this unfortunate man has come to, after lying and deceiving others his whole life. Your Excellency was incorrectly informed about this priest, and I did not want to interfere and disclose the full truth, inasmuch as I had not been asked. Fr. Mieżwinski has been associated with me for twelve years, so I have been able to come to know him well. He was an unbelievably arrogant person—the most insignificant paternal correction would drive him into a rage—he would cause a scandal with his foul curses.

His visits in the villages were only a diversion for him—they had nothing of the nature of a "mission." On account of his renegade behavior he has brought the faithful nothing but evil. Thus I have only Fr. Georgij Jurkiewicz from Khabarovsk. As for Nikolsk-Ussuriisk—Orthodox priests have taken over the church in which Your Excellency celebrated Mass because of an oversight on the part of the local Catholics, who failed to submit a request to the local authorities that the church be given to them.

And Blagoveshchensk, where there are approximately 1,500 Catholics, now has only a small chapel.

Atheistic propaganda has led to massive devastation among the young people, thus leaving parishes empty. As for me, thanks be to God, Mass attendance on Sundays and holy days is significant. In May I made a canonical visitation of the whole diocese. I visited Khabarovsk and Blagoveshchensk and spent more than a week in each city. I spent a whole month traveling.

In addition to my episcopal duties during this visitation, I also spent a lot of time in the confessional, hearing confessions until late in the evening. The Good Jesus blessed me with a large number of people who came to me for confession. Among them were Catholics who had not been to confession for dozens of years. In general, the visitation was necessary—and it yielded good results. But only God knows whether this will continue....

I have been summoned several times to the GPU, but so far I remain among the living. God has preserved me, because I am now the only bishop in all of European Russia as well as all Asian Russia.

Now Your Excellency knows our situation—and therefore, expressing my highest respect, together with my faithful flock I entrust us all to your blessing and divine prayers.

Eternally grateful,
Servus in Christo
Karol Sliwowski, Bishop

Margin note: Fr. Georgij Jurkiewicz is going to Sakhalin next week, then after his return he will go to the vicinity of Blagoveshchensk, where there are numerous Catholics who have their own chapel. They number approximately 1,500 souls.

In 1925 Bishop Sliwowski made his last visit to Harbin, this time for the dedication of the new church in honor of St. Josaphat. It was a joyous and blessed trip, but the bishop's joy was short-lived. There now began a new and difficult period in the ministry of a Catholic priest in a country under a Communist regime. Nothing had come of the Vatican's intention to create a Catholic Vicariate of Siberia because Fr. Gerard Piotrowski, O.F.M., who had been designated the Apostolic Vicar of Siberia, was simply not allowed into the country. He continued teaching at St. Charles Seminary in Harbin, where he also served as head of the seminary.

In August 1928 a small group of seminarians who had completed St. Charles Seminary in Harbin departed from Harbin for Poland, where they would continue their studies at the seminary in Lublin. Brother Zachariusz Banaś, of the order of the Bernadine Fathers and one of the teachers at the seminary, accompanied the seminarians. They arrived in Vladivostok on a Japanese steamer and in two days they were to set out across Russia by train for Poland. Brother Zachariusz first of all hurried to the Catholic church, hoping to see anyone, if only someone on the technical staff. Near the church Brother Zachariusz met a Mr. Wiburski, a technical worker of the Roman Catholic Vladivostok parish. Going into the Wiburskis' apartment, which was located on the semi-basement level of the three-story parish house, Brother Zachariusz gladdened the Wiburskis with the news that their son, Stanisław Wiburski, was progressing well in his seminary studies and upon completion would be ordained a priest.

Concerning the fate of the elderly Bishop Sliwowski (who was now eighty-three years old), Brother Zachariusz learned that he was alive, but for all practical purposes lived under house arrest. Even though he continued to live in his own brick house, he had only one half-empty room where he was practically under the observation of the young people who had been moved into his home—i.e., "under house arrest." The parish was now led by a young priest, Fr. Georgij Jurkiewicz. They had also moved him out of the parish house and forced him to live in a tiny little room in the Kuzmins' house; furthermore, they had moved an old gloomy criminal type, recently released from prison, into the passage leading into his room—and he kept track of who came to the young priest and for what purpose.

On September 15, 1928, Kazimierz Symonoliewicz, the Polish consul in Harbin, arrived in Vladivostok on business. He asked a student-Orientalist named Waldemar Pelc who had gone to Harbin to study to call on the Vladivostok bishop Karol Sliwowski and find out how he was doing. With the greatest caution, the student went to the house, the location of which had been described to him in great detail. In his report, the student noted that the bishop continued to live in his own brick house on the second floor, but that they had allotted to him one almost empty room without any signs of the presence therein of a clerical personage. When the student went up the stairs, he noted that young people stood below, near the stairs, watching him, as though on guard.

The outer appearance of the bishop, seated in an armchair in the empty room, horrified his visitor because this high-ranking clerical figure looked like an impoverished, dilapidated old man in wretched civilian garb. Seeing the student, the bishop was very frightened and began to wave his hands and asked in a whisper that the unexpected visitor leave. When the student quietly told him who it was that had sent him in order to find out how to help him, tears fell from the bishop's eyes. Sighing and crying, he gave thanks for those good intentions. But at the same time the bishop warned that any help for him would be looked upon with hostility.

In the autumn of 2002, Fr. Marian Radwan, a professor at Lublin Catholic University, kindly gave to the archives of the Vladivostok Roman Catholic parish of the Most Holy Mother of God a copy of a letter handwritten in 1988 by another professor of Lublin Catholic University—Waldemar Pelc. In this historical document are described the touching moments of the meeting of the student-Orientalist with the unfortunate Bishop of Vladivostok.[80]

Recalling the details of his visit to the elderly bishop, Professor Waldemar Pelc writes in part:

> . . . If I am someday in heaven, then undoubtedly I will be given a "plus" for that visit to Bishop Karol Sliwowski. I recall that in the course of five minutes I had to quickly and insistently annihilate those mountains of lies which the bishop had been receiving from the Soviet press—after all, this was thc only source of news available to him in 1929 [sic]. It was the first year of an independent Poland, the year of the International Fair in Poznań, and it was only two years before the Great World Congress. This was my, this was our youth—it was the enthusiasm of a free human being in a free government! Enthusiasm and a love for Poland were simply bursting from my heart. All this I tried to convey to the bishop.
>
> Now I know that I gave him to drink a fortifying cup of joy. God knows, perhaps this was the last joy in the holy life of this pastor and martyr. The bishop gave me a rosary and blessed me. And when I stand before God at the Final Judgment, I will ask to testify on my behalf the one who will already be St. Karol, Bishop of Vladivostok.

In 1928 the Polish government and Polish hierarchy decided to encourage the spirit of the Bishop of Vladivostok and on November 10, 1928, they awarded him *in absentia* a medal commemorating the Rebirth of Poland, but this award was seen by the Soviet regime as a very belligerent act and a torrent of accusations came rushing down

80 Letter of Professor Waldemar Pelc, Archives of the Roman Catholic parish of Most Holy Mother of God, Vladivostok.

on the head of the old man—they disparaged him without mincing words. The sick old man only wanted to live and pray in some quiet little corner, where others would not be watching him, their eyes full of hatred. But all the bishop's requests to be moved somewhere else were ignored. They said the city was full of refugees and it was time to forget any dreams of a "good apartment." But at the end of June 1930 they put the old bishop in a simple wooden cart, they piled boxes with his church vestments into the cart as well and they took him to the little village of Sedanka outside the city.[81] Fortunately, Mrs. Kazimira Piotrowska, who rented an apartment there in a summer house, right away began to look after the bishop. Thanks to her good heart, the bishop was surrounded by attention and care to the end of his days.

In 1931, Brother Zachariusz Banaś, returning from Poland to Harbin, again stopped in Vladivostok, since he had an assignment from the Vatican to find Bishop Sliwowski, to give him some money and to find out the details about his life. This assignment was not easy because as soon as the train arrived in Vladivostok Brother Zachariusz acquired a "sticking friend" who, while showing a tiresome kindness, followed Brother Zachariusz' every step. Suspecting that this "sticking friend" worked for the NKVD, Brother Zachariusz began to play the role of a dim-witted provincial who was only interested in the old architecture of Vladivostok, and the "friend" finally left him in peace. Early on the morning of March 13, 1931, Brother Zachariusz, taking great precautions, set off for the church, and suddenly he saw Fr. Georgij Jurkiewicz walking along the road. He called out to the priest and the priest very concisely explained that he could not invite a guest to his apartment because he was constantly being followed—at home and on the street—and he was sure they were going to arrest him in the near future. Then he told him that the Wiburskis still lived in the same apartment and that Elżbieta Karlowna would be able to tell him about the life of

81 Ks. J. Urban, *Walka z antychristem* [The Struggle with the Anti-Christ], Kraków, 1930, p. 14. Syg. 155.44, Biblioteka Narodowa, Warsaw.

Bishop Sliwowski in his Sedanka exile because she often visited the bishop and brought him things from the parishioners. And with that, they parted.

Circling through the streets to make sure that he had no "tail," Brother Zachariusz hurried to the Wiburskis. He found Elizbieta Karlowna at home with her daughter, and she was glad to hear the news that her son had practically completed his studies at the seminary in Lublin and would soon be ordained a priest. Elizbieta Karlowna was very, very distressed that she could not offer such a dear guest more than a cup of tea; but Brother Zachariusz assured her that he had had a fine breakfast at the hotel. Then Elizbieta Karlowna explained to her guest in great detail how to get to Sedanka and how to find the house where the exiled bishop lived. Warmly taking leave of his hostess, Brother Zachariusz set off for his hotel and began to prepare for his trip to Sedanka. He understood that it was a dangerous venture and if an "inspector" were to find him in the bishop's apartment, he would kill not only him, but Bishop Sliwowski as well.

In the morning of the following day, having changed into simple old clothes, Brother Zachariusz went to the train station, bought a ticket, and stepped onto the platform where the suburban train was soon due. There were a lot of passengers on the train—all the seats were taken—and Brother Zachariusz, looking at the people around him, assured himself that he did not stand out. Opening the newspaper he had bought at the train station, he pretended to be very absorbed in his reading so that no one would attempt to engage him in a conversation. Reading the pages of Brother Zachariusz's journal, one can feel the nervousness and tension that filled him on that trip. He was risking his freedom and his life. He had no fear, but only concern about finding the house in which the exiled bishop lived.

When the train got to Sedanka station and he stepped down onto the platform, the ticket controller, checking his ticket, reminded him that the return train to Vladivostok left at exactly 5:00 p.m. Falling in line with a group of women who were leaving the train, Brother Zachariusz hurried after them. After a short time the women turned to the side, explaining to him where he had to go. Soon he came to an alley on which stood a house and in the window appeared a woman's face—then the woman came to the porch and said in Polish that her name was Kazimira. Inviting him into the house, Kazimira told Brother Zachariusz that Fr. Georgij Jurkiewicz, who had come the evening before to give the bishop Holy Communion, had told her to expect him. She invited him to be seated, then went to the next room to ask the bishop whether he was able to get up and come see his guest. She soon returned with a joyful smile and told him that the bishop had gotten up and would certainly come out to visit with such an important guest.

And the bishop did in fact come out from his room. He was wearing a civilian suit with a tie and a skullcap and on his finger he wore his episcopal ring. Brother Zachariusz was struck by the bishop's skin, now yellowed, with large brown spots. As was the custom, they recited the *Benedictus*, then warmly kissed and sat down at the table. Brother Zachariusz asked permission to smoke and offered the bishop a package of cigars. This gesture so moved the bishop that he began to cry like a little child, saying through his tears how attentive the brother had been—remembering how much he loved to smoke cigars. The bishop still remembered that once a railroad worker from Harbin had brought him a package of cigars, as a present from Brother Zachariusz.

When he had calmed down, the bishop invited his guest into his "office." This was a compartment approximately 2 square meters for the bishop's bed, his suitcases, a wash basin and, in the right-hand corner near the window, a cupboard. Showing the cupboard to his guest, the bishop opened both front panels and before Brother Zachariusz' eyes appeared a beautiful small altar. "This is my episcopal cathedra…" he said with bitterness. Later he told him that this wonder had been made for him by his Chinese cook, who had worked for him for many years. His name was Mu Ha. The bishop no longer had the means to pay him, but this faithful Chinese nevertheless did not leave him and often brought him something to eat. The "watchmen" wanted to frighten him off, but the Chinese answered them that he had served this priest for many years and now that the priest was old, ill and fallen into misfortune, he would not abandon him, despite any threats.

After tea, the bishop and Brother Zachariusz were alone in the bishop's "compartment" and Brother Zachariusz asked whether the bishop had written to the Holy Father to ask for money and the bishop confirmed that he had, since he had been forced to do so. But when money came from the Vatican, it was taken for the Red Cross, the Red Army, postal expenses, airplanes, charitable works—and for him there wasn't even enough left for bread. Once it even turned out that they claimed he owed money! And again they pressed him "Write to the Pope! He has lots of dollars, let him send you money!"

Upon hearing this bitter and sad tale, Brother Zachariusz said that they would need to come up with a channel for sending the bishop money without its falling into others' hands. The bishop said the most reliable way of sending money was by way of the Austrian consul, a Catholic—or by way of the Chinese. At the end of this conversation, Brother Zachariusz gave the bishop a significant sum of money from Fr. Gerard Piotrowski, the Apostolic Delegate. The bishop carefully counted the money and said that it would last him a long time. The bishop and Brother Zachariusz then returned to the main room where Kazimira invited them to the table. Brother Zachariusz then pulled from the "secret" pockets of his jacket a package with sausage and various sweets. All these happy events so touched the bishop that he could not hold back his tears and he began to pray as he wept, "O God, O merciful God!"

This scene was so emotional that it forcefully seized Brother Zachariusz' heart and he could not hold back his tears, knowing that he was seeing the bishop for the last time. He was powerless to help this old man in any way. The bishop continued sobbing and said through his tears, "The Holy Father remembers me and is concerned about me! And a brother for the sake of seeing me has undertaken a trip so dangerous that if they seized us here we would be sent to the gallows or a dark basement...."

It was getting close to 5:00 p.m. and Brother Zachariusz had to hurry to catch the five o'clock train since he was to leave for Harbin that night. When he returned to the hotel, he began to prepare packages with Easter presents for the bishop, Fr. Jurkiewicz and Elizbieta Wiburska. As they had arranged, Elizbieta Karlowna Wiburska late that evening waited for Brother Zachariusz at the Vladivostok train station, and he presented the "holiday packages" to her.

Sitting in the train en route to Harbin, Brother Zachariusz again and again recalled the details of his meeting with Bishop Sliwowski, sadly realizing that he had seen him alive for the last time....

27. Testimony of Eyewitnesses

We learned many of the details of the life of Bishop Sliwowski in Sedanka from the former Vladivostok parishioner, Regina Stańko, a retired military doctor now living in Tomsk. Her father, Stanisław Stańko, a railroad worker, was not afraid of visiting the exiled bishop in Sedanka and conversing with him at length in Polish. The Stańko family at that time lived in First River; their house stood above the lake, not far from the sea. In their small compound the Stańkos kept chickens, geese and a cow. The mother entrusted little Regina with taking fresh milk to the bishop in Sedanka and the little girl was thus always a welcome guest. Regina several times witnessed the "searches" of the bishop. Then some serious and dour people came to the little summer house and they moved the priest's vestments from one place to another, counting and re-counting his things and meticulously inventorying his books. Of course these "inspectors" found nothing illegal among the bishop's possessions, but during these inspections the bishop always experienced deep emotional anxiety and was shamed to the point of tears....

Regina's accounts greatly assisted the present-day parishioners in establishing the chain of events of those days.

On the morning of January 5, 1933, Regina as usual brought the bishop fresh milk, but at the doorway she was greeted by the weeping Kazimira. Sobbing, she said: "He doesn't need milk. He doesn't need anything. He's dead!" Regina recalls that the funeral took place the following day, January 6, 1933. They carried the coffin with the body of the deceased bishop on a sleigh to the nearby Sedanka cemetery. The coffin had been soldered because Kazimira intended to take the bishop's body to Poland. The deceased bishop was accompanied by the parish elder, a small group of parishioners, several children and Regina and her parents.

Maria Switecka, at that time a 17-year-old girl, who had served the bishop as a maid, described the bishop's funeral to us somewhat differently: "The bishop lay in an open coffin, dressed in a white chasuble and a gold beret, on his finger was his episcopal ring and alongside him in his coffin lay his crosier. They sang his funeral in the old chapel without a priest and they buried him next to the chapel." Maria remembered that the German consul attended the funeral and burial. Three days later robbers dug up the grave, opened the coffin and stole the crosier and episcopal ring. The bishop's body was re-buried in a simple wooden coffin somewhere between the chapel and the school. (Author's Note: The school was the bishop's manor—today it is the Orthodox Martha Mary Convent.)

Regina also told us that during the summer vacation of that year she lived at Mrs. Piotrowska's in Sedanka and every day they went to the bishop's grave. Simple wildflowers grew on the grave and, as she recalls, an iron cross with a small plaque stood over the grave. On the plaque were written in Polish the bishop's name and the dates of his birth and death. Regina sent our parish two photos of the grave. Having buried the bishop, Mrs. Piotrowska, not expecting to get permission to transport the bishop's body, departed for Poland, after having distributed to the parishioners the last of the bishop's possessions....

In spite of the fact that the head of the family, Stanisław Stańko, was arrested and sent to the Siberian labor camps, and his wife and two children banished to Tomsk, in this family even during times of severe hardship, the bishop's valuable silver keepsakes were preserved inviolable. In 1995 Regina Stańko conveyed these heirlooms to the Vladivostok Roman Catholic parish.[82]

When the sorrowful news of the bishop's death reached Harbin, Fr. Władisław Ostrowski, now the Harbin Vicar Delegate, commemorated the courageous bishop of Vladivostok by erecting a simple Christian monument in St. Stanisław Church, since that was where his consecration as bishop had been celebrated. The journal *Tygodnik Polski* described the dedication of the memorial: "In the middle of the church, among flowers and burning candles, lay a large crucifix and on it they placed the symbols of the bishop's authority.... Fr. Władisław blessed the cross, praying on his knes before it. Most of the congregation wept and all fervently prayed for the soul of the Polish bishop who had died in exile, in Siberia, and had been buried without the proper Christian rites..."[83]

After the prayers, they placed the cross before the entrance to St. Stanisław Church.

28. Last Catholic Priest of the Vladivostok Diocese

Even before Bishop Sliwowski had fallen seriously ill, Fr. Georgij Jurkiewicz had become the head of the Vladivostok parish, and it was this pastor who was the last Catholic priest to serve the church of the Most Holy Mother of God in Vladivostok. He was born April 5, 1884, in a petty bourgeoise family of the little village of Timkowicz, in the Kopylsk region of Minsk *gubernia*, and he had two brothers and a sister. The parish has no other information about his family. The little village of Timkowicz is noteworthy in that in olden times it had seven Orthodox churches, St. Michael's Catholic Church, three synagogues and a mosque! This information, found in the diocesan archives, was published by a local historian, Fiodor

82 M. I. Efimova, "Xranitel'nica istoricheskix cennostei," *Sibirskaia katolicheskaia gazeta* ["A Keeper of Historical Treasures," The Siberian Catholic Newspaper], 2000, No. 9, pp. 20-22.

83 *Tygodnik Polski*, 1933, No. 560, p. 4.

Abramczyk. In his opinion, St. Michael's Catholic Church was an architectural wonder of past centuries.

Thanks to archival documents that His Excellency Bishop Kirill Klimowicz conveyed from Irkutsk to Vladivostok, we have been able to study the historical chronicle and learn that 400 years ago Timkowicz was a significant settlement and the church there was built by the contributions of peasants, merchants, noblemen and Prince Sapegi. During times of numerous wars, the church was significantly damaged, and a well-known artist of that period, Franciszek Bruzdowicz, who used Belorussian folk motifs in his work, undertook the artistic restoration of the church. When one stepped over the threshold into the church, one fell, as it were, into a world of colorful Biblical depictions. The Franciscan church in Kraków is adorned with similar paintings. The historian Żeskar in his *Handbook of Belorussian Churches* notes: "The Timkov church is rich in form, aesthetic harmony—a living celebration of polychromatics. It was for Belorussia and Lithuania what the Franciscan church designed by Stanisław Wyśpianski was for Kraków—a joyful hymn of folk art." In 1976 and 1979 this architectural monument was studied by researchers of the Institute of History, Ethnography and Folklore of the Belorussian Academy of Sciences, who measured and photographed the church. Their materials, however, were not included in their *Monuments of Belorussian History* because in 1986 the Timkov church burned to the ground.

It was in this small but famous little village that the Belorussian boy Georgij Jurkiewicz was born and grew up. After completing school in Timkowicz, Georgij entered the St. Petersburg Seminary, and then in 1910 he was ordained a priest. His first assignment was in western Siberia—the Catholic parish in Krasnoyarsk. Two years later he was transferred to the Far East, to Khabarovsk, where he became the chaplain for the Khabarovsk Cadet Corps, the catechism teacher at the girls high school and the vocational school, and the head of the Khabarovsk Roman Catholic parish. In addition, he was also responsible for the care of the Roman Catholic parish in Nikolaevsk.

Fr. Jurkiewicz first came to Vladivostok in 1921 in connection with the dedication of the new brick church. On account of the fighting along the Khaborovsk-Vladivostok rail line, he had to make the trip via the Sungari River to Harbin, then by rail to Vladivostok. Dean Sliwowski liked this young, energetic, highly educated priest and he invited him to serve as vicar of the Vladivostok parish. But the official transfer of Fr. Jurkiewicz to Vladivostok did not occur until 1923.

Judging by the information of long-ago parishioners and their photographs, Fr. Georgij was very handsome: brown-eyed, tall, slender, with curly brown hair. He also had a fine voice and willingly worked with the parish choir, sometimes even singing in the choir himself. Fr. Jurkiewicz also gave a lot of attention to the parish children, preparing them for their First Holy Communion—and the children loved him! Since Dean Sliwowski was now getting on in years, Fr. Jurkiewicz made the pastoral visits to those Catholics living outside Vladivostok. When Bishop Sliwowski was exiled to Sedanka, Fr. Jurkiewicz was permitted to visit the bishop twice a week to hear his confession and bring him Holy Communion.

The repeated inspections of the bishop's residence and constant following of Fr. Jurkiewicz indicated that some sort of repression was impending—and on December 1, 1931, that which all the Catholics of Most Holy Mother of God parish most feared finally happened: Fr. Jurkiewicz was arrested. They placed him in an investigatory isolation unit of the Vladivostok District Branch of the Plenipotentiary Representative's Office of the Far East OGPU.[84] The priest sat in this investigatory isolation unit for two months and seven days. They accused him of spying activities and having connections with Polish and Japanese diplomatic workers—and also of systematic work against the new Soviet authority. In particular, they cited him with agitating his parishioners against the Soviets and condemning those Catholics who supported the Soviets. In addition,

84 M. I. Efimova, "Oni pogibli za Xrista" ["They Died for Christ"], published by Most Holy Mother of God Parish, Vladivostok, 2000.

they accused him of speculation in foreign currency and gold, since during their search of his apartment when he was being arrested they found gold and silver coins from the tsarist period, as well as yens and dollars.

The documents that we studied concerning the criminal proceeding against Fr. Jurkiewicz reveal that at the first interrogations the arrested priest denied everything, but it seems that the interrogation was conducted using such harsh methods that the arrested priest eventually admitted to almost all the accusations. One can propose that some of the accusations were based on denunciations made by people close to the priest; for example, he admitted that he had in fact buried part of the coins in the garden plot of unsuspecting neighbors—his parishioners Karl and Stefania Niklan-Zawistowski. But did someone know of this secret? How else could the investigators have found out? They took the arrested priest 26 kilometers, and he pointed out the place of the secret burial. However he stubbornly insisted that he had never been involved in currency speculation—and that the found coins were his personal savings. Where was he to keep his savings? There was no savings bank, banks in general were almost not functioning, and practically all people who had rings, earrings or broaches "saved" them in their gardens. It was dangerous to leave any jewelry in the house since at any moment representatives of the new power could appear at citizens' apartments and take from the family anything that had even the least value!

As for the accusations of espionage, Fr. Jurkiewicz categorically denied them all. Of course he knew a lot of Poles—they were his parishioners. And he also met with several Poles at Polish House. And he had known the attorney Mr. Chencynski, the Secretary at the Polish Consulate, since the time when Mr. Chencynski and his wife had been his parishioners in Nikolaevsk. When Fr. Georgij visited that city as part of his pastoral work, he stayed at the home of the Chencynskis. And now in Vladivostok their acquaintance continued on the same basis. Fr. Georgij did not deny his acquaintance with many Polish parishioners who worked at Polish House. But at the same time he asserted that he absolutely did not have any similar acquaintances with Japanese.

But no matter how hard it was for Fr. Jurkiewicz to endure these interrogations, he did not implicate anyone else. The investigation concluded February 12, 1932, and Fr. Jurkiewicz was convicted by a three-man panel ("troika") under the auspices of the Plenipotentiary Representative's Office of the Far East OGPU to ten years' deprivation of freedom under Articles 58-6 and 59-11, and sent to the Siberian labor camps. It was not until much later that the priest's parishioners were able to find out his exact address.

The Vladivostok parish took this tragic event with great grief, since now the parish had been completely orphaned—Bishop Sliwowski was under house arrest in Sedanka and Fr. Georgij had been imprisoned and exiled. In order to continue the life of their parish, the elder Marcin Pietrowicz Malinewski and a group of parishioners did not abandon their church. Without a priest, they could not have Mass, but the faithful gathered in their beautiful cathedral and simply recited their prayers. Naturally, there followed several unpleasant events—the first of which was that the Catholics had to pay taxes for the use of the land on which the church stood, since it no longer belonged to them. What could they do but pay—collecting what small amounts they could from all the parishioners, whoever had any means. Nor did the parishioners leave their young pastor Fr. Jurkiewicz in his misfortune, and when he was in prison they brought him food. But the parishioners were categorically refused any meetings with the imprisoned priest….

After rehabilitation [in the 1950s], it became possible to inspect the materials of the investigatory organs that had sent the priest to prison, and then to exile. Thus the present-day parish was able to find out why Fr. Georgij Jurkiewicz had been so severely punished. Above all, the priest was accused of connections with employees of foreign diplomatic offices; in particular, his frequent meetings with the Polish consul Mr. Karczewski and the Secretary of the Consulate, Mr. Chencynski.

The priest's explanations were very simple and truthful: by the duties of his office he had to receive Catholics who sought to confess their sins. The priest had known Mr. Chencynski since the days of his pastoral visits from Khabarovsk to Nikolaevsk. He had stayed at the apartment of his parishioners, the Chencynskis, and of course he had heard the confessions of both Mr. Chencynski and his wife. When the Chencynskis moved to Vladivostok, where he became the Secretary of the Polish Consulate, they were once again Fr. Georgij's parishioners. When a guest of the Chencynskis, Fr. Georgij made the acquaintance of Consul Karczewski, whose wife was a devout Catholic, one of his parishioners, and accordingly he heard her confession.

Attending evening events at Polish House from time to time, Fr. Jurkiewicz naturally met many compatriots there and was thus acquainted with Messers. Tomaszewski, Klaszewski, Przyjecul and other Poles—but these were simply secular acquaintances. And he firmly denied the accusation that he had "cursed" the Bolsheviks from the pulpit. That he had never done! Then they brought forward the accusation that he kept foreign currency for speculation and that on December 1, 1931, when searching his apartment, they had found tsarist-minted gold valued at 100 rubles and other silver coins worth 250 rubles. The investigation brought to light that Fr. Jurkiewicz had entrusted this money to citizen Biron for her to hide. On a second search, they found another three gold 10-ruble pieces baked into a loaf of bread.

After a series of harsh questionings, Fr. Jurkiewicz told the investigators that he had buried some of his savings in the garden plot of Mrs. Niklan, and he had hidden the rest of his savings—dollars, yens, English pounds, and Russian "gold rubles"—in Mrs. Gluhowska's apartment. Trying to prove his innocence, he told the investigator that he had to hide that part of his savings that was in foreign currency in secret places and that these savings were his own personal valuables. But Fr. Georgij firmly assured the investigator that he had never been involved in currency speculation and he had no intention of doing so, as he was a priest. As for his acquaintance with Polish families, they were either connected with church matters or were purely secular acquaintances—as a priest, he had never been involved in any spying activities.

But all his clean-hearted explanations did him no good. The investigator firmly insisted on his interpretation of the facts, accusing Fr. Jurkiewicz of spying connections with the Polish and Japanese consulates. He also asserted that the priest had hidden the foreign currency as a speculator. These indictments led to a sentence of ten years in the Siberian labor camps and confiscation of all his property.[85]

Fr. Jurkiewicz's arrest and exile to the labor camps caused panic and fear among his parishioners. It is possible that those parishioners who had denounced him feared being discovered and hid in their homes—others collected money and brought food, which the parish elder then brought to the priest in prison. After Fr. Jurkiewicz was sent to the labor camp, he let them know of his whereabouts, and the parish elder continued to send modest food packages and small amounts of money to the priest in the labor camp.

Fr. Jurkiewicz served his sentence in a Siberian camp and it is thought that the camp was located near the Yaya station, since letters from him came from this station. The previously mentioned parishioner of Fr. Jurkiewicz, Regina Stańko, has informed the present-day Vladivostok parish that after her father's arrest her family was sent to Tomsk. There they received a letter from Fr. Jurkiewicz, in which he asked them to send him woolen leggings and pork fat. Despite their financial hardships, Regina's mother fulfilled the priest's request. Regina does not recall the exact date of this letter, but thinks it was in 1938 or 1939. The parish elder, Marcin Pietrowicz Malinewski, also received letters from the prisoner. Here is one of them:

March 21, 1935.

85 Excerpt from a protocol of the PP OGPU DVK, February 6, 1932. Archives of Most Holy Mother of God Parish, Vladivostok.

Most respected M. P.! I wanted to write you back on March 7 but I was too late for the post. I cordially thank you for your letters and the money. I am sincerely glad that you have recovered enough to return to work. There is nothing new in my life—day after day passes so monotonously that there is nothing to write about. And to go on and on about my illnesses is boring and of little interest. There is no cure for aging, and in old age all ailments and illnesses remind one of oneself, especially chronic illness.

I've not received any letters at all lately—even my aunt and Anna have stopped writing, and there is no one else from whom I any longer expect letters. It's sad that Efrosina Osipovna's health has worsened—don't forget that in addition to rest she also needs medical assistance. [Efrosina Osipovna was Marcin Pietrowicz's wife.] Winter is passing, and already one can catch the smell of spring in the air.

I send my heartfelt greeting to all, and I wish all the very best—especially health.

Sincerely,
Jurkiewicz

We have indirect evidence from Regina Stańko concerning Fr. Jurkiewicz's being in the concentration camp in 1940. Regina writes that her mother encountered in Tomsk a former imprisoned parishioner who had seen Fr. Jurkiewicz in the camp—missing one eye, frightfully aged and exhausted. To our inquiry to the Information Center of the Ministry of the Interior, Russian Federation, Kemerovsk District, came the response that the imprisoned Georgij Ludwigowicz Jurkiewicz had died June 4, 1942, in a camp in the Novo-Ivanosk section in the Mariinsk region of Kemerovsk District. From this one can conclude that he had not been released at the end of his sentence term, December 1, 1941. This bureau had no further information concerning the cause of death, place of burial or other details. Apparently, the priest's remains lie in peace somewhere in one of the numerous common, nameless graves that are abundantly scattered across our Siberian lands....

29. They Died for Christ

The death of Bishop Sliwowski and the arrest and exile of the vicar Fr. Jurkiewicz had left the Vladivostok Roman Catholic parish without a leader. But nevertheless parishioners faithful to God came to the church to read religious books and pray. After the appearance of the new rules, the community of believers had to pay a tax for the use of their own church and this tax was regularly increased. In the 1930s, the required tax payment rose to such an amount that it could not be paid by the Catholics and they were forced to abandon their church....

But the parishioners did not betray the Faith of Christ; they continued praying in their homes and sometimes they gathered together in one or another of their homes. This did not go unnoticed, and soon the authorities arrested, tried and then shot some of the most staunch Catholics. Who were these executed Catholics?

Antonij and Walerij Gerasimuk

Antonij Iwanowicz Gerasimuk was born in 1878 in a peasant family of the village of Werszbic, in Helmsk *gubernia* (today, Lublin), where he completed the village school. The parish has no other information about Antonij's family and how he ended up in the Far East. In Vladivostok he had a large family: his wife Waleria Gerasimuk (b. 1876), daughers Janina (b. 1902), Maria (b. 1910), Nina (b. 1916) and a son, Walerij (b. 1914). Antonij's children are not noted in the parish registry, so it is likely that the family moved to Vladivostok from other places in Russia. Waleria Gerasimuk and her husband were very devout Catholics. They regularly attended Mass with their children and they contributed as much as they could to the offertory collection, and when the church was taken from the Catholics, at Waleria's initiative the faithful sometimes gathered in the Gerasimuk home to pray together.

The large and friendly Gerasimuk family at first lived in their own wooden three-by-four-sazhen home at No. 34 Krugovaia Street. Around the house the family had a large vegetable garden and they kept chickens, geese and piglets. But in 1936 the family had to sell the house because they could not pay the large tax on "personal property" and they moved to a more modest dwelling. The head of the family—Antonij—was a fine musician. He played several wind instruments and thus worked as director of the "Electromortrest" orchestra at the Ilich Club. He had a lot of friendly contacts with musicians in the city, especially those who attended the Catholic church. The Gerasimuk children all studied music, and the son, Walerij, sometimes played with his father and other musicians in wind ensemble concerts at the Ilich Club.

In 1931, Walerij Gerasimuk finished the seven-year school and at the age of seventeen volunteered to serve in the Red Army. At first he was stationed in Voroshilov (today known as Ussuriisk), then they transferred him to the naval squadron in Vladivostok. He finished his service in 1935 in military unit No. 3179. After demobilization this former Red Sailor began to work as a driver, then he went to work at Voentory. Soon he became acquainted with a very sweet girl, Faina. They married and at the end of 1936 the young couple had a little girl, whom they named Lidia. The child's godmother was the wife of Jan Strudzinski, whom the Gerasimuks knew from church. The Strudzinski family was very well off and Mrs. Strudzinski often helped the poorest parishioners. When Antonij Gerasimuk ended up in the hospital with a serious illness, the Strudzinskis brought him food parcels. To thank their benefactors, Walerij Gerasimuk paid them a visit on July 18, 1937. On July 19, 1937, a tragedy occurred: Antonij and his son Walerij were arrested by the OGPU....

From Lidia Gerasimuk's letters we know that the blow that befell the family was so unexpected and so terrible that it brought the rest of the family into complete confusion. Faina loved her husband dearly and went several times to the jail to find out about the fate of her husband and her father-in-law—but it was useless. The family received no news of the arrested men. Finally, Faina received a postcard which suggested that she formalize a divorce from her husband at the Civil Registry. There she saw on a table a packet with a black band, which could only mean one thing: that she had already become a widow, and her tiny Lidochka was from this day forward an orphan. But concerning her father-in-law there was no news. Nor was it known what kind of death Faina's husband had died—but the city was full of dark rumors that an epidemic of typhus had broken out in the jail and that they had attached iron weights to the feet of the dead and even the half-dead and thrown their bodies into the sea....

Sigizmund Brzeziński

Sigizmund Brzeziński, arrested September 2, 1937, was born in 1892 and came from the peasants of Suchaczewsk district, Warsaw *gubernia*. His father, Władisław, had died young, and his mother remarried and had four daughters by her second husband. Sigizmund finished the parish grade school in the village and because the family was very poor he was not able to continue his schooling. He helped his stepfather. In 1913 he was called up into the tsar's army and sent to the Far East. Here he decided to fulfill a long-time dream—to get a high school education. Late evenings and sometimes well into the night the persistent soldier sat at his textbooks, studying the various subjects of the high school curriculum. In three years Sigizmund mastered the four-year course of studies, passed the exams and received the corresponding document. This achievement was immediately reflected in his service position: he was appointed clerk (in those days this was a very important post).

The year 1917 and the revolution brought Poland its independence, and in Vladivostok a Polish Committee was set up and Mr. Poplawski was named its president. Later this Committee became the Polish Consulate, and all Poles were offered the opportunity to document their citizenship at the Consulate. Sigizmund Brzeziński was among the first Poles to officially formalize his Polish citizenship: he was issued Certificate No. 54. But for unknown reasons, in 1927 Sigizmund turned in his certificate and took Soviet citizenship.

Demobilized from the army in 1918, Sigizmund began to work in various organizations as a manager. In two years he married the charming 16-year-old Polish girl, Sofia Duchnik. She came from a very poor family that lived in the village of Aleksandrovsk on Sakhalin Island; there were nine children in the family. When the father, Michal, died, the family moved to Vladivostok to live with the grandfather. The mother re-married. Because of the extremely difficult situation of the family, the grandfather gave the children to various relatives; he sent Sofia to be raised in the family of Dorota Anna Grochowska, whose husband was a sailor and was constantly at sea. Dorata Grochowska sent Sofia (who was a wonderful helper at home) to study at the Polish school, and when they closed this school, Sofia continued her studies at the Russian school.

Recalling those difficult times, the venerable Sofia Michajlowna told us that in their family, as in many other Vladivostok families, there were problems with clothing, shoes and food. But the family lived very amicably. Sofia was infatuated with music—she learned to play the violin and she loved to sing, both at home and in the parish choir. There is a rare photograph that has been preserved in her family, showing the head of the Vladivostok parish, Fr. Karol Sliwowski, and Fr. Władisław Mieżwinski and a group of children who have just received their First Holy Communion. In this photo, Sofia, in a white dress, veil and crown, is standing behind the shoulders of Fr. Sliwowski. Sofia married young, and like all teenage girls she was always singing something. Her husband, Sigizmund, also loved music and there were often duets in their home: Sofia played the violin part and Sigizmund played the violincello. There were four children born into this poor but happy family: Bronisław, Gennadij, Adel and Stanisława. The father of the family had to work constantly to earn a living wherever he could—days he worked as a manager, evenings he and other musicians played at dances in the clubs. At this time in Vladivostok, paper money with little purchasing power was in circulation and thus sometimes foreign currency circulated in the market, even though it was illegal. In 1930 Sigizmund was arrested and they found some foreign currency on him. The GPU then conducted a thorough investigation, accusing him of "speculation in foreign currency." However, taking into account his family situation and the fact that he had tuberculosis, they released him from prison. And now in 1937 he was once again arrested....

Jan Strudzinski

Also part of the group of those "stubborn Catholics" who refused to forget their Faith was Jan Jeronimowicz Strudzinski. He came from the Radom district of Warsaw *gubernia*, where he was born April 5, 1878. He had two brothers—Jósef and Antonij. His father—Jeronim Strudzinski—worked as a watchman for the landowner, since he himself did not have his own land. All three sons completed the parish grade school and then went to work for the landowner. When Jan turned twenty-one, he was drafted into the tsar's army and sent to serve in the Far East, at the Vladivostok garrison. There he rose to the rank of junior noncommissioned officer and then he married a local resident, Elena Francewna Baranowska. After he was demobilized he stayed to work in Vladivostok and from 1906 to 1927 he worked as a customs inspector.

Like all Poles, Jan Strudzinski was a very devout Catholic and he was a parishioner of the Vladivostok Roman Catholic parish. Attending church, he formed friendships among his co-religionists; his closest friend was his fellow parishioner, Marcin Malinewski. It was this friend who had given him a recommendation for a job as a caretaker at the Workers Society of the Japanese Bank on Suyfunskaia Street. In 1922 the workers at the Japanese Consulate took over this Society and thus Jan Strudzinski automatically became a technical worker of that consulate. Working for the Japanese gave Jan a good, stable income and thus he was able to help his fellow parishioners. For example, when Antonij Gerasimuk fell sick and ended up in the hospital it was Strudzinski's wife, Elena Francewna, who brought food to the patient (in those times, they did not feed patients at the hospital). As a sign of their gratitude, the Gerasimuk family asked Elena Francewna to be godmother to Antonij's granddaughter, Lidia.

Marcin Pietrowicz Malinewski

Marcin Pietrowicz Malinewski became the elder of the Vladivostok Roman Catholic parish at the end of January 1933 after the sudden death of the prior elder, Julian Niewero. Marcin Pietrowicz also came from the western *gubernia*s of Russia. He was born in the village of Nogaczowka, Winnitsk district. He had two sisters—Rozalia and Petronela. Called up to the army in 1902, Marcin landed in the Far East and served there as a gunner until 1906. He married Efrosinia Osipowna Mogulewska, who suffered a serious illness after their marriage and remained paralyzed. Her mother cared for her, while Marcin had to look for work that would feed two unfortunate and powerless women. Naturally, this difficult family situation weighed heavily upon him and as a very devout person he prayed fervently, entrusting his prayers to the Divine Mercy.

Despite the threat of arrest, the elder Malinewski did not abandon the arrested Fr. Jurkiewicz in his misfortune; he brought parcels for him while he was at the investigation prison and after the priest was sent to the labor camps, the elder collected food and money from the faithful and sent them to the unfortunate Fr. Georgij. This support helped Fr. Georgij survive in the "hell" of the Siberian camps. Nor did the elder cease caring for the church building, and when the authorities increased the tax on the parishioners to 3,800 rubles, Marcin Pietrowicz sought ways to get it lowered. He was actively assisted by a Mr. Bernadski, an experienced attorney and former parishioner of Fr. Sliwowski who had been a judge prior to the Revolution. But this was all in vain—on July 7, 1935, the Vladivostok Executive Commission for the Examination of Religious Questions adopted the decree "Concerning the Abrogation of the Agreement with a Group of Believers of the Roman Catholic Church and the Liquidation of the Functions of the Church Building." It was noted that the "group of believers had scattered." In accordance with the decree "Concerning Religious Associations," adopted April 8, 1929, by the All-Union Central Executive Committee and the Council of Peoples Commissars of the Russian Soviet Federated Socialist Republic, it was proposed to give the building to the District Archive Bureau, to be used free of charge.

Thus the majestic cathedral, built exclusively with money from Catholics, was taken from them. And all the arrested Catholics were shot at 6:00 p.m. on February 3, 1938.[86]

❋❋❋

Many decades passed before the names of those innocent men killed at that time were cleansed of slanders and accusations: on July 30, 1959, by verdict of the Pacific Fleet Military Tribunal that they were all "rehabilitated." In the 1990s, on the outskirts of Vladivostok, at the place of the executions and burials of all executed citizens, by the efforts of the relatives of those innocently killed people, a very modest Memorial monument with a cross was erected. To this place came all those who had lost their arrested relatives and neighbors in the 1930s; here they held communal prayers for the memory of murdered priests, both Orthodox and Catholic. To our great sorrow, this monument was vandalized by hooligans: the marble cross and the commemorative plaque were literally shot at several times, then completely smashed….

A second Memorial—a stone monument to the people who perished in the NKVD torture chambers—was built in Vladivostok near Youth House in the Second River section of the city. All those who walked the way of the cross of the repressions, and their children, grandchildren and relatives come here, bringing flowers and

86 M. I. Efimova, "Oni pogibli za Xrista."

prayers…. For this sorrowful monument, a red stone was especially chosen, symbolizing the blood shed by guiltless, murdered Russians….

Roman Catholic Church, Transfiguration of Our Lord, Blagoveshchensk, 1896

Chapel built of logs, Immaculate Virgin Mary, Vladivostok

Bishop Jan Cieplak, Vicar General of Mogilev Archdiocese, 1919

Blessing of cornerstone, Vladivostok, 1909. Procession of the faithful led by Bishop Jan Cieplak, to place where the cornerstone had been laid in 1908

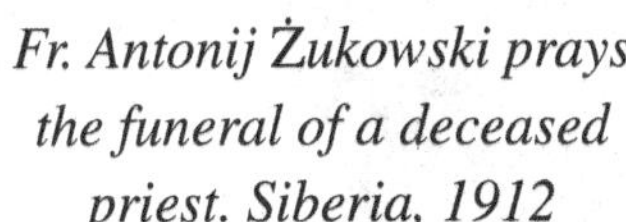

Fr. Antonij Żukowski prays the funeral of a deceased priest. Siberia, 1912

Fr. Karol Sliwowski, head of the Vladivostok Roman Catholic parish

Eugenij Ayewski, former Vladivostok Boy Scout, now an architect in Warsaw. 2002

Pavel Stanisławowicz Tenczinski, parishioner, Vladivostok Roman Catholic parish, and chief doctor of the city hospital. Assisted in the work of Dobrochinnost' Society

Anna Belkiewicz, organizer of the Committee for the Rescue of Polish Orphans

Edward Sienkiewicz, 1919. Businessman, philanthropist, parishioner

Polish orphans with their caretaker, Maria Miecznikowska, at the dacha owned by the Sienkiewicz brothers, Sedanka, 1920

Polish children and medical staff of the hospital of the Japanese Red Cross. Tokyo, Japan

A Japanese nurse at the hospital of the Japanese Red Cross, with a Polish orphan who was saved from a serious illness. Tokyo, Japan

Dr. Josef Jakubkiewicz

American "Polonia" festively greets a group of Polish orphans in Seattle

Vladivostok dean Karol Sliwowski and Fr. Julian Bryllik with children of the Vladivostok parish. Next to Fr. Bryllik is Lucia Oranska, recently deceased; Stanisław Zeliński is seated at Fr. Sliwowski's feet. 1920

Procession—(1) Bishop de Guébriant (in civil attire); (2) Fr. Władisław Mieżwinski; (3) Fr. Aleksandr Ejsymontt; (4) Fr. Sliwowski (hidden by the Host)

Architect's sketch, Catholic Church, Nikolsk-Ussuriisk

First liturgy in the new stone church, Vladivostok, October 2, 1921

Vladivostok bishop, Karol Sliwowski, Vicar of Eastern Siberia

Dean Karol Sliwowski, Fr. Władisław Mieżwinski and a group of children after their First Holy Communion. Among them are Sofia Brzezińska (standing above Dean Sliwowski), Stanisław Zeliński (seated at Dean Sliwowski's feet) and Eugenij Ayewski (seated at Fr. Mieżwinski's feet)

House with annex, where Bishop Sliwowski lived his last years. Sedanka, 1930

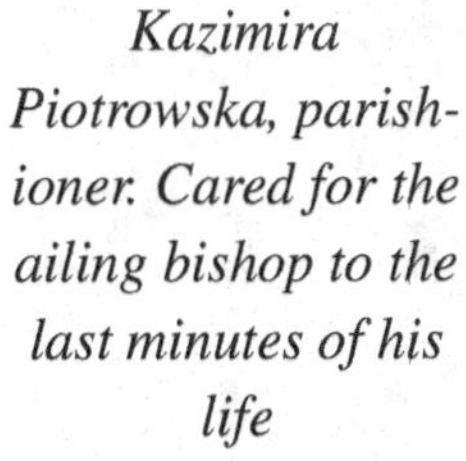

Kazimira Piotrowska, parishioner. Cared for the ailing bishop to the last minutes of his life

Regina Stańko, a retired military doctor

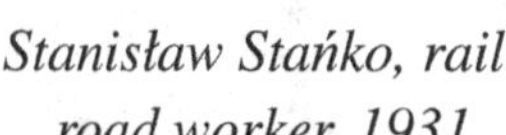

Stanisław Stańko, rail-road worker. 1931

Grave of Bishop Karol Sliwowski in the old Sedanka cemetery. The bishop's grave has been irretrievably lost.

Fr. Georgij Jurkewicz, last head of the Vladivostok Roman Catholic parish

Building where Fr. Georgij Jurkewicz rented a room and where he was arrested, 38 Volodarskaya Street, Vladivostok

Brzeziński family: Sofia, Sigizmund and children: Bronisława, Gennadij and Adele

Marcin Petrowicz Malinewski, last elder of Vladivostok Roman Catholic parish. Shot by firing squad, February 3, 1938.

IV

Harbin Catholics and Their Churches

But the just shall inherit the land
and shall dwell therein forevermore.

Psalm 37:29

1. Birth of the City of Harbin

Soon after the conquest of Siberia and the annexation of the lands of the Amur and Primorye regions and Central Asia, Russia turned all its attention to somehow incorporating Manchuria within the borders of the Russian Empire, as "Yellow Russia." This territory, situated between Great Hingan, the Amur, the Eastern Manchurian Mountains and the Great Wall of China, was abundant in mineral deposits. At the beginning in the seventeenth century, this territory was part of China, but then Manchuria seized China and placed a representative of the Manchurian Tsing dynasty on the throne. The reign of this dynasty (1644-1911) brought China to complete political and economic catastrophe. As a result, the previously sovereign lands of China were turned into semi-colonial possessions of Holland, France, Great Britain, Germany, Russia, Japan and even Italy. “Foreigners,” inspecting China’s mineral wealth, had to obtain concessions for mining the minerals. The Russian Empire worked systematically toward strengthening its influence in China, and the construction of the Chinese Eastern and South-China railroads served as a “prelude” to its expropriation of Chinese territories. Both these rail lines were part of the plan for the construction of the Trans-Siberian Railroad in 1896.

Russia entered into negotiations with China for the construction of the Chinese Eastern Railroad, which, by way of a spur from Chita to Vladivostok, would shorten the route of the proposed Trans-Siberian Railroad by 500 kilometers. The head of the Russian negotiators was Sergei Witte—a dynamic, highly educated defender of Imperial Russia, who had introduced into politics the fashion of “peaceful” penetration into China. China, on the other hand, was represented in the negotiations by the greedy and corrupt 72-year-old Li Hung-chan, a defender of the interests of the Tsing dynasty, the last of China’s imperial dynasties. A secret agreement that gave Russia significant rights in China, including the right to build a railroad, was signed on June 3, 1896, in Moscow, and the East Siberian Railroad Joint Stock Company was formed September 8, 1896.

The projected wide-gauge rail line had important strategic, political and economic significance: it provided the opportunity for the economic exploitation of Manchuria and northern China and it was also an important factor in the Russian-Japanese controversies. The Board of Directors considered two variants of the project and decided on the “northern variant,” which would pass through the fortress “Echo” above the Mutandzian River and through the cities of Acheng, Hulan and Tsitsikar, down the valley of the Ula River, the Great Hingan mountain massif to Haalar and the Manchurian border station. A special geological-engineering expedition, led by the engineer Adam Szidlowski, was sent on March 8, 1898, to explore this route, and on April 11, 1898, the expedition came to the shore of the Sungari River. Here, eight kilometers from the shore of the river, not far from a tiny Chinese village with the Mongolian name "Ha-La Bin," the expedition set up its base in the ruins of a wine and vodka distillery. The run-down building was quickly repaired and made habitable. Thus when the steamer *Odessa* arrived with a contingent of engineers and officials on board, there awaited them a base ready for beginning work. And this is how the city of Harbin was founded. Harbin later became the central station of the Trans-Siberian Line and the Chinese Eastern Line.

The completion of construction had been planned for 1897-1900, but for various reasons this deadline was not met. There were huge damages to the construction during the Boxer Rebellion (1897-1901), a Chinese patriotic outcry against the hated "foreign devils." The railroad ties and rails were destroyed along portions of the rail line that had already been laid, as well as steam engines and train cars. Many railroad workers perished—which is evidenced in the Harbin cemetery where over the graves of Poles stand little plaques with the same inscription "Died during the construction of the railroad." It took Russian troops, brought in from Khabarovsk, to quell the patriot Boxers. But hardly had they finished with the consequences of the Boxer Rebellion when a terrible cholera epidemic broke out in Harbin.

Taking into account all these complications that threatened the railroad workers, the builders had to introduce certain changes in the project: all buildings at the stations would now have thick walls, solid windows and doors; the workers were given weapons and ammunition; and further, there would be cannons at every station. On short stretches of double track they built fortresses, set back 47.5 meters from the tracks and surrounded by ditches. Close by they built brick barracks for soldiers and stables for horses. In addition, they established a Railroad Guard Corps. Approximately fifteen percent of the Corps officers were Poles.

At the very beginning of the construction, the Polish engineer Jokisz had developed a "Plan for the Construction of the City of Harbin." The plan was adopted by the city magistrate, and the vice-burgomeister, the Pole Eugenij Dynowski, was responsible for its implementation. Together with the development of the "capital of the Chinese Eastern Railroad" there was the building up of the territories lying along the railroad in the "belt of alienation" protected by Russian guards. As the laying of the railroad progressed, more and more guards were needed, and therefore (in accordance with the treaty with China) the Board of Directors of the Chinese Eastern Railroad established a Corps of Border Guards. Poles were emigrating to the Far East from Poland, which at that time was experiencing a high rate of unemployment. Several hundred of these newly arrived Poles became part of the Corps of Border Guards.

Any large construction project requires the development of an infrastructure and the construction of the railroad was no exception. Business people began to arrive in Harbin; large industries opened offices. The Pole Czajewski founded a vodka distillery in Harbin; Wroblewski started a beer brewery. The Rynowski-Kowalski firm started up the first steam-driven mill; Bogdan Bronewski built a large sugar factory, the equipment for which was supplied by the Polish firm of Szpońtański, Borman and Sweda. A factory for making Krasiński steam boilers could also be found in Harbin. All this activity led to the fact that in three years there were already several thousand Poles involved directly or indirectly in the construction of the Chinese Eastern Railroad in Harbin and the surrounding areas. One should note that even Russian authors, who considered Harbin only a Russian enclave in China, acknowledged that the Poles played a significant role in this grand construction project. For example, P. V. Malikov writes that "the Poles worked on the Chinese Eastern Railroad in various capacities, among the technical and engineering personnel, and they were essentially the main contingent."[87] But although Harbin "had a Polish accent," it was not a Polish city. The main component of the population was, of course, the Chinese, who controlled the small businesses, the trades and services. Second place was undoubtedly held by the Russians who were in charge of

87 Ibid., p. 115.

the management and supervision of the line, the administration and border security services.

While involved in the construction of the Chinese Eastern Railroad, the Russians were also trying to get a concession for the construction of the South China Railroad. Russia needed this second concession in order to gain influence over the Yellow Sea. In December 1897 Russian military vessels, within the context of "friendship" with China, without any notice, occupied Port Arthur and Dalian.

This considerably complicated and aggravated Russian-Chinese relations and so the Russian Ministry of Finance, to facilitate negotiations, "showered" gold and Li Hung-chan received a "gift" of 609,000 rubles, while the Russian press sparkled with news about the heartfelt friendship of Russia and China. Then a Russian delegation headed by Prince Ukhtomski was sent to China. He did not spare any "sweet beautiful phrases" about the friendship of the Russian and Chinese peoples, and the prince bestowed medals and diplomas on the members of the Tsing dynasty. This "diplomatic work" of the Russian mission was not in vain—soon Russia had in its hands a document allowing it to rule the Liaodong Peninsula between the Gulf of North Korea and the Yellow Sea for a period of twenty-five years! The territory was 225 kilometers in length and varied in width from 80 to 130 kilometers, and it included the cities of Port Arthur and Dalian. The treaty was very advantageous for Russia if only for the fact that, according to the data of the engineer-geologist Bogdanowicz, the peninsula was a huge gold-bearing province. But this turned out to be harmful to the railroad enterprise because "wild" gold seekers dug up the railroad bed and threw rails and ties all over the place in order to get to the gold. Russia was not to rejoice for long in its acquisitions in the Far East, as Japan began a war in 1904.[88]

---

88 Zofia Lech, *Syberia Polską pachnąca* [Siberia Has the Scent of Poland], Verbinum Wydawnictwo Księży Werbistow, Warsaw, 2002.

The first president of the Railroad Construction Society, Siu Dzin-chen, died during the Boxer Rebellion, and China did not seek to replace him; therefore, from 1901 the engineer Aleksandr Jugowicz occupied this position. Mr. Jugowicz was at the same time the director of the concession for the Ussuriisk Railroad. Nicholas II granted this engineer more authority than any governor of the Russian Empire had ever had! For example, Mr. Jugowicz was able to allow the Guard Corps of the Trans-Amur Railroad, without any coordination with the Chinese authorities, to go deep into Chinese territory. This situation was very convenient for Russian military, geologic and topographic contingents.

In 1903 the Polish writer and traveler Wacław Siroszewski passed through Harbin. The city struck him with its "disconnectedness" and lack of architectural organization. He wrote thus of his impressions: "Harbin is a city of railroads. It is the junction of the Manchurian, southern and eastern rail lines. The railroad station is huge, but filthy.... The city does not have a water system—but it has an opera theater. It is easier to find champagne than a glass of clean water...." There was one other way in which Harbin differed from other cities: there was no international conflict in the city right up to the Russian-Japanese War in 1904-1905. It is also interesting that Harbin continued to develop economically even during the Russian Revolution because the Chinese authorities defended Harbin against the Bolsheviks.

2. *Building and Dedication of St. Stanisław Church*

Life in the Polish enclave in Harbin developed in the religious as well as the social spheres. During the early years, the Catholics turned to the French Catholic missions for their spiritual needs. (The French missionaries had served in Manchuria since the fifteenth century.) The prayers at the French mission were of course either in French or Latin. The Polish diaspora in Harbin decided to build its own church. A Church Building Committee was set up to raise the necessary funds. The cornerstone for the new church was placed on November 7, 1906.

The builders erected this first Catholic Church rather quickly; the means for its construction were collected from amongst the whole community, with the well-off Catholics making substantial contributions. It was dedicated in honor of St. Stanisław on August 1, 1909, by Jan Cieplak, Archbishop of Mogilev, who at that time was in the Far East making his visitation of Roman Catholic parishes on the fringes of the Empire. Unfortunately this historic building was demoslished during the Chinese Cultural Revolution in the 1970s.

3. Fr. Antonij Konstantin Maczuk

Fr. Antonij Maczuk, the first priest to serve St. Stanisław church, was born in 1866 into a petty-bourgeoise family of the small village of Kryniczyn in the Kovensk *gubernia*.[89] Upon completing the classical high school, Antonij enrolled in the Mogilev seminary. He was ordained in 1888, and in 1889 he began his priestly service in various parishes of the Mogilev archdiocese. In 1905 he was transferred to Tula as chaplain of the local parish and on January 9, 1907, he was given the assignment to serve as chaplain of St. Stanisław parish in Harbin. Heading for Harbin at the direction of the Consistory, Fr. Maczuk sent back the following report:

> In keeping with the Consistory's directive of January 16, 1907, and in light of the unclear situation with respect to the status of the Harbin church, I respectfully ask the Consistory to clarify the following: Is there a Roman Catholic church in Harbin? If so, in what does its property consist?
>
> Fr. Antonij Maczuk

89 RGIA, f. 826, op. 1, d. 1363, l. 152.

In his next letter to the Consistory, Fr. Maczuk informed them that he had received from the military chaplain Fr. Przyluski only the bare essentials for celebrating Holy Mass and the sacraments—there could be no talk of an "inventory list." Thus Fr. Maczuk had to set about acquiring on his own the necessary church vessels. But he was not destined to continue his ministry in the Catholic parish of Harbin: Bishop Stefan Denisewicz, Apostolic Administrator of the Mogilev archdiocese, transferred him to the post of head of the Gorbachevo-Obytsk parish in Polotsk, Vitebsk *gubernia*.

In the summer of 1908 a mission of Redemptorist Fathers visited St. Stanisław parish, and the Harbin parish commemorated this unexpected but joyful event in a special way: they erected in the church garden a large wooden cross on which they placed a plaque with the names of the Redemptorist Fathers and all the parishioners in attendance at the church on that day.

From some archival documents it seems that after the departure of Fr. Maczuk a Fr. Lew Swiatopolk Mirski served the parish. But we have been unable to locate a concrete document confirming his service. There is, however, a document dated November 27, 1909, with the following remarks:

> I am informing the Consistory that Fr. Władisław Ostrowski, curate of the Krasnoyarsk church, and Fr. Lew Swiatopolk Mirski, chaplain of the Harbin chapel, have been reassigned: they will change places with each other.
>
> Bishop Denisewicz
> Apostolic Administrator
> Mogilev Archdiocese

Our parish unfortunately has no other information concerning the service of Fr. Mirski in Harbin.

4. *Fr. Władisław Ostrowski*

After the departure of Fr. Antonij Maczuk, the Harbin Roman Catholic parish was headed by Fr. Władisław Ostrowski, a very experienced priest formerly assigned to the Roman Catholic parish in Kazan. Fr. Ostrowski was a very gifted person, an excellent preacher and a defender of the spiritual life. He was a talented organizer; he was a patriot; and he was a man with a deep awareness of the necessity of his ministry, to which he devoted all his life's energy. Having taken the Roman Catholic parish of Harbin under his management, Fr. Władisław was able to make it the main center of the spiritual life of the large Polish colony in the Far East.

In his care for the Harbin church, Fr. Władisław managed to use donations from the parishioners to erect three Gothic altars and a confessional in the church. In addition, at the main altar there hung a beautiful painting of the Sacred Heart of Jesus, and at the side altar, paintings of the Most Holy Virgin Mary of Ostra Brama and St. Joseph. There were also statues of St. Anthony of Padua and St. Władisław.

Fr. Władisław was born into a family of the small landowning nobility in Mogilev on the Dniestr. The boy finished the Mogilev high school and then studied at the Mogilev Archdiocesan Seminary. On March 3, 1899, he was ordained to minor orders; he was ordained to the priesthood on March 4, 1900, by Bishop Karol Niezialkowski. His first assignment was the city of Mogilev on the Dniestr, then Smolensk and Wiatka. From May 1901 he served as vicar at the Roman Catholic parish in Kazan, where the pastor at that time was Karol Sliwowski. Thus when Fr. Władisław arrived in Harbin in early 1910, he was already a very experienced preacher and a distinguished public figure. It was at his insistence that there was established in Harbin a St. Vincent de Paul Society, whose members were active in philanthropy, culture and scholarly activity. A Polish grade school named in honor of St. Vincent de Paul was founded and solid contacts with cultural institutions in Poland were established.

❁❁❁

Right after the beginning of World War I, after the Germans seized the territory of the Congress Kingdom in 1915, crowds of Polish refugees swarmed to Harbin, and with every passing year there were more of them. But the number of refugees markedly increased after the October Revolution and then after the annihilation of Kolchak's power in Siberia.

Practically speaking, the entire Polish colony in Harbin was dragged into political "games," and the colony was divided into two camps. The repatriation of Poles from Harbin to Poland began in 1920. Throngs of local Poles and refugees filled the office of the Polish Consulate. Wealthy Poles traveled on their own money by decent steamships; workers on the Chinese Eastern Railroad also joined the crowd for repatriation. The remnants of Polish military units left for Poland on the steamers *Yaroslav* and *Voronezh* that had been chartered for them.

But for ordinary citizens and persons not of means, repatriation was very difficult. Passage by rail through Russia was closed, passage by sea was enormously expensive, and there were extremely few free tickets for the steamers. Nevertheless, the *Brandenburg* set sail in May 1920, carrying several hundred Poles, and small groups of repatriates were transported by Japanese vessels. But by the end of 1920, all financial resources had been exhausted and large-scale repatriation came to an end.

Despite the massive exodus of Poles, those remaining in the Polish colony continued to survive. For the very poorest Poles, who had not the means for repatriation, the Harbin Red Cross Society set up a shelter in the former barracks of the Russian Army. The high school continued to function, with 200 students who were being taught by well-established teachers.

Fr. Władisław was a persistent priest. Acknowledging that a single person could not resolve all the problems arising in the Harbin Roman Catholic parish, he decided to establish close ties with the Apostolic Administrator. To this end, he set off for Europe. But all the suggestions of the anxious priest were left abandoned on paper, both at the Vatican and in Poland. Only Bishop Edward Ropp and Bishop de Guébriant paid attention to Fr. Władisław's earnest proposals. Bishop de Guébriant's visit to Harbin and Vladivostok in 1921 was the result of Fr. Władisław's visit to Europe. The distinguished guest agreed with many of Fr. Władisław's suggestions and he gave particular attention to the establishment of junior seminaries where it would be possible to prepare future Catholic priests. In addition, the Vicar Apostolic came to the conclusion that the number of Harbin Catholics had grown significantly and that St. Stanisław Church could no longer accommodate all of them. Accordingly it was time to consider building a second church in Harbin.

This wish of the archbishop was fulfilled thanks to the good will and assistance, primarily, of the Vice-Director of the Chinese Eastern Railroad, Stefan Offenberg. The management of the Chinese Eastern Railroad gave the Catholics for the construction of a new church a beautiful plot of land in the business district of Harbin, where the majority of the railroad workers lived.

The solemn dedication of the cornerstone of the future church took place September 3, 1922, and in 1925 a beautiful church was completed and named in honor of St. Josaphat. Harbin Catholics, however, gave it their own name—"the church by the wharf."

5. *Creation of the Apostolic Vicariate of Siberia*

The tumultuous times and revolutionary events in Russia introduced adjustments to the plans of the Vatican's Apostolic Administration. It was difficult to lead parishes in a country where representatives of the Apostolic Administration had no right to enter and from which local religious persons no longer had the right to leave. But nonetheless the Vatican persistently tried to resolve this problem and Pope Benedict XV by an Apostolic Letter dated December 1, 1921, severed the entire Asian part of Russia from the Mogilev Archdiocese, establishing a new Vicariate of Siberia. This vicariate was bounded on the west by the Caspian Sea and the Ural

Mountains; on the north by the Arctic Ocean and Bering Strait; on the east it reached to the shores of the Pacific Ocean; and on the south it extended to Persia, eastern Turkestan, Manchuria and the Amur and Primorye regions. Fr. Gerard Piotrowski, a representative of the Franciscan Fathers in Nanking, was named the head of this huge Vicariate of Siberia. The Soviet government, however, categorically and permanently forbade the entry of this Catholic official into Russian territory.

Today we understand how absurd and impossible was the Vatican's decision to send a Vatican official into a Communist country! But in those now distant days Vatican officials—and others as well—stubbornly believed that Soviet power in Russia would not last long. Inasmuch as the Soviets would not allow Fr. Piotrowski to enter Russian territory, the Congregation of the Propagation of the Faith selected Harbin as his seat, and Fr. Piotrowski arrived there February 2, 1925.

Fr. Gerard was a practical man. During twenty years of missionary work he had acquired considerable experience in establishing convents for nuns and missionaries, as well as hospitals and orphanages. He had served as a procurator in Shanghai and Hong Kong. In Hong Kong he had established a convent of missionary Sisters where girls of various nationalities studied. It is interesting to note that the majority of girls from Orthodox families willingly converted to the Catholic faith and they were then able to marry Catholics.

From the moment of his arrival in Harbin, Fr. Gerard became aware of the story of Fr. Ostrowski's life and his "miter-mania"—that is, his long-standing, burning desire to be named a bishop. Having invested so much energy in the foundation of Catholic parishes and then convening a Catholic Congress in Harbin, Fr. Władisław was certain that he would be named bishop—but the bishop's miter was given not to him but to the Vladivostok dean, Karol Sliwowski. But this did not dampen Fr. Władisław's zeal. He reasoned that since Archbishop Derbini headed the movement for the conversion of Orthodox to Eastern Rite Catholic, he [Derbini] could establish an archimandrate for Eastern Rite Catholics, of whom there were many in Shanghai, Manchuria and in all of China—especially in the French, British and American concessions. Large numbers of Russians worked there as well.

Fr. Władisław called Archbishop Derbini's attention to the fact that although there were many people of the Orthodox faith living in Manchuria, neither the Orthodox clergy nor their bishop, Bishop Innocent, had been able to get permission to open an Orthodox seminary. The main reason for this was that the Chinese did not recognize married clergy! After all these communications, Fr. Ostrowski awaited the developments of events in accordance with his plan—and therefore he decided to settle the newly arrived Fr. Gerard close to himself in the very uncomfortable, small wooden building used for the grammar school, where he also intended to house future seminarians. Fr. Gerard's neighbor turned out to be a widow with a hysterical sister. Naturally, the new arrived cleric was unpleasantly surprised, wondering why Fr. Ostrowski had not given him a place in the brick parish building which had central steam heat and all the necessary amenities.

Fr. Gerard had to endure it while he looked around and became acquainted with many Poles. These people helped him find a separate residence with central heating—the former residence of the Soviet consul. The beautiful building was purchased and Fr. Gerard settled in at 89 Grand Prospect in Modziagov, three kilometers from Old Harbin. Not far from him was the mission of the Franciscan Sisters of Mary of the White Missionaries. The mission was located in the beautiful park of General Dmitri Leonidovich Horvath, who had gathered a significant military force during the Civil War in Russia, created his own bank, the Russian Bank of General Horvath, and issued his own bank notes! Right from the beginning of his undertakings he had received the support of Japan. But then he had come to realize the futility of his opposition to Soviet power—he dismissed his forces, gave his luxurious park to the Franciscan Sisters and gave his palace to be used as an orphanage and hospital. Having completed these charitable acts, he departed for Japan.

6. *Opening of St. Charles Vladivostok Minor Seminary in Harbin*

When Fr. Marius Kluge arrived in Harbin from Vladivostok with four seminarians, news of the opening of a seminary spread instantaneously throughout Harbin and all the railroad settlements. Fr. Marius proposed naming the new seminary the St. Charles Vladivostok Minor Seminary. News of the opening of the seminary attracted many candidates, so there were enough seminarians. With respect to the teaching staff, however, the situation was more complicated. Fr. Gerard sent a request for assistance to the Provincial [of his order], Fr. Benedict Wezitsula, in Lwow. A volunteer who agreed to work in the Harbin seminary was immediately found—Fr. Paulin Wilczinski, the vicar of the Radecznetski Convent and head of the Radecznits Collegium. There were others who would have wanted to go to faraway Asia, but some feared the frigid Siberian winters, others asked for guarantees of a high salary—but it was impossible to even speak of any such guarantees. Thus for the time being only Fr. Paulin Wilczinski went to Harbin. This was in 1925.

Soon the administrative offices of the Vicariate were set up in the building on Horvath Avenue that also housed the St. Charles Vladivostok Seminary. The activity of this Vicariate was limited to the allocation of material assistance to the Roman Catholic missions working in Siberia and in purely religious issues. Vicar Gerard Piotrowski tried again to get into Siberia in 1926, but representatives of the Bolshevik power categorically and permanently forbade his entrance onto Russian territory. Practically speaking, the connection of Siberian and Far Eastern Catholics with the Administration of the Vicariate of Siberia had been definitively broken. Given this state of affairs, the Vicar of Siberia had to limit himself to professorial/pedagogical and religious activity, serving as a professor and the head of the St. Charles Vladivostok Minor Seminary.

There were some changes in the Harbin convent of the Ursuline Sisters: it split into two groups. The larger group of Ursulines followed Sr. Emmanuila Labujewska and continued to adhere to the Latin Rite; they organized a boarding school on the edge of the city.

The second group of Ursuline Sisters, under the leadership of Mother Alozia Śliwowska, affiliated themselves with the Greek Catholic Rite and organized a boarding school for Greek-Catholic pupils. After 1945, when Soviet troops entered Harbin, the majority of Poles had the opportunity to be repatriated to Poland. Both the Latin and the Greek Catholic Rite missions, colleges and high schools were closed. The Ursuline Sisters and other religious were expelled from Harbin. Mother Alozia Śliwowska returned to Kraków where she supported herself giving private lessons; she also worked as a translator in the metropolitan curia. Soon she fell sick and peacefully died. Her body was buried in the Kraków cemetery. Unfortunately, during the following decades her gravesite was lost, and when visiting the cemetery in recent years we were unable to locate the grave of Sr. Alozia Śliwowska. Mother Agnia Sofia Malczewska, whose acquaintance we made at the Ursuline convent in Kraków in 2002, despite her very venerable age and blindness, has an excellent memory and with great pleasure she told us about herself and about Mother Alozia Śliwowska in pure "gentry" Russian.

7. *Fr. Antonij Leszczewicz*

A small mission parish had been established at Manchur Station, approximately 850 kilometers from Harbin, where many Catholic railroad workers lived. In 1917, the young priest Antonij Leszczewicz was transferred from Chita to serve St. Stanisław parish, from where he was right away sent to serve in this mission parish for approximately five years.

Antonij Leszczewicz was born September 17, 1890, in the village of Abramowszczyna, Vojstemsk district, Vilensk *gubernia*. The boy's father, Ioann Leszczewicz, and his mother, Karolina Sadowska, were of the petty nobility. Antonij at first studied in a private high school in Vilensk *gubernia*, and then from 1906 to 1909 he was at the Roman Catholic Boys High School at St. Catherine Church in St. Petersburg. He completed his religious education in the Mogilev Archdiocesan Seminary and was then ordained to the priesthood in

April 1914. He began his first assignment in June 1914 as vicar of the Irkutsk Roman Catholic Church. A year later he was named head of the Roman Catholic Church in Chita where he served two years. The local parishioners dearly loved their young pastor—a good, attentive and very kind-hearted man. When it became known in Chita that this pastor was being transferred to Harbin, the Mogilev archdiocese was flooded with petitions and requests that this beloved pastor be allowed to remain in Chita.

But the parishioners' pleas went unheeded and Fr. Leszczewicz left first for Harbin and then from there to Manchur Station. A cozy little Catholic church had been built there, with a school and house for the priest next to it. The young and attentive priest quickly established friendly contacts with his new parishioners. He served in Manchur Station approximately five years, after which he was called back to Harbin and entrusted with the new parish, St. Josaphat.[90]

Of great significance to Fr. Leszczewicz and the other Harbin priests and parishioners was the question, to which diocese did the three Harbin parishes belong? According to long-standing church law, they ought to be considered parishes of the Mogilev archdiocese, but the deep political changes that had occurred in Russia precluded that possibility. In such a situation, according to laws in use in the Catholic Church over the course of several centuries, geography would be the determining factor—and thus the Harbin parishes would be part of the Diocese of Jilin. This historical detail forced the Harbin Catholics to direct the following letter to Bishop Sliwowski in late 1923:

Your Excellency!

90 He served in Harbin until December 1937. He returned to Europe in early 1938, and after celebrating his twenty-fifth anniversary as a priest, he petitioned to be admitted to the Marians of the Immaculate Conception. He completed the required novitiate and was accepted into the order. He was martyred by the Nazis in Rosica. The cause for the canonization of Blessed Antonij Leszczewicz is under way.

With great joy we, the Harbin parishioners whose parishes encompass Harbin and the territories of the entire Chinese-Russian Concession, have learned that by decree of the Apostolic See a diocese has been formed in Vladivostok under your leadership. At the same time we have some anxiety with respect to the news that there has not yet been a decision to join the Harbin parishes to the Diocese of Vladivostok, and that that decision will be made in Rome. Thus we turn to You, Worthy Pastor, and ask that you hear our request and support it before His Excellency, the Apostolic Delegate [to China] Archbishop Costantini.

We ask that Archbishop Costantini support our request at the Apostolic See, namely that the Harbin parishes be included in the Diocese of Vladivostok. We offer the following in support of our request:

1. From the moment of its organization in 1908 our parish has always belonged to the Archdiocese of Mogilev, like all the parishes in the Amur and Primorye regions.
2. St. Stanisław church was dedicated by Bishop Jan Cieplak; thus from the beginning of its construction the church was always considered a parish church of the Archdiocese of Mogilev.
3. The parishioners of the Harbin parishes are predominantly Poles. The occasional German, Irish and Lithuanian Catholics comprise not more than one or two percent of the number of parishioners.
4. All historical and cultural societies associated with the parish have been created primarily by Poles.

5. The pupils at the local Genrich Sienkiewicz High School and the St. Vincent de Paul grade school are 100 percent Poles.
6. Since there are French missionaries near Harbin, in Funandzian and other places outside the boundaries of the Concession, who tend to the pastoral needs of Chinese Catholics and European Catholics who live outside the bounds of the rail line territories, assigning our entirely Polish parishes to the Diocese of Vladivostok ought not provoke any misunderstandings.
7. Even if the number of Poles were to decrease in the future, the Poles would still comprise the largest ethnic group, since there would always be commercial bonds between Harbin and Poland.

We humbly ask You, Worthy Father Bishop, to take all these enumerated arguments and present them, if necessary, to the Papal Delegate.

Parish Council
Harbin—October 29, 1923

We do not know whether the Harbin Catholics ever received a definite response to their letter. No documents on the questions have been found. We only know that in addition to Fr. Antonij Leszczewicz there was one other priest who served in Harbin, Fr. Aleksandr Ejsymontt.[91]

91 The Marians of the Immaculate Conception had a novitiate in Harbin and several members of their community served in Manchuria through the 1930s. For more information, see *The Marian Martyrs of Rosica*, ed. Rev. Jan Bukowicz, MIC (Stockbridge, MA: Marian Press, 2000).

8. Fr. Aleksandr Karl Ejsymontt

The next priest to serve in Harbin after Fr. Leszczewicz was Fr. Aleksandr Karl Ejsymontt.[92] He was born in 1883 on the "Kolubyszki" Estate in a family of the landowning gentry in the Grodnensk district, Grodnensk *gubernia.* His parents were Aleksandr Kazimierz Ejsymontt and Anna Ejsymontt, neé Bulkiewicz. The child was baptized in the church of the Bernadine Fathers by Fr. Jósef Sawrimowicz. After completing the six grades of the local Grodnensk high school, Aleksandr enrolled in the Mogilev seminary. He completed the seminary in 1906 and was ordained a priest by the suffragan bishop of Kovensk, Bishop Cyrtowt. He was given his first assignment May 26, 1906, when he became the vicar of the Catholic parish in the town of Mozyr and the religion teacher in the Mozyr high school. On April 18, 1909, he was named vicar of the Catholic parish in the town of Orlov, and then in the autumn of 1910 he was once again transferred, this time to Khabarovsk.

The arrival in the Far East of such a highly educated priest elicited a lively interest among the leadership of the high schools and various educational institutions. The young priest very soon received several offers. The archives include invitations to teach at the Count Muravyev-Amursky Khabarovsk Cadet Corps, the Khabarovsk Nikolaevsk city grade school, and the Khaborovsk Aleksandrovsk girls high school.

Fr. Ejsymontt most likely felt some satisfaction in being so much in demand in the Far East, and he therefore conscientiously carried out his ministry in the Roman Catholic parish and his responsibilities as a teacher. But when he requested permission to go on vacation, his request was refused and instead he was discharged. Why was such a diligent and industrious Catholic priest so precipitously dismissed?

---

92 RGIA, f. 826, op. 1, d. 1482, l. 3.

Bishop Cieplak received this explanation in response to an inquiry he had sent to the Ministry of Internal Affairs: The ministry had received information that the chaplain of the Khabarovsk parish, Fr. Ejsymontt, in the current year, before Easter, had refused to hear the confession of a Mrs. Sotnikova, referring to the fact that her husband was not Catholic, but Orthodox. Upset by this claim, the priest wrote the following explanation: he would agree (referring to the Pope) to hear Mrs. Sotnikova's confession if she would first divorce her Orthodox husband and then re-marry him—but not on Russian territory.[93]

Upon learning all this, the metropolitan of the Mogilev Archdiocese wrote the following to the Ministry of Religious Affairs: "From the explanations of Fr. Ejsymontt, I have concluded that his conversation with his parishioner, Mrs. Sotnikova, took place in the confessional, and under this circumstance I can make no further questioning. It is in no way possible to verify the extent to which Mrs. Sotnikova's accusations are credible. I have once again appealed to Fr. Ejsymontt with a request that he help Mrs. Sotnikova, and I only hope that she will be satisfied."

Fr. Ejsymontt did all that the representatives of the consistory advised him to do, but nonetheless he was not allowed to remain at his post in Khabarovsk.

For what was Fr. Ejsymontt being punished? It turns out that the dark shadow of a misdeed committed back in 1906 when he was

93 There may be more than one explanation for what is going on here. But one can suppose that since it was illegal for Catholics to marry Orthodox on Russian territory without prior permission from the highest church authorities, Mrs. Sotnikova, in marrying an Orthodox, had presumptively converted to Orthodoxy. It was therefore not appropriate for her to request the sacraments of a Roman Catholic priest—nor would it have been appropriate for a Roman Catholic priest to administer them to her. Perhaps in a moment of exasperation, he proposes an absurd solution: she should start over! Divorce her husband and then marry him outside Russia. Her marriage would then be legal, she would still be Catholic, she could receive the sacraments.

serving as the religion teacher at the Mozyr girls high school was still hanging over him. There, at his own initiative, Fr. Ejsymontt had arranged in his own apartment several meetings of pupils from the boys high school and pupils of the private girls high school. He had not informed his school supervisor about these meetings—and they considered this a terrible offense, for which the trustee immediately recommended that the priest be dismissed from his position.

But the Mozyr-Reczinsk dean, Genrich Gumnicki, came forward on the priest's behalf. He wrote that as in previous years, students met in the priest's apartment on December 8 because every priest must make efforts to establish contact with his pupils, since the spiritual direction and moral education of children depend on such contact with priests. And it was necessary to have these "unofficial" meetings because in the classroom one only talks of the development of the pupils' academic knowledge.

Fr. Ejsymontt was also blamed for an incident on January 12, when his pupils visited him to find out whether a party that the landowner, Mrs. Sniadska, had promised to arrange was going to happen. The children learned from the priest that permission for the party had not been granted—and they then left his apartment right away. Dismissed from his job and very upset, he went to take the cure at the baths at a resort in Japan, but upon his return they continued to "get" accusations, and there is no knowing where it all would have ended, but the events of 1917 completely turned upside down all the frightening paragraphs of the accusations, and Fr. Ejsymontt was able to quietly depart to serve in Harbin.

When Bishop Cieplak sent him an order to manage the chapel in Nikolsk-Ussuriisk, Fr. Ejsymontt responded to the bishop with a lengthy letter in which he explained in detail the reasons for his refusal of this assignment. In the first place, he had found satisfactory work in the Harbin parish. In addition, he had been invited to teach catechism in the Harbin high school for children of railroad workers, and that now gave him privileges to purchase food inexpensively in the special shops for railroad workers, as well as free rail passage.

Fr. Dominik Mikszys also gradually made his way to Harbin. As far back as 1905 he had been sent as military chaplain for the front-line Manchurian Army. Having served some time in Nikolsk, Fr. Dominik had experienced for himself the "expansionist instinct" of Mr. Steckiewicz and he had therefore decided to leave for some other parish. When the Mogilev archdiocese transferred him from Nikolsk-Ussuriisk to Nikolaevsk, he ignored his superiors and on his own "transferred himself" to Harbin, inasmuch as there was enough work there for several priests. Another priest who abandoned Nikolsk-Ussuriisk and made his way to Harbin was Fr. Jan Dyrijallo[94], who had been thoroughly disgusted by the activities of the magnate Steckiewicz and his attempts to turn the local Roman Catholic parish into his own obedient vassal.

94 RGIA, f. 821, op. 1, d. 1782, l. 1.

V

The Transfer of the Vladivostok Catholic Church Building to the Archive Bureau

After the remaining Catholics had had to abandon it, the Vladivostok Catholic Cathedral stood closed. But in 1935 the authorities agreed to transfer the building of the former Catholic church to the Archive Bureau for the storage of historical documents relating to Primorye. Document No. 370 was the official document describing the transfer: "Resolution of the Presidium of the Primorye Executive Committee of the Councils of Workers and Peasants and Peasants' Deputies, concerning the presentation to the Archive Bureau of space for the storage of archives and office space: the building of the former Polish church, located at 22 Volodarskaia Street, together with the one-story little house ("watchman's cabin") belonging to it and the plot of land is presented to the Primorye Archives to be used free of charge."

This document was signed by the deputy president of the Territorial Executive Commission, Comrade Pervukhin. On September 3, 1935, the Presidium of the Vladivostok City Council issued the following Resolution No. 78:

Comrade Fadeev (Zav. Norgo) is ordered within three days to turn over to the Primorye Region Archive Bureau the building of the former Polish church with all its auxiliary structures.

On October 17, 1935, an order was issued for the transfer by Government Securities to the Archive Bureau for use of the building of the Roman Catholic church and the "watchman's cabin" associated with it. In the conveyance it was documented that:

> 1. The Gothic-style brick building of the former Roman Catholic church, 17 by 19 sazhens, was valued at 50,000 rubles in 1926 values.
>
> 2. Condition of the building: in the large hall, the sanctuary and the two adjoining rooms, as well as in the choir, there is wooden flooring, painted, in good condition, but there is no floor where the altar was, nor in the room on the southwest corner next to the choir. The stairs going up to the attic have been built only up to the door going to the choir; going up further there are two old steps that would not provide a safe access to the attic. Five of the interior wooden doors are banged up on one side, and the bases and door jambs of these doors are also partially banged up and ruined. On the door going from the choir to the southwest room, the inside lock is broken and the door jamb is damaged.
>
> 3. The outside door from the east side, leading into the room next to the sanctuary, is damaged on the outside, and in this same room the window frames of two windows are damaged.
>
> 4. Grilles have been placed on the building's twenty-four windows (including the upper windows).
>
> The one-story wooden "watchman's cabin" is 60 square meters and has a kitchen. Condition of the cabin: Dilapidated, with half-rotted logs in the walls.

> The logs of the walls on the northwest corner and the entire northern wall to a height of one meter from the foundation are almost completely rotted. The foundation on the southwest side has cracks on the outside. The ceiling over the kitchen is collapsing on account of the decay of the beams and boards. The roof is covered with rusted zinc and leaks in several places.
>
> Chulkov
> Inspector of Government Revenues
> K. Stoliarov
> Manager, Primorye Archive Bureau

Despite the significant defects in the church building, the Archive Bureau had to accept the building in an "as is" condition, without appropriate repairs for the safekeeping of important archival documents of Primorye. Over the course of fifty-eight years the Archive Bureau used the building of the Catholic church, which had been built solely for Catholics and solely with the financial contributions of Catholics….

VI

Renaissance

1. First Attempts at Restoration of the Roman Catholic Parish in Vladivostok

After the beginning of the new epoch of Russian life that historians called "perestroika," there began in Vladivostok the restoration of old and the formation of new religious communities. The Jewish community and synagogue were restored, the Muslim and Lutheran communities were reborn. The Roman Catholic parish was also among the Christian communities hopeful of restoration, especially since there were still surviving members of the long-ago parish: Olimpiada Talko, Jadwiga Czarnecska, Lucyja Orańska, Julia Riabowa, Jadwiga Zelińska and several other former parishioners.

Polish Catholic priests began to visit Vladivostok; among the first of them were Fr. Jan Gajek and Fr. Ignatsyj Paulus. Because the parish had not yet been formed, these priests met with believers first at the apartment of Anastasia Potapenko, and then later at the Palace of Pioneers. The real pioneers of the restoration of the Roman Catholic parish in Vladivostok were Andrei Popok and Anastasia Potapenko.

In his lengthy letter to the Vladivostok Roman Catholic parish, Andrei Popok, who now lives in Ukraine, provided the parish with his recollection of his efforts to recreate the parish:

> I made the first attempt to locate like-minded people back in 1988, i.e., right after my arrival in the Far East after my completion of the Kiev Army-Navy Political Academy. Of course at that time I had no thoughts of creating a Catholic parish—I only wanted the company of like-minded people, i.e., people who were close in spirit—nothing more. But this attempt, as was to be expected, ended in failure. Most likely, at that time my personal contacts were limited and unvaried. In addition, one could see some fear expressed in the caution of those with whom I had occasion to speak on this topic, and also there was my military service—after all, I was at that time the First Secretary of the May 1st Union of Communist Youth!
>
> Upon my arrival in Vladivostok, I learned that there was a church building, which now housed the Regional Archive Bureau. Going there several times, I thought that most likely it would be possible to revive the activity of the parish, and this thought would not leave me any peace. But it was only in 1991 that I was able to realize this idea when, after unsuccessful attempts to find co-religionists, I placed an announcement in the newspaper *Konkurent*. The announcement read: "All who are not indifferent to the fate of the Catholic Church of Vladivostok are invited to respond." The announcement was published in Issue No. 16 of *Konkurent*. At that time, Igor Davidov, a former cadet of the Military High School who had become a Seventh Day Adventist, supported my initiatives. A week after the publica-

tion of my announcement, Anastasia Potapenko responded, and on the following day we met and agreed that in subsequent announcements we would give her home telephone number. Soon the following Poles responded: Jadwiga Francewna, Jadwiga Leonowna, the Switalskis, and others.

The "Founding Meeting" of the future Catholic parish took place August 25, 1991. I had maintained close contact with Monsignor Jan Krapan, the pastor of St. Alexander parish in Kiev, and that parish had sent me its parish charter, which we then used as a model for our own. We also received from Fr. Krapan all kinds of help, including supplies of Christian literature. The whole process of registering the Vladivostok Roman Catholic parish dragged on for almost six months—it was completed January 4, 1992.

Prior to the arrival of Fr. Myron Effing in November 1991, the parish resembled a "club" for those who shared an interest in things Catholic, and we met in the Regional Center of Popular Culture. We read Sacred Scripture, we planned future work, we discussed plans and problems and naturally we dreamed of the day when the Catholic church building would once again be the Lord's House. The soul of our group was without a doubt Jadwiga Francewna Zelińska, may she rest in peace.

2. *Arrival of Fr. Myron Effing and Fr. Daniel Maurer*

In 1991, when news of the collapse of the Soviet Union and the return of their religious freedoms to the peoples of Russia shook the whole world, Fr. Myron Effing traveled as a tourist to Russia's Far East in order to become acquainted with its unique natural environment and also to try to find any Catholics there. Bishop

Joseph Werth, S.J., at that time the Acting Apostolic Administrator of Asian Russia, supported Fr. Myron's plan. Upon his arrival in Vladivostok, Fr. Myron placed an announcement in the local paper that Mass would be said at the gates of the former Catholic church. Approximately thirty people responded. Naturally, both Andrei Popok and Anastasia Potapenko were there, along with many long-time staunch Catholics: Jadwiga Zelińska, Jadwiga Switalska, Regina Piwinska, Nelli Wojcechowski, Wita Ramm and others. Because Fr. Myron at that time did not know Russian, Igor Davidov served as translator.

Visiting the Catholics, the priest saw how fervently they prayed, with tears in their eyes, evidence that the Faith of these people, despite several decades of repression and punishment, had not died out. Fr. Myron conveyed his impressions to Bishop Werth, who subsequently appointed Fr. Myron Effing the head of the Vladivostok Roman Catholic parish. Thus Fr. Myron's second visit to Vladivostok could already be described as a pastor's visiting his flock.

Fr. Myron was born February 7, 1941, in Evansville, Indiana. His parents had four children. The young Myron went to the parish schools and then he attended Indiana University, where he received a bachelor of science degree in physics. In 1962, after he had graduated from the University, he entered the novitiate of the Canons Regular of the Holy Cross (Croziers) in Hastings, Nebraska. The following year he became a monk, making his first vows, and began his studies at the Major Seminary in Fort Wayne, Indiana. Upon completion of his seminary studies, Brother Myron enrolled in the graduate program at Cornell University in Ithaca, New York, and earned a master's degree in astronomy.

On May 27, 1972, in Fort Wayne, Bishop Leo Pursley ordained Brother Myron a priest of the Order of Canons Regular of the Holy Cross, and the young pastor began to teach his favorite subjects—physics, astronomy, geology, chemistry—at two minor seminaries near South Bend, Indiana, and Onamia, Minnesota. In 1985, Fr. Myron established a new group of canons—Canons of Jesus the Lord—on the island of Guam. He was joined by one of his former pupils, Daniel Maurer. In 1985, Fr. Myron was named rector of the Seminary on the island of Guam and at the same time he served as director of a Catholic school with 400 students. In addition, during the course of the year he also taught astronomy at the local university. In 1989, after a four-year term of teaching on Guam, Fr. Myron moved to the city of Modesto, California, and there for two years he taught Bible studies in a Catholic school and served as chaplain at the state university.

On his second visit to Vladivostok Fr. Myron was accompanied by Brother Daniel Maurer. Brother Daniel was born March 5, 1951, in Hart, Michigan, one of three sons of Roger and June Maurer. His resume shows that he received a solid liberal arts education. In his childhood he went to St. Joseph School in St. Joseph, Michigan. From 1965 to 1969 he was a student at the Minor Seminary of Our Lady of the Lake in Syracuse, Indiana, where he studied Latin and French. He became a candidate for the monastic order of Canons Regular of the Holy Cross.

From 1969 to 1973 he studied at Michigan State University in the College of Social Sciences, Department of East Asian Studies. At MSU he studied French and Chinese and upon completion of the course of studies he received a bachelor's degree in liberal arts. From 1973 to 1975 he was Director of Admissions at Wauwausee, a college preparatory school in Syracuse, Indiana.

After a year of graduate studies, he entered the Order of Canons Regular of the Holy Cross; he completed the novitiate and additional studies in philosophy and theology. He then transferred to the Congregation of Augustinians of the Assumption of the Virgin Mary. This required additional studies, after which he served as a missionary for the order in Mexico City. In 1988 he joined Fr. Myron and his studies then focused on ordination to the priesthood. He was at last ordained on September 21, 1992, in the Cathedral of the Most Holy Mother of God in Vladivostok by His Excellency Joseph Werth, at that time the Apostolic Administrator of the Catholic Church in Asian Russia.

The solemnity of Fr. Daniel's ordination made a huge impression on all the parishioners of the Vladivostok Roman Catholic parish. After all, most Catholics were witnessing this solemn and emotional ceremony for the first time in their lives. Fr. Daniel's parents had traveled from the United States for the ordination. Following the wondrous ceremony, the overwhelmed parishioners were invited to a festive banquet in honor of so important an event for the parish.

After his ordination, Fr. Daniel was named vicar of the Vladivostok Catholic parish, and in 1993 he became the pastor of St. John the Evangelist parish in Bolshoi Kamen, Primorye. Unfortunately, this parish has not been active since 2001, when parishioners departed for other regions of Russia. But for ten years, beginning in 1996, Fr. Daniel was head of Holy Trinity parish in Romanovka.

Fr. Daniel literally transformed the musical life of all Christian communities in Vladivostok. First, he established the St. Augustine Russian Liturgical Music Society. This society composes, translates and collects and distributes free of charge liturgical music and texts in Russian for Catholic parishes of the Latin rite. Second, Fr. Daniel had the marvelous idea of conducting a Christmas Festival of Christian Choirs. In 1999 Fr. Daniel began professional organ and choral concerts with vocal soloists. And the parish organist, Marina Omelchenko, founded the Queen of Angels Chamber Ensemble, which performs more than fifteen concerts as well as a music festival each year in the church.

Fr. Daniel had to "start from zero," teaching the parishioners liturgical choral music—but first of all, they needed to get the church building returned to the Catholics. They once again said Mass at the gates of the church, and now a group of Catholics had been formed; they were familiar with the order of the Mass and they could be called parishioners. Their devotion convinced Fr. Myron that he was needed here, in Vladivostok, in order to return the church to the faithful, to revive divine worship, to marry young couples, to baptize children and bury those whom the Almighty had called to Himself.

While the question of the return of the church to the Catholics was being decided, the faithful rented a hall for their worship, first at the Palace of Pioneers, then at the House of Trade Unions and finally at the Palace of Trade Unions. Steadily the number of parishioners grew; many young people joined the parish—the children and grandchildren of the "veterans" of the long-ago parish, as well as members of western European families—Poles, Ukrainians, Lithuanians—who had emigrated from the western *gubernia*s of Russia. It was not easy for the priests because they had to re-awaken in the memory of the elderly parishioners all the rubrics for the Catholic Mass as well as instruct the young parishioners who were coming to a Catholic church for the first time in their lives.

3. *Return of the Catholic Church to the Faithful*

In the middle of September 1993 the Primorye Council of Peoples Deputies returned the building of the former Catholic church to the Vladivostok Catholic community. The transfer was conditional upon the Catholic community's agreement to undertake and complete a thorough restoration of the building as a historical and cultural landmark. The fact that the building had been divided into several floors was a problem for both the priests and the parishioners, as the first Masses were said on the top floor, where the tops of the highest windows were beneath the floor! The first floor was little more than a garbage heap and it seemed to the parishioners that they would never be able to clear it out. But they did! They cleared out the garbage and cleaned the walls and floors. Then all liturgies, weddings and baptisms took placed on the first floor, from where one could look up and see the iron beams undergirding the upper floors.

When Fr. Daniel began to address the parish's "musical problems," he began by teaching the parishioners to sing psalms and other choral religious music *a capella*, but soon he purchased a synthesizer and on August 15, 1992, the feast of the Assumption of the Most Holy Virgin Mary, the parish choir performed for the first time with musical accompaniment. The parish's first musician was Anna Gafurova, a graduate of the piano program at the local conservatory and a charming and talented girl whom many young people liked. Soon one of them, a young American, offered Anna "his hand and his heart." The first Catholic wedding, celebrated in 1994, gladdened all parishioners, but the choir was soon saddened because Anna left the parish and went to the United States with her husband.

The next serious musician in the parish was Marina Omelchenko, a graduate of the piano program at Vladivostok Art Institute. Marina was a wonderful pianist, but unfortunately she was not a director. Fr. Daniel thereupon offered the position of choir director to Ekaterina Jankina. This immediately resulted in a quality of choral performance of liturgical music that was beginning to sound quite professional. But once again the choir was out of luck—Ekaterina and her sister left for South America. Then a student of the Art Institute, Svetlana Naumova, who had a wonderful voice, began to direct the choir, with Marina Omelchenko the main accompaniest. When American Catholics donated an organ to the Vladivostok parish, Marina decided to further her musical education and soon she was a graduate student in the organ program at Moscow Conservatory.

The development of the organist's skills were paralleled by the development of the choral music. Svetlana Naumova worked very diligently with the choir, and gradually she brought them to the highest levels of performance. At that point it became possible to offer concerts of choral and organ music, which for several years now have enjoyed enormous popularity in Vladivostok. At these concerts local well-known singers are often featured as soloists, and from time to time famous maestros from the capital have also performed. In 2000 Svetlana Naumova and Fr. Daniel founded the Professional Concert Choir, and right away the regular concert attendees began to consider this choir one of the best in Vladivostok!

Beautiful concerts of choral music are also conducted at the parish at Christmastime, and the choirs of several denominations gladly participate. They all sing of God, of God's Mercy—and the audience experiences a great feeling of joyous satisfaction, because we all need peace and tranquility.

4. Arrival of New Catholic Priests

In May 2003 the clergy at Most Holy Mother of God parish was increased with the addition of Fr. Sebastian Marian De'Silva. Fr. Sebastian was born April 9, 1955, in Mangalore, India. At the age of fifteen he moved to the missionary diocese of Meerut, which is in northern India near New Delhi. In 1972 he entered the seminary of St. Albert College in Ranchi and on May 15, 1981, he was ordained a diocesan priest in his native city of Mangalore. Fr. Sebastian subsequently served in five parishes of the Diocese of Meerut.

At the invitation of Fr. Myron, Fr. Sebastian came to St. Joseph parish in Irkutsk in 2003, then he was sent to the Roman Catholic parish of the Most Holy Mother of God in Vladivostok, where he was joyfully welcomed by both clergy and parishioners. He quickly learned Russian and assumed all priestly responsibilities. The parishioners of the Vladivostok Roman Catholic parishes love this good-natured and very polite priest. In April 2007 he was appointed pastor of Our Lady of the Pacific in Nakhodka.

In 2004 two more priests came to Primorye: Fr. Bartolomej Szost and Fr. Krzysztof Terepka both came from Poland, and they both served in Nakhodka at Our Lady of the Pacific parish, Fr. Bartolomej as pastor and Fr. Krzysztof as his assistant. In 2007 they had to return to Poland.

Nativity of Christ parish in Ussuriisk has Fr. Dominic Kim, O.F.M., as its pastor and three Sisters of the Order of St. Paul of Chartres assist him: Sr. Teresa Kann, Sr. Theophilus Kim, and Sr. Maria Nam. Fr. John Gibbons, O.F.M., and two brothers—Mario Neygi and Corrado Khvanbo—are also at Nativity of Christ parish. Fr. Gibbons also serves as pastor of Annunciation parish in Arseniev.

A member of the Vladivostok parish, Oleg Yelchaninov, has entered the monastery and is now in Slovakia at the Abbey of the Canons of St. Norbert where he is completing his theological education.

Fr. Myron Effing, as dean, is responsible for the Primorye, Amur and Khabarovsk Provinces and the Jewish Autonomous District. In addition to this huge territory, Fr. Fyron is pastor of both the main parish of the deanery, Most Holy Mother of God, and St. Joseph, which is located in the Second River section of Vladivostok. Fr. Myron also has to contend with numerous financial and construction matters associated with the Vladivostok parishes. The construction of the Pastoral Center is coming to completion and then work will begin in the church building on the removal of the coverings of the second floor so that it will be possible to completely recover the natural grandeur, height and beauty of the sanctuary. In addition, there are plans for erecting the two bell towers, as had originally been intended when the church was first built.

5. *Transformation of the Vladivostok Cathedral and Return of the Crucifix*

The external appearance of the Catholic cathedral has steadily been transformed and improved since 1994.[95] And even though it still does not have its two Gothic bell towers, each brick of the walls of the cathedral has been cleaned and polished and thus it shines like a mirror. The beautiful Gothic windows, which in the 1930s were blocked with ugly hinged window panes and prison-like grilles, now have highly artistic stained glass. Each window portrays a Biblical theme: the Annunciation, the Visitation, the Nativity, the Presentation, the Coronation of the Virgin Mary and others.[96]

Fr. Myron and Andrei Vdovichenko, the superintendent of the building, formulated the ideas for the windows; the Belorussian specialists Aleksei Ivanovskii and Vladimir Ivanov executed the designs.

---

95 Since a bishop presided at the church in earlier years, the church is properly called a cathedral.

96 M. I. Efimova, "Dukhovnaia sila vitrazhei," *Sibirskaia katolicheskaia gazeta*, No. 10, p. 8.

Although there are still iron coverings over the first floor, the completion of the priests' house is drawing near. The church furnishings and the two organs will then be moved temporarily into the priests' house so that the work in the church can be completed. The parishioners now try to imagine how beautiful and grandiose the graceful and lofty sanctuary will be, with its snow-white clusters of columns and wondrous stained-glass windows once the repairs are fully completed!

When the Vladivostok Roman Catholic parish began having Mass, it had only one piece of religious art, which Fr. Myron brought to the very first Mass at the gates of the cathedral—a small statute of Our Lady, Mystical Rose. This statue had been brought to Andrei Popok from Germany and it was the first and for a long time the only piece of sacred art at all the liturgies.

Meanwhile the parishioners learned that one of the main artifacts of the church—the marble crucifix—was in the Vladivostok Art Institute, where it served as a visual aid for art students. There then began the lengthy process of getting this sacred piece of art returned to the Catholic church. At first there were numerous negotiations with the director of the Institute, but these always ended with a firm refusal—they said the crucifix had never belonged to the church—it had been found in a cemetery, buried in a deep grave. It seemed that all the parishioners' efforts would be in vain. But fortunately, a very modest but extremely necessary document was found in the regional archive: a receipt signed by the former Director of the Art Institute stating that he had received the marble crucifix as a study aid. This was a stroke of good fortune. Finally the crucifix would be returned to its home.

There were later others—for example, the beautiful icon of the Most Holy Mother of God of Vladivostok, a gift from the Byzantine Catholic monks to commemorate the return of religious freedom to Russia. The icon, "written" in the style of ancient Christian images, was made for Russian Catholics by Fr. Damian from Transfiguration of Our Lord Monastery in Redwood Valley, California. The icon was acquired and bequeathed to the parish by Mrs. Angela Walsh

Wozniak—may she be praised in heaven! High over the tabernacle is a huge statute of the Mother of God holding the Child Jesus—a gift of Sisters from Fremont, California, whom the parishioners faithfully remember in their prayers. Along the inside walls are hung twelve small icons of the Lord's Passion, as well as a canvas painting of the Virgin Mary done in Florentine style by a local parishioner, Yu Men Hu.

The relics of St. Thérèse of Lisieux, a French Carmelite nun canonized in 1925, less than thirty years after her death, were in Vladivostok for four days in 1999, and this event made an unforgettable impression on the parishioners. The pilgrimage of the saint's relics throughout Russia had been organized by Fr. Michael Shields of Magadan. On this occasion, Divine Liturgy was celebrated in the Cathedral of the Most Holy Mother of God, and after communion, the parishioners surrounded the reliquary containing the saint's relics—which had now completed their pilgrimage through all of Russia, reaching the shores of the Pacific Ocean in Primorye. The nuns who were accompanying the relics spoke to us of St. Thérèse as of one still alive—and Vladivostok parishioners, old and young, stood and sat around the reliquary as though enchanted.

It was with just the same tenderness and reverence that Vladivostok Catholics welcomed the statue of Our Lady of Fatima which made a pilgrimage journey through all the parishes of Siberia and the Far East.

Time passed, and the transformation of the parish was reflected not only in the walls and the stained-glass windows, but also in its most important asset—the parishioners. At the beginning of the restoration of the parish there were no more than twenty parishioners who from their childhood remembered both the prayers and the "rules of conduct" in church. These were mostly Poles and Belorussians, western Ukrainians and Lithuanians. Some of them are shown in an old group photograph that was saved by the Brzeziński family. The photo shows the brother of Pani Jadwiga - Stanisław Zeliński who was arrested and shot.... Nor did fate spare Jadwiga, as she died in our times in terrible suffering. The parishioner Jadwiga Czarnecka has died, Franczeska Romana has died—and the Lord has gathered many other parishioners to heaven. Anatoli Petrovich Stashkov, Fr. Myron's personal driver, has also died. He had driven the priest along many roads of Primorye, visiting Roman Catholic parishes of the region. His widow has published a little book of poetry dedicated to her beloved husband. May the glory of the Lord be upon all the departed!

6. *Acquisition of New Historical Documents*

In 2000 the archives of Most Holy Mother of God parish were supplemented with important historical materials which the author managed to locate in the archives of the Bernadine Fathers in Kraków. The materials were primarily manuscripts of Fr. Zachariusz Banaś, who described with great detail his meeting with the bishop of Vladivostok, Karol Sliwowski, in his Sedanka exile. Fr. Wecław Murawic, director of the archives, and Susanna Kazanowska, archivist, not only allowed the author to become well acquainted with all the historical documents of interest to us in the archives of the Bernadine Fathers, but they also allowed the author to copy excerpts from the documents and suggested to her where she might find even more detailed historical documents about Bishop Sliwowski—namely, the archives of the Ursuline Sisters.

In spite of the fact that during our first visit to Kraków the archives of the Ursuline Sisters were under repair, the director, Sr. Iwona Naglik, managed to find for us photos of the bishop of Vladivostok and parishioners taken in the early 1920s. These photos were sensational for our parish—in them our parishioners from the Usas family—Julia and Alla—immediately recognized their close relatives. They also saw their grandfather, who was holding a little girl in his arms—their aunt, who was still living. When Fr. Myron learned about this still-living aunt, he set off right away to the village of Preobrazhenie, where she was living, hoping to learn from her some historical information about the life of the former parish. Alas! The little girl was now more than ninety years old and blind.

She poorly—or perhaps not at all –remembered her relatives and the events of so many decades ago. In addition to their grandfather, Julia and Alla recognized several other relatives—aunts and uncles who had long since died.

Some of the photos showed the interior of the wooden "barracks" church, which allowed us present-day parishioners to see all the church furnishings and, most important, to see for ourselves that the large marble crucifux and a whole assortment of church furnishings had in fact belonged to the Vladivostok Roman Catholic parish.

The memoirs of Andrei Usas, which have been given to the parish, have immense historical value. Andrei Usas was one of the military builders who were sent from Kovno (today Lithuania) for the construction of the forts of the Vladivostok fortifications, and he was one of Bishop Sliwowski's parishioners. He built Seventh Fort, which is fourteen kilometers from the city, between the Second River and Sedanka railroad stations.

The parish archives have other photographs of Catholic families, for example, photos of the large Kaczanowski family which came to the Far East from the Ukrainian village of Wasilkowa in the Kiev *gubernia* and settled near the Chinese border in the village of Novo-Kievka. It was a large and friendly family. They built a house and laid out a decent garden that was a reliable source of food for the family. In the family photo given to the parish archives we see the head of the family, Peter Benediktowicz Kaczanowski, and his wife, Teklia Kazimierzowna, and their children: Edward, Michal, Stefan, Maria and Petronela. In our times there are still many Kaczanowskis living not only in Primorye but also in other parts of the country. Tatiana Kaczanowska has given her whole life and all her energy to "Dalzavod" (a ship repair facility). She is now a pensioner and a member of Most Holy Mother of God parish. Her cousin Victoria Saks is involved in charitable and social works; in addition, she has become, as it were, the Kaczanowski family chronicler, with a valuable collection of historical materials.

The activity of the present-day members of Most Holy Mother of God parish has with time become quite varied—but it is primarily charitable works. Various groups of parish volunteers have been formed—one is devoted to helping elderly or very seriously ill Catholics and non-Catholics; another tends to the needs of families in dire need; and yet another provides hot meals to homeless children. There are many volunteers with artistic talent and they put on delightful children's costume plays on Biblical themes. In a word, there is enough work for each parishioner! The priests—Fr. Myron, Fr. Daniel and Fr. Sebastian—continue to seek out Catholics who live in Primorye and establish mission parishes where they live. Such parishes have now been established in the cities of Nikolsk-Ussuriisk, Lesozavodsk, Arseniev, and Nakhodka and the village of Romanovka, in addition to parishes that were re-established and have been turned over to the care of other priests (Immaculate Conception parish in Khabarovsk and Transfiguration in Blagoveshchensk).

7. *Sisters of Mercy of St. Anne*

The Sisters of Mercy of St. Anne, from Spain, devote much heartfelt warmth to the little Catholics.[97] This order was founded in Saragossa at the beginning of the nineteenth century, and Fr. Juan Bonal Cortad and Mother Maria Raphels Brunes are considered its co-founders. The order began as a charitable community concerned with patients in the Main Royal Hospital in Spain. Abandoned children also came under the Sisters' care, and gradually the activity of the order expanded beyond the bounds of the Iberian peninsula.

Today the Sisters of Mercy of St. Anne serve on five continents, in thirty-one countries, and in all they number approximately 2,700 Sisters! When the Claretian Father José Cristo Rey Garcia Parades, who had served a whole month in Siberia, returned to Spain from this "mysterious Siberia," his enthusiastic stories about Siberia and its peoples fascinated the Mother Superior. Thus in 1997 she

97 *Sibirskaia katolicheskaia gazeta*, 2003, No. 5, p. 18.

sent to this mysterious Siberia a "landing party" of Sisters: Mother Julia Rumbreras, Sister-Secretary Anna Fernandez, and Sr. Alicia Gonzalo. This was the same day that the new cathedral was dedicated in Novosibirsk. They became acquainted with Bishop Werth and took his advice to base themselves in Vladivostok, where the climate was not as severe. On August 2, 1998, the "Spanish landing party" arrived in Vladivostok: Mother Superior Julia Rumbreras and Sisters Alicia Gonzalo and Madvi Menon. They were later joined by Srs. Maria Eugenia Lazaro and Rosario Vicente. The community was soon officially registered and the Spanish Sisters began their ministry on another continent. Unfortunately, the Primorye climate had a harmful effect on Sr. Madvi Menon and she had to return to Spain, but the order sent Sr. Purificación Belido in her place.

The sweet, affectionate, attentive and kind-hearted Spanish Sisters have been very well received by the Vladivostok parish. Right from the beginning the youngest parishioners and children became very attached to the Spanish Sisters; and it is as though there were no "language barrier" at all, especially since the Sisters set themselves to an intensive study of Russian and quickly became proficient. And perhaps it was because a mutual love for liturgical music, understood by Catholics of all countries, united them all.

Several years passed and there were some changes in the Sisters' community: Sr. Purificación Belido took a leave of absence; Sr. Rosario went to the Philippines; a Russian parishioner, Olga Nemchinova, has become a sister; and two other parishioners, Oksana Gorelova and Marina Malinina, are preparing to take vows. Marina is the head of the parish Sunday school. The little children simply adore their teacher—as soon as they get to church with their parents they hurry to her class and follow after Marina like little ducklings!

The Sisters work hard, putting warmth and cordiality into the spiritual life of the parish; they are the core of the choir; they care for seriously ill people in the hospice; they look after the very elderly parishioners who haven't the strength to get out of bed; and of course they are very affectionate toward all the parish children. In addition, Sr. Alicia teaches Spanish at the Foreign Language Institute of Far

East State University and Sr. Maria Eugenia taught Spanish in the Institute of International Relations at FESU. The Sisters also organized the Juan Bonal Youth Center for young parishioners and the Center is very popular among Catholic youth. Are the Sisters satisfied with their stay in Russia? Here is their answer: "We accept as a gift of God that we were sent to this country, to this city, to these people, and that we have the opportunity to warm this cold land with the fire of the universal, boundless mercy that we receive daily, as God's gift!"

8. Fraternal Gift of Polish Catholics

One cannot forget the friendly, fraternal gift that Polish Catholics gave to the Vladivostok Roman Catholic parish. It all began after Fr. Myron's return from Novosibirsk, where he had attended the dedication of the new Catholic Cathedral of the Transfiguration on August 10, 1997. Our pastor was captivated by the gesture of good will on the part of a Polish priest, Fr. Edmund Cisiak, who had brought to Novosibirsk—hitched to his car—bells for the bell tower of the new cathedral. Everyone of course was happy for the Novosibirsk Catholics, and then a timid idea was born: might the Polish Catholics also give such a gift to the Vladivostok church? They wrote a diffident letter to Fr. Edmund Cisiak, not especially hopeful of the outcome—but soon the telephone at the Vladivostok church rang and Fr. Edmund in an everyday, business-like voice advised that a collection for bells for the Vladivostok cathedral was already under way and that the casting of the bells would be done by the well-known Filczinski Company! They just needed to know what names the Vladivostok Catholics wanted to give the bells. Fr. Myron gave him the names for the bells and the parishioners began to await the results, still doubting the reality of receiving such a miraculous gift.[98]

98 The bells were named Our Lady of the Siberians, St. Joseph, St. Gabriel and St. Raphael Kalinovsky (a Siberian saint).

It later became known that the collection for the bells for the Far East Catholics was undertaken throughout all of Poland; everyone contributed whatever he could, no matter how little. Here is what Mrs. Danuta Grabowski from the Polish city of Ełk wrote to our parish: "We decided to help in the construction of the bells. We organized a collection at the "Siberian Union" and we were able to raise the significant sum of 600 złotys. We passed along the information about your problems with the bells to the Union of the National Army, where they collected 180 złotys, and the pensioners of Solidarity in Ełk collected 70 złotys. In all, we collected 850 złotys in Ełk, the equivalent of $243." Reading these words, one cannot but recall the parable of the widow's mite….

In 1999 the bells were ready and they were taken to the city of Radom, so that during his visit to that city Holy Father John Paul II would be able to bless this gift of solidarity on behalf of the Poles—and so it happened! And then there was the question, how to transport this valuable gift, blessed by the Pope, to the other end of the continent, to the Far East. Fr. Edmund's idea—of transporting the bells himself to Vladivostok, as he had done with the bells for Novosibirsk—could not be carried out because at that time there was no direct road from Moscow to Vladivostok. Several other ideas were considered, and finally the problem was solved by two Polish Scouts, Marek Wolosza and Pszemysław Macionszek. This team got their valuable cargo by car traveling the highway as far as Chita, where the highway ended. Then the bells were packed into containers and sent by rail to Vladivostok. One might think that here our story would end—but there arose before the community still one more obstacle: Her Majesty the Customs Office! Not taking into account the fact that this was not simply "cargo," but humanitarian aid from Catholics of Poland to Catholics of Vladivostok, the Customs Office required payment on the "merchandise" by the full value of its weight! What could they do but pay. But now the wonder-bells peacefully wait in the vestibule until the bell towers are built for them. Then Vladivostok Catholics will hear the sound of these wonderful bells!

9. Dedication of the New Cathedral in Irkutsk

In early September 2000 an important and happy event occurred for all Catholics in Siberia and the Far East. On May 31, 1998, the Polish priest Jerzy Mazur had been raised to the rank of bishop at a solemn ceremony held in Novosibirsk. A year later, on May 18, 1999, the Apostolic Administration of Siberia was divided. Henceforth Bishop Joseph Werth would preside over the Apostolic Administration of Western Siberia, with its seat in Novosibirsk, and Bishop Jerzy Mazur would preside over the Apostolic Administration of Eastern Siberia, with its seat in Irkutsk. The energetic Bishop Mazur turned the dedication of the new Catholic Cathedral of the Immaculate Heart of Mary into a special church celebration, to which he invited a large number of Catholic clergy of Russia, Poland and other countries. The Polish Catholic Church was represented by the Primate of Poland, Jósef Cardinal Glemp, and the apostolic nuncio from Warsaw, Archbishop Jósef Kowalczyk. Russian Catholics were represented by the apostolic nuncio Archbishop John Bukovski, SVD, of Moscow. From Vladivostok parish came the pastor, Fr. Myron Effing; the vicar, Fr. Daniel Maurer; the wonderful parish choir; and many parishioners who wanted to make a pilgrimage to Irkutsk to participate in so important a church celebration. But it was not only a festive celebration. It was also a time of deep sorrow, as one day was entirely dedicated to the memory of those Catholics who had perished in the prisons and camps of the Gulag. After Mass at the Cathedral of the Immaculate Heart of Mary, representatives of many Roman Catholic parishes of Siberia and the Far East came forward to read the names of those members of their parish who had been killed. Miroslava Efimova of the Vladivostok parish told the story of those Catholics of the Vladivostok parish who had been shot in 1938 for no other reason than the fact that they loved and honored God....

Near the wall of the new cathedral is a special chapel of Reconciliation and Peace with a four-meter statue of the Risen Christ. At the foot of the statue is laid out a symbolic cemetery in which they have buried fourteen urns filled with earth from the Gulags, where the earth was saturated with blood and human misery. The statue of the Risen Christ here depicts the hope for resurrection of all the innocents murdered….

After the celebration in the new cathedral, the pilgrims made several excursions through Irkutsk and its surroundings. First of all they went to the very old and beautiful Catholic Church that had been built by the first Catholic priest of Siberia—Fr. Krzysztóf Szwermicki. During the years of the battle against religion the church was taken from the faithful and turned into the Philharmonic Concert Hall. Only on the lower floor havc thc Irkutsk city authorities now allowed a small worship space, where the Roman Catholic parish of the Assumption of the Virgin Mary meets. The pastor of the parish for many years was Fr. Ignacij Paulius, SVD. Vladivostok Catholics know this priest well, as he was the leader of all the pilgrims who went from the Russian Far East to Poland during Pope John Paul II's visit to Poland in 1997.

10. The Parish's Work with Children

Meanwhile the Vladivostok Roman Catholic parish of the Most Holy Mother of God continued its soul-saving activity, giving great attention to the younger generation of Catholic families. As far back as 1994 the parish organized pilgrimage hikes for the parish youth; Jury Belozerov, a parishioner and teacher of biology at Middle School No. 28, led these hikes. With his extensive experience in working with children, Jury has now for several years organized trips for the youth along various routes. For example, they go along the road from Nikolsk-Ussuriisk to Lesozavodsk. They pitch tents for their overnight stops and of course they cook their food over campfires. There's usually singing around the campfire. Along this route there are places where the road and the campsites are right near the river. Of course the children love this kind of bathing! Another favorite hike is the "geographical route"—climbing up Mt. Pedan. This great beauty, which rises in the Partizansk region of Primorye, attracts all mountain climbers. School children, students and all rock climbers of the region know this mountain well.

Most Holy Mother of God parish usually organizes summer religion outings, when the children go with a catechist to a camp outside the city. The typical programs of the summer camps include sports, walks, hikes, and, when possible, swimming. Last year Fr. Myron encouraged the organization of a Scout troop, which Denis Bondarev leads. In 2004 the Scouts took a lengthy, complicated hike, camping along the way, praying, and eating food that they themselves prepared over a campfire.

Another area of work with the parish children is their preparation for Christian holidays. Getting ready for Christmas, for example, the Sunday school children try to make beautiful Christmas tree decorations and those who are older love decorating the trees and making gifts for their friends and relatives. Usually long before Christmas the children prepare for the main moment of the festivities, when they, dressed in Palestinian costumes, process into the church carrying the Infant Jesus and place Him in his humble cradle in the manger. The impressions of these activities stay with the children the whole year—and perhaps even for their whole lives….

No less interesting are all the events connected with Easter. Of course in all the Christian families they make beautiful, sweet paskha and painted eggs, and the children inspect all these wonders and decide which of the Easter baskets is the best looking and most beautiful. Near the altar they place a table that is quickly transformed into a beautiful Easter "flower bed," decorated with a variety of Easter breads and baskets with painted eggs.

One must not forget one other holiday—Palm Sunday. If we are fortunate and the weather is warm and sunny, the procession of priests and parishioners will remind one of a garden made of fluffy palm branches in the hands of the parishioners and the light blue sky completes the beautiful springtime composition.

The parishioners also have unforgettable impressions of the weddings of Catholic couples—when the bride appears in a marvelous white gown, like a storybook fairy, and the groom in a suit, dressed like a prince! The organ plays and the choir sings, joined by the wedding guests of the young couple. It seems in moments like these unseen angels flutter about the church! Members of the older generation remember with sadness their own wedding festivities, at times when one could not even dream of having a church wedding.

And then too our children married in the Orthodox church in accordance with its rituals. A church choir sang in the choir, and if there was no choir, then the church grandmothers, the Keepers of the Faith of Christ, sang with their discordant voices. Now in our church an organ plays at weddings and littlc girls in white dresses carefully carry the long lacy train of the bride's gown.

In addition to festivities there are also sorrowful events, because the parishioners of the older generation—and sometimes young Catholics as well—die and the parish sees them off on their distant journey, as is done in Catholic churches. In the vestibule of the church stands the open coffin with the body of the deceased and all relatives and friends in attendance bid farewell to their dear one. Then they carry the closed coffin into the church and they place it at the foot of the altar. Then the funeral Mass begins. The organ plays, the choir or a soloist sings, and then after the Mass they take the coffin to the cemetery. One must credit our priests, Fr. Myron, Fr. Daniel and Fr. Sebastian, with the fact that there has never been an instance when they have refused to preside at the funeral and burial of a deceased Catholic—even if the deceased had never attended church, even if a typhoon or winter blizzard raged outdoors….

11. Caritas—A Ministry of Mercy

One charitable work of the Roman Catholic church of Vladivostok that is carried out under the aegis of Fr. Myron deserves to be described in detail. As is known, Caritas International, an international conference of more than 120 independent national organizations, was established with the blessing of the Holy See. These national organizations have as their goal "bringing mercy and social justice to the world." Caritas International extends its activity to all regions of the world: Africa, the Near and Middle East, Northern Africa, Europe, North America, Latin America, Asia and Oceania. The first Russian office of Caritas opened in Moscow in 1991. By a decree of the Roman Catholic Apostolic Administration for the coordination of charitable activity in the territory of the Asian part of Russia, Caritas was established in Novosibirsk in December 1991, and in Vladivostok in 1993. The Caritas-Primorye branch was registered March 31, 1995, as an organization intended to coordinate the charitable activity of Catholic parishes and groups of citizens in the Far East. By that time the parishioners of the Roman Catholic parish already had experience carrying out charitable activities—for example, children's early morning care, the collection of clothing for large families and assistance to the elderly at home. A more serious problem now confronts Caritas-Primorye—assisting the development of charitable activities in Khabarovsk Province, the Amur region, Kamchatka Peninsula and Sakhalin Island. At the present time, all the charitable work of Caritas is in one of three main areas—medical, social and spiritual—and this activity extends beyond Vladivostok. Residents of very impoverished regions now receive assistance from Caritas—Popov Islands, Reineke, Romanovka, Noveneshino, Bolshoi Kamen and Kamen-Rybolov.

Today groups of Caritas volunteers are working in all Roman Catholic parishes of the Far East: in Yuzhno-Sakhalinsk they visit children's institutions; in Nakhodka they help lonely pensioners; in Khabarovsk they participate in the rehabilitation of women prisoners; and in Blagoveshchensk they tend to the needs of large families. In recently established parishes in Arseniev, Lesozavodsk and Ussuriisk there are already Caritas volunteers. In doing works of mercy for others, people come to better understand one another, they come to know their strengths and their weaknesses—and in the future they can choose for themselves a suitable line of work, for which they can better plan the necessary steps.

Every year Caritas-Primorye conducts meetings and seminars for volunteers; it also distributes instructional materials for the exchange of opinions and the development of joint plans of work in order to help groups better organize their charitable activities. In conjunction with the American organization "Healing the Children," Caritas-Primorye began in the spring of 1995 to help send sick children to the United States for medical care if they were unable to receive treatment in Russia.

The needs of the socially undefended population in Russia are now great, but the head of Caritas-Primorye, Anastasia Potapenko, believes that neither financial difficulties nor a lack of experience will be obstacles for the development of charitable activity, since the people are in such great need of such help.

The head of the charitable programs of Most Holy Mother of God parish is Lilia Timofeevna Silina. Since 1991 she has devoted all her learning and her whole heart to this good work. The parish program has the following components: aid to solitary elderly citizens of little means; abandoned children; children who are HIV-positive or have other infections; assistance to those departments of the Vladivostok hospitals that take mentally ill citizens into their permanent establishments. At the present time, the following programs are carried out by the parish:

> Free dinners for the poor, served in the cafeteria of Factory No. 178 four times a week—Mondays through Thursdays. There are usually approximately 30 people each day. In 2004, dinners were served on 191 days; 5,223 persons were fed, including 260 hot meals that were delivered to homes by volunteers.
>
> Assistance to the Department of Nurses' Care based at City Clinical Hospital No. 4. The assistance rendered is varied, involving several areas of work: (1) supplemental nutrition; (2) helping with the seriously ill—feeding the sick, providing spiritual com-

fort; (3) medical equipment for care of the sick: radiation for air disinfection; mattresses and mattress covers; rocking chairs, walkers, crutches, disposable diapers, bed lines, over-the-bed tables, movable wash stands, etc.; (4) furnishings—hospital beds (regular and multi-purpose), night stands, chairs, cupboards for instruments.

Assistance to City Children's Hospital No. 3, including purchase of water heaters, electric radiators, children's beds, washing machines and other items.

In 2004 Caritas purchased children's food for approximately 50 children a month at Children's World. The food, selected for the age and illness of the children, included milk products and a variety of cereals, meat, yogurt with fruit, juices and fruit for children and infants. In 2004, food valued at 382,097 rubles was purchased for the children. And, as the head of this humanitarian program, Lilia Timofeevna Silina, believes, the poor and suffering always need to be helped.

The Women's Support Center is also of great significance for the province and the city of Vladivostok. The third branch of the Women's Support Center is located in the Second River section of the city. It provides counsel with respect to "crisis pregnancies." In 2005 it worked with single mothers, mothers of large families, under-age girls and others for the preservation of the lives of unborn children. In all there were thirty women who were directed to the Women's Support Center. In November 2005 the administration of the Vladivostok Regional Council made an appeal on behalf of the Women's Support Center that resulted in a citywide collection of new clothing and shoes.

In 2005 there were 337 doctor's visits (86 for a first visit, 269 for repeat visits). As a result, forty-three women saved the life of their future child; eleven women received assistance under the program of "Aid to New Mothers"—baby food, disposable and cloth diapers, and baby clothes. During their visits, those pregnant women in a difficult situation were counseled by volunteers in more than 300 counseling sessions.

For several years now Alcoholics Anonymous has been active within Most Holy Mother of God parish. It conducts meetings every Saturday evening for anyone who hasn't the power on his own to free himself from dependency on alcohol. At these meetings they ask neither name, nor specialty, nor employment—since they are all equal with respect to this disease. The leader of this society is Sergei Nikolaevich Jakovlev, a consultant with the Regional Sanitarium for Programs of Recovery and a doctor of biological sciences. This program has allowed many people to free themselves from "the green snake" and live normal worthwhile lives with their families.

12. Parish Library

Most Holy Mother of God parish has a parish library that was founded February 13, 1994, when the pastor invited parishioners who wanted to organize a parish library to meet with him. Two parishioners responded: Elena Shaposhnikova and Miroslava Efimova. Two years later, Miroslava turned her focus to the creation of the parish archives, beginning with the collection of archival documents in Vladivostok, then in the archives in St. Petersburg, Moscow, Minsk, Warsaw, Kraków and Lublin. Elena continued to expand the parish library. Now the main and auxiliary collections of the parish library include more than 1,500 titles of books and brochures. The library also holds several years of newpaper files of *Svet Evangeliia* [Light of the Gospel] and *Sibirskaia katolicheskaia gazeta* [The Siberian Catholic Newspaper], and the magazines *Simvol* [Symbol], *Istina i zhizn* [Truth and Life] and *Tvoi Blagovest* [Your Good News]. Thanks to Fr. Myron's initiative, the library's holdings have been systematized under nineteen headings and ninety subheadings, such as the Bible, Sacred Scripture, spirituality, Christianity, theology and philosophy, as well as historical, reference, artistic and children's literature. A display of "New Acquisitions" is provided weekly for readers.

The library has a separate section for books in English, German, Spanish, Polish, Lithuanian and Ukrainian. This literature is of most interest to foreign volunteers who come to Vladivostok. The library also has approximately 300 videocassettes and 135 CDs for DVD players.

The library collection is increased by catalogue purchases, but also by books donated by parishioners. The library accepts money contributions from parishioners, which then allows it to purchase new literature at bookstores. The librarians give particular attention to the Roman Catholic parishes of the province, creating for them a selection of books, magazines and religious articles, such as icons, medals, crosses and rosaries.

The library is open every day and is now staffed by two librarians, Elena Shaposhnikova and Tamara Gubareva. On Sundays, feast days or any other days when members of parishes in other cities are in Vladivostok, two volunteers help the librarians—Masha Churusova and Galia Romanova. During organ concerts the librarians prepare small displays for the attendees, where they can purchase cassettes and CDs of organ music, small, artistically crafted icons, medals and commemorative postcards with views of the church and its stained-glass windows. In chatting with concert attendees, the librarians talk about the history of the church, Sunday liturgies and religious holidays and they answer numerous questions. In addition, the librarians regularly, before Mass, give a short announcement about interesting materials in new issues of *Light of the Gospel* and *The Siberian Catholic Newspaper* as well as new books and brochures that parishioners can get in the library.

With the permission of Fr. Myron, the library is also used by instructors and students of the institutions of higher education in Vladivostok, as well as by anyone who is interested in questions of Christianity, theology, philosophy and the history of world religions. In addition, the librarians help parishioners build their own collection of books on spirituality and Christianity.

13. Parish Archives

The collection of archival documents related to the activity of the Roman Catholic parish from 1863 down to the present day was begun soon after the reestablishment of the parish. The first archival documents, which were located in the Primorye Archives, were studied and carefully analyzed. At this stage of the work, we had as our scholarly consultant Nellia Grigorievna Mis, the most qualified regional expert on the Primorye, a geologist by specialty, who seems to know absolutely all that one can know about our province. The most valuable artifacts for present-day Catholics were the registry books of the earlier parish, which we considered a chronicle of by-gone days. Because of their aged condition, the registry books could not be photocopied—we had to copy them out by hand. This effort, which required accuracy and a good command of the language, was carried out by Anastasia Pankevich, Antonina Efimova and Miroslava Efimova. Then all the hand-copied parish registry books were printed and bound, and now they are preserved in the parish archive as a chronicle of former years. The dates of the significant events in the lives of members of the Polish diaspora in by-gone historical periods are specifically noted in the parish registry books.

Also of huge historical value are copies of documents concerning the activity of Catholic priests who served in the parishes of the Amur, Khabarovsk and Primorye regions, and also on Sakhalin Island. Documents about these priests give us not only data about one or another event, they also allow us to see, as it were, each chaplain, to understand his character and his aspirations. Not every one of them was an angel—a burdensome lot of difficult experiences and cares befell many of them, especially those who remained faithful to God and the Church during the period of the brutal revolutionary years. We obtained copies of archival documents concerning these Catholic priests from the archives in St. Petersburg, Minsk, Vitebsk, Warsaw, Kraków and Lublin.

There are no stories in this book that have been "invented" by the author—if something seems unlikely, one must keep in mind that in those long-ago times unlikely events were everyday occurrences, and Catholics who survived until our own day in their unpretentious stories have confirmed all these "unlikely" events. Unfortunately, the eyewitnesses of the events are going to God, taking with them all the sorrow and pain of the drama played out in their lives.

❁❁❁

So this is how the present-day Vladivostok Roman Catholic parish of Most Holy Mother of God lives and grows. The older parishioners grow old and go to God, but every year young couples marry, they form new families and children are born—because the Lord and the Faith are always with us!

St. Stanisław Catholic Church, Harbin, dedicated in 1909

St. Josaphat Catholic Church, Harbin, 1922

Fr. Gerard Piotrowski, Apostolic Administrator, Vicariate of Siberia

Opening of St. Charles Vladivostok Minor Seminary in Harbin, 1924. Fr. Gerard Piotrowski (center) and Brother Zachariusz Banaś, Bernadine Order (to the right of Fr. Piotrowski)

Vladivostok Minor Seminary. Seated (left to right): Brother Zachariusz Banaś, Lawrenti Butkman (teacher), Gerard Piotrowski (director), Brother Paulin and Fr. Antonij Leszczewicz. Standing: Seminarians. Harbin, 1924

Mother Agnia Sofia Malczewska and the author, Miroslava Efimova. Ursuline Sisters Convent, Kraków, 2002

Church and priest's residence, Manchur Station

Fr. Antonij Leszczewicz with children on their First Communion. Manchur Station

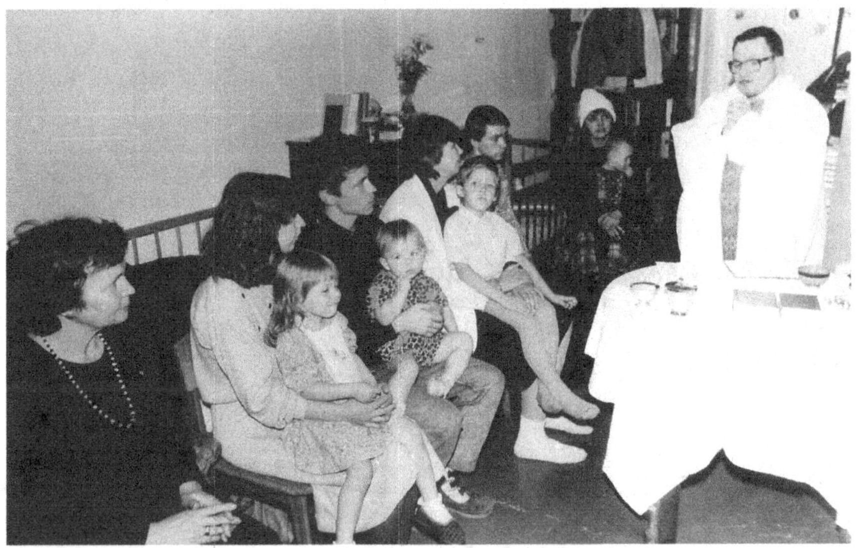

Fr. Ignatsyj Paulius says Mass in apartment of Potapenko family. Vladivostok, 1991

Fr. Sergiusz Gaek says Mass at Pioneer House. Vladivostok

Fr. Myron Effing, head of Vladivostok Roman Catholic parish

Fr. Daniel Maurer, parochial vicar, Vladivostok Roman Catholic parish

Fr. Myron Effing says Mass at gates of former Catholic Church, 1991

Memorial Cross, Vladivostok

After Mass at House of Unions (left to right): Julia, Lima, Nelli, Fr. Myron, Miroslava, Antonina, Fr. Daniel, Malvina, Alla

Wedding of Anna Gafurova (the parish's first organist) and Adam Jones (from the United States)

Marina Omelchenko, main accompaniest for Masses

Combined choir of Christian denominations, Vladivostok, 2006

Fr. Sebastian Mariann d'Silva, newly arrived from India

Fr. Myron says Mass at St. Joseph parish, Vladivostok

Left to right: Aleksei Ivanovski and Vladimir Ivanov, the craftsmen responsible for the beautiful stained glass windows, and Andrei Udovichenko, parish plant supervisor

The return of the Crucifix to the church

Vladivostok Catholics venerate the relics of St. Therese of Lisieux

Anatolii Stashkov, Fr. Myron's personal driver

Sr. Iwona Naglik, director of the archives of the Ursuline Sisters in Kraków

Kaczanowski family, parishioners of Bishop Sliwowski

Sisters of Mercy of St. Anne

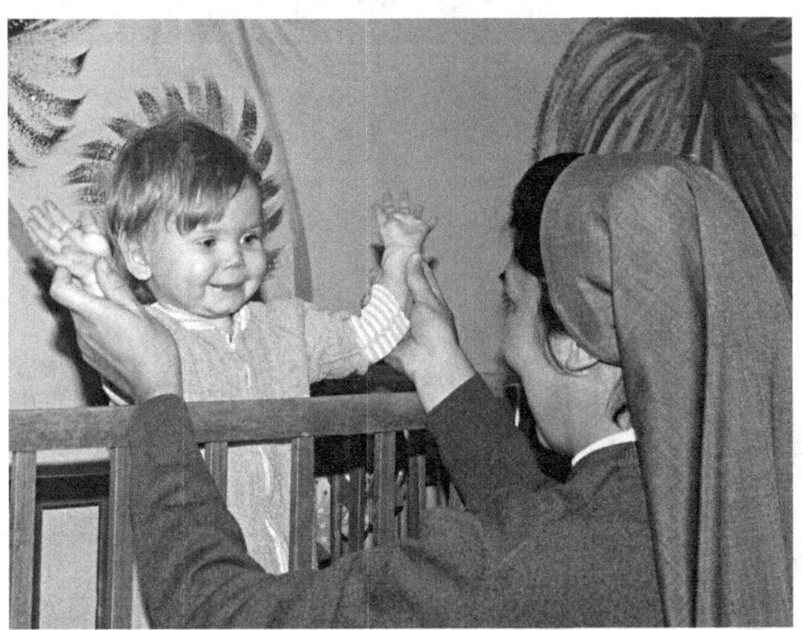

Sr. Rosario Vicente at the orphanage

Fr. Edmund Cisiak. Poland

A little parishioner loves to sit next to the big bell!

Bishop Jerzy Mazur shows Catholics the key to the new cathedral

Library, Mary Mother of God Cathedral parish, Vladivostok

About the Author

Miroslava Igorevna (Tukalevska) Efimova was born in the little village of Belaya Tserkov, Ukraine, in 1929. Her father was inducted into the Red Army before the outbreak of World War II, and once the war began Miroslava, her mother, grandmother and little brother were evacuated to Balashov, and then in 1942 to Kazakhstan. Her uncle, an agronomist at a collective farm near Irkutsk, Siberia, invited them to join him with the promise that they at least would not starve. But conditions were worse than the family expected, and they returned to Yaroslavl to stay with an aunt. After the Red Army had expelled the Germans from Kiev, the family returned to their home, only to be sorely disappointed by the ruins they found. After the war, her father was transferred to Khabarovsk.

Miroslava completed her high school education in Khabarovsk and then enrolled in the Far Eastern Technical Institute in Vladivostok, where she would study in the mining department, working toward a degree in geology. Her parents returned to western Russia, but Miroslava remained in Vladivostok. In her last year at the institute, she married a student from the electro-technical department, Vladilen Fyodorovich Efimov, and after Miroslava's graduation with a degree as a mining engineer the young couple had a son, Vladislav, and later a daughter, Anastasia (and Miroslava now has several grandchildren). Meanwhile, Miroslava had continued her education, eventually defending her dissertation.

Although she returned to the Ukraine for a brief period of her professional life, Miroslava lived and pursued her career in geology and mineralogy with the Soviet Academy of Sciences in the Russian Far East and in North Korea. In 1992 she became involved in the re-establishment of the Roman Catholic parish in Vladivostok and over the following years, having retired from her geological career, she contributed her expertise on the Russian Far East and her research skills to the collection and publication of a variety of materials on Roman Catholic life in the Russian Far East from the 1860s to the present. The present work represents the culmination of all those efforts.

Old Russian Units of Measure

arshin—28 inches
sazhen—7 feet
verst—0.66 mile
desiatyn (agricultural)—3.6 acres
desiatyn (state)—2.7 acres
pood—36.11 pounds

Russian Far Eastern Federal District

Capital: Khabarovsk
Population: 6,796,041

Subunits of the Far Eastern Federal District:

Entity	Population	Capital	Population
Primorsk Krai	2,071,210	Vladivostok	594,701
Khabarovsk Krai	1,436,570	Khabarovsk	583,072
Amur Oblast	902,844	Blagoveshchensk	219,221
Kamchatka Krai	358,801	Petropavlovsk	198,028
Magadan Oblast	182,726	Magadan	99,399
Sakhalin Oblast	546,695	Yuzhno-Sakhalinsk	170,000
Jewish Autonomous Oblast	190,915	Birobidzhan	77,250
Chukotka Autonomous District	157,000	Anadyr	11,038
Sakha Republic	949,280	Yakutsk	210,642

Population figures are from 2002.

The Russian Far East. Used with permission of Stanford University Press and Manoa Mapworks, Inc.

Present-Day Roman Catholic Parishes in the Russian Far East

City	Parish	Pre-Revolution Founding	Post-Soviet Founding or Re-Founding	Currently in Care of:	2006 Members
Vladivostok Deanery					
Vladivostok	Most Holy Mother of God[1]	c. 1891	1992	Frs. Myron Effing, CJD and Daniel Maurer, CJD	400
Vladivostok	St. Joseph	---	2002	Frs. Myron Effing, CJD and Daniel Maurer, CJD	70
Nakhodka	Our Lady of the Pacific	---	1996	Fr. Sebastian D'Silva	85
Bolshoi Kamen	St. John the Evangelist	---	1992—inactive	n/a	n/a
Lesozavodsk	Visitation	---	1999	Franciscan Fathers	40

Arseniev	Annunciation	---	1999	Fr. John Gibbons, OFM	
Romanovka	Most Holy Trinity	---	1996	Fr. Christopher Teleba	60
Ussurisk	Nativity of Our Lord[2]	c. 1902	2000	Fr. Dominic Kim, OFM	
Khabarovsk	Immaculate Conception of the Virgin Mary	c. 1909	1993	Fr. Marcelo Brandan, IVE and Fr. Jose Lopez IVE	50
Khabarovsk	Most Holy Trinity	---	2001	Fr. Marcelo Brandan, IVE and Fr. Jose Lopez IVE	70
Khabarovsk	St. Benedict	---	2001	Fr. Marcelo Brandan, IVE and Fr. Jose Lopez IVE	50
Blagoveshchensk	Transfiguration of Jesus	c. 1896	1994	Frs. Thomas Klavon SVD and Harold Jude SVD	50

Svobodny	Divine Mercy	---		Frs. Thomas Klavon SVD and Harold Jude SVD	40
Komsomolsk-on-Amur	Holy Family of Nazareth	---	1998	Fr. Marcelo Brandan, IVE and Fr. Jose Lopez IVE	
Nikolaevsk-on-Amur	Sts. Cyril and Methodius[3]	1867	2001	Fr. Marcelo Brandan, IVE and Fr. Jose Lopez IVE	20
Magadan Deanery					
Magadan	Nativity of Our Lord		1991	Frs. Michael Shields and David Means	250
Ola	Holy Family	---	1999	Frs. Michael Shields and David Means	50

Ola	Holy Family	---	1999	Frs. Michael Shields and David Means	50
Sokol	Blessed Charles de Foucauld	---	2005	Fr. Milosz Krakowski	15
Petropavlovsk	St. Terese of the Child Jesus	---	1999	Fr. Christopher Koval	80
South Sakhalin	St. James	---	1993	Fr. Lawrence Jong, KFMS	20
South Sakhalin	Assumption	---	2001	Fr. Lawrence Jong, KFMS	140
Korsakov		---	2004	Fr. Lawrence Jong, KFMS	20
Kholmsk	Sts. Andrew Taegon and Paul Hasan	---	2004	Fr. Lawrence Jong, KFMS	20
Aniva				Fr. Ferdinand Gosselin, MM	

(Footnotes)

1 We are not sure of the name of the pre-revolutionary parish in Vladivostok. The three churches (the wooden church that burned down in 1902, the temporary barracks church, and then the brick church dedicated in 1921) had various names referring to the Blessed Virgin. The very elderly people referred to the name of "Most Holy Mother of God" when interviewed in 1992.

2 The pre-revolutionary parish in Nikolsk-Ussurisk was named St. Nicholas the Wonderworker.

3 The pre-revolutionary parish in Nikolaevsk-on-Amur was named Sts. Peter and Paul.

Printed in the United States
By Bookmasters